REVELATION ROAD

REVELATION ROAD

One man's journey to the heart of the apocalypse – and back again.

Nick Page

**HODDER &
STOUGHTON**

Scripture quotations are taken from the New Revised Standard Version of the Bible, copyright 1989 by the Division of Christian Education of the National Council of the Churches of Christ in the USA. Used by permission. All rights reserved.

First published in Great Britain in 2014 by Hodder & Stoughton
An Hachette UK company

First published in paperback in 2015

1

ISBN 978 1 444 74967 0
Ebook ISBN 978 1 444 74968 7

Typeset in Sabon MT Std by Palimpsest Book Production Ltd, Falkirk, Stirlingshire

Printed and bound in the UK by Clays Ltd, St Ives plc

Hodder & Stoughton policy is to use papers that are natural, renewable and recyclable products and made from wood grown in sustainable forests. The logging and manufacturing processes are expected to conform to the environmental regulations of the country of origin.

Hodder & Stoughton Ltd
Carmelite House
50 Victoria Embankment
London EC4Y 0DZ

www.hodderfaith.com

'For some time now it has seemed to me that the two questions we should ask of any strong landscape are these: firstly, what do I know when I am in this place that I can know nowhere else? And then, vainly, what does this place know of me that I cannot know of myself?'

ROBERT MACFARLANE

'Travelling outgrows its motives. It soon proves sufficient in itself. You think you are making a trip, but soon it is making you – or unmaking you.'

NICOLAS BOUVIER

'In a time of universal deceit telling the truth is a revolutionary act.'

GEORGE ORWELL

Contents

The Cave

The sky is a pale, washed-out white, turning apricot at the crest of the hills across the bay. The sea is the colour of steel.

I leave the apartment, struggling, as usual, to close the door. At this time of day, even Shakira isn't interested in saying hello. She avoids eye contact, unlike the many cats who fill the terrace where the dirt track joins the streets of the upper town. They eye me warily as I walk by.

At the house with the pink flowers I turn right, into the alley where everyone parks their scooters. Then right again at the end, along the backs of houses, shuttered and sleepy, until I reach a long, narrow, steep flight of steps. Cut through the courtyard of the Proton supermarket, then out through the backstreets of Skala, past gardens lavish with pomegranate, fig and lemon even this late in the year.

Now the way starts to rise. Crosses the winding coil of the main road for the stone path ahead. This was the old route, I think. The donkey track. Geil came this way, and Guérin and Georgirenes. And the man himself? Maybe. The sun is rising now and the path is steeper. A small dog joins me for part of the way but then veers off, sniffing some other prey. At the end of the rough cobbles, a small wooden sign offers a choice: Straight ahead for Chora and the monastery; turn left for the Apocalypse.

Left it is, then.

The dry grass on either side of the path is the colour of spun sugar. The earth beneath has been caramelised. Now the track takes me into dark green woods. I plunge through cool, welcome pools of shadow. Ahead and far above, I glimpse Chora through the trees, the dark, fortress-like monastery guarding the white houses as it has done for a thousand years. Below that, clinging to the hill is the gateway, the rambling hotchpotch of buildings that houses the Monastery of the Apocalypse. And at the far side of those buildings, a cupola, a stone bell tower and the barrel vault of the small church of St Anne.

Even at 7.30 in the morning the heat is intense. It bounces off the rocks, filling the air with the incense of heat and pine and dust.

The sea looks smooth, now, still and silver-grey. It looks – as the man himself wrote so many years ago – like a 'sea of glass'. Maybe he was out early in the morning, too. A hooded crow rows gracelessly across the sky. Far off, the pale shadows of distant islands hover, grey like ghosts.

It's really hot now and I am turning into a great globule of sweat, loosely held together by skin. Half man, half jellyfish. A steady climb now through shaggy, dusty pines and pale eucalyptus. Here the trees thin and the ground to the left of the path falls away, revealing the detritus of sudden winter rains: dried-up river beds, great, landslid boulders, misplaced in the dirt.

And then, a clearing. A flight of whitewashed steps leading to a cluster of buildings, a small, chocolate-coloured door in a white wall.

Inside, darkness. Eyes adjust slowly. Go to the counter, fish in the pocket for the two-euro coin. Got to pay the ferryman.

Another door takes me out into a maze of stairways. Here the sky appears as a bright-blue square framed by high walls as I descend through sudden terraces and small landings, plunge in and out of pools of sunlight, staircase after staircase, until finally, switchbacked and vertigoed, I reach a small chapel.

A moment. A breath. A beat.

And then go in. Enter the Cave of the Apocalypse.

ENGLAND

'An idea, to be suggestive, must come to the individual with the force of revelation.'

WILLIAM JAMES

1 An Apocalypse in Chipping Norton

I went to Chipping Norton because I was wrongly informed.

I had been reading the book of Revelation, or *The Apocalypse of St John* to give it its older, Greek title. It's a curious, unsettling book, a record of a vision, or visions, given to a man called John on Patmos, an island in the Aegean sea, and addressed to communities living in what then was the Roman province of Asia. Scholars argue about the date – actually, they argue about everything to do with this book – but the general consensus is that it was written during the reign of the emperor Domitian, around AD 92.

So, the youngest book of the New Testament, and the oddest as well. This is a book which opens with a vision of a white-haired man with a sword sticking out of his mouth, before charging on into a landscape of dragons and whores, cities real and imaginary, angels, beasts, trumpets, scrolls (edible and inedible), horsemen, earthquakes, thunder, lightning, and tiny locusts with beards.

Faced with such weirdness, I was looking for new ways to explore the book, to get beneath its skin. And that's why I ended up in Chipping Norton. In Peter Levi's beautiful book *The Hill of Kronos*, he takes a trip to Patmos:

At mid-afternoon the hills were green and stony, in the evening they turned yellow and the sea glittered darkly. Samos appeared on the horizon in a milk-white mist. In the evening a harbour was a spring of warm yellow lights. In the morning at the top of the island the wind and the sea gave the whole place the sensation of the bridge of a petrified ship, but at mid-day it was like two or three hills from somewhere like Chipping Norton towed out to sea and abandoned for thousands of years.

3

Chipping Norton? That's not too far. I would go and experience it for myself.

On reflection, probably what I'd missed here was the 'abandoned for thousands of years' bit. Chipping Norton may be many things, but it is not abandoned. On the contrary, it has been embraced by quite a lot of people, such as David Cameron, Jeremy Clarkson, and a lot of other well-heeled businessmen, financiers, media-execs and People Who Work in PR who have fled London by means of the M40.

Frankly, as a way of trying to understand Revelation, Chipping Norton was a bit of a let-down. For one thing, it was raining; for another, as I quickly realised, nobody in Chipping Norton has ever had a revelation about anything. Unless it was some kind of divine command to buy a new Audi, or perhaps to relaunch the Tory party.

I took refuge from the rain in a charity shop. The one thing about posh market towns is that you do get a better class of hand-me-down in the charity shops. Never know when you're going to come across a pair of Gucci wellies or a slightly used black Labrador. And there I saw it. Proust was transported back to his childhood by a madeleine. (It's a cake. Apparently.) For me it was a blue-covered paperback: *The Late Great Planet Earth*.

*

It's 1972. I am in the attic room at home. Probably wearing flares, platform heels and a tank top. Bowie is playing on the record player. 'Five years, that's all we've got . . .'

There is the book on the bookshelf: *The Late Great Planet Earth* by Hal Lindsey. A deep, dark-blue cover, with the earth in the middle, looking small and marbled and vulnerable.

In the febrile, doomwatch days of the cold war, Lindsey dealt in a brand of speculative fiction masquerading as carefully worked-out predictions which showed clearly and incontrovertibly that we were absolutely, definitely, 100 per cent in the middle of the end times. Lindsey had read Revelation – and other predictions in the Bible – and finally worked out what they all meant. John's description of a mountain falling into the sea? That's a nuclear bomb, the fallout from which would poison the water, while its mushroom cloud darkened the sun and the moon. Armageddon? Clearly a battle in the

Middle East, which would draw in the Soviet Union and lead to a complete economic meltdown, food shortages, and the unfortunate demise of a quarter of the human population. When Revelation talked about a 200 million-strong army of horsemen from the east, Lindsey saw the army of the Peoples' Republic of China. Where John describes horses with the heads of lions, and mouths which issue forth fire and smoke and brimstone, Lindsey saw mobile rocket launchers. (And he provided plenty of detail: chapter 12 has a fascinating account of 'the Armageddon campaign' – complete with maps.)

The ten-headed beast from the sea was the European Economic Community. This had six members at the time Lindsey was writing, but he confidently predicted it would grow to ten, at which point this 'revived Roman empire' would be taken over by the antichrist or 'Future Fuhrer' who would become 'ruler of the European confederacy'.

Lindsey was confident. Lindsey was concerned. Lindsey was completely wrong. Everything but the most obvious of Lindsey's predictions has failed to materialise. Far from having ten nations, the EU currently has twenty-seven and is ruled by no one (except perhaps Angela Merkel, and she's not anyone's idea of the antichrist). He also predicted that Christ's visible return would occur 'within forty years or so of 1948'. That is, by my calculations, er, hang on . . . 1988. Whoops. I must have missed it.

Meanwhile, the cold war has ended. The Soviet Union has collapsed. And we're all still here.

And yet the curious thing is, despite the fact that none of his predictions have actually come true, despite the fact that John's language is taken far too literally at times, and symbolically at others, depending on what he wants to prove, Mr Lindsey still presides over a significant publishing and media operation. His believers still have faith in him.

But that is the thing with the true believers. They remain undeterred, whatever tiny obstacles appear in their path. Like a complete lack of proof.

Lindsey's approach was nothing new. The technique of trying to find parallels for John's prophecies in contemporary historical events had been invented some 800 years earlier by a medieval monk called Joachim of Fiore. But Lindsey caught the *zeitgeist* perfectly. Apocalypticism goes hand in hand with anxiety and in the 1970s everyone was scared. (Fear still drives his sales. Apparently, sales of the book increased by 83 per cent in the summer of 1990, when the USA and other nations invaded Iraq. An executive from Lindsey's publishers said, 'Often times we see during a crisis that people more actively turn toward God and things spiritual.')

Fear. That's what it's all about.

In the seventies, fear of reds under the bed and nuclear meltdown. In the nineties, fear that Saddam Hussein would drag the world down into the worst fulfilment of Lindsey's fantasies. Fear of what the world had become. Lindsey was writing for an audience who feared that they were out of date. Post-hippies and pre-punk, surrounded by the wreckage of the Vietnam war and the death of the American Dream, many people looked on in bewilderment. America was no longer Mom, Dad and Apple Pie. In Britain, upper lips were no longer stiff and the empire on which the sun never set was experiencing something of an eclipse.

Apocalyptic fervour feeds on a mix of power and powerlessness: it grows where some people have immense power and others feel they can do nothing about it. And in such circumstances, the power-less turn to Revelation. This – *this* – will prove that they were right all along.

Today, the fear remains. Sure, the cold war thawed, but other dangers still send icy shivers down the spine. Global warming. Government surveillance. Norovirus, bird flu. War in the Middle East. The collapse of the banking system. Power and privilege grav-itating to the '1 per cent'. Simon Cowell, *The Only Way Is Essex* – there's more than enough fear out there to go around.

And nowadays, the latest Hal Lindsey-style pseudo-prophet doesn't even need to publish a book. The all-encompassing reach of the internet means that you can spread your latest theory about Revelation with the click of a mouse. End-time fever has been democratised. All you need is a Bible and a blog.

Back in the 1970s I never did get to the end of *The Late Great Planet Earth*. I was too busy reading my Marvel comics, which, though no less concerned with the end of the world, were, I felt, marginally more believable. But as the years went by, Lindsey's book became a symbol of the problems with Revelation. The Apocalypse, to put it bluntly, was a nutter-magnet. The blend of obscure imagery and cryptic narrative made it a book to be avoided.

*

Re-reading Lindsey's book in a Chipping Norton café made me sad more than anything else. Not because Lindsey is so spectacularly wrong, nor even because he prefaces his failed predictions with classic weasel words, the small-print 'terms and conditions' so beloved of end-time prophets – 'I believe that these forecasts are based upon sound deductions; however, please don't get the idea that I am infallibly right in the same way that a Biblical prophet speaking under the direct inspiration of God's Spirit was.' No, the reason I was sad was because he's right – but in completely the wrong way. Revelation does claim that God is active and in charge of human history. Revelation does claim that the Lamb of God will have the victory. But it is not the victory that Lindsey describes. It will not arrive through Armageddon and antichrist and locust-like attack helicopters.

And the big problem with this kind of interpretation is that it pushes Christians and non-Christians alike into the opposite error: the mistake of thinking that Revelation is *only* metaphor, *only* picture language, or that its metaphors are ultimately unknowable, impenetrable. So they don't read Revelation at all.

I was re-reading the Apocalypse because I was convinced that it meant *something*. It had something to say to the people to whom it was addressed – Christians in Ephesus and Smyrna and Philadelphia and Pergamum. They heard this message and realised there was stuff you could do. A book that was purely about the end of the world, a book which was merely about events two thousand years after they were dead – well, what use would that be?

The name is the clue. 'Apocalypse' does not mean 'the end of the world'. It means 'unveiling', disclosure, a revealing of something hidden. It's one of the most misused of all biblical terms. Today, when we hear the word 'apocalyptic', we think of something catastrophic, something terminal. We think of survivalists, bunkered in the middle of nowhere, stocked up on supplies and ammo, waiting for 'the apocalypse'. There is an entire genre of 'post-apocalyptic' fiction and movies, most of which depict the world after some kind of meltdown, one featuring bombs and disease, or zombies moving around very slowly and yet still managing to catch and eat people. These things are not post-apocalyptic.

A *real* post-apocalyptic film would show what happens 'after the unveiling'. In that sense, the most literally post-apocalyptic movie in the world is *The Wizard of Oz*, where the curtain is drawn back to reveal that the Great and Powerful Oz is really a bumbling man from Kansas. That's apocalypse. The hidden truth has been revealed.

But maybe a better example is *The Matrix*, where that famous piece of furniture, Keanu Reeves, plays Neo Anderson. (The name is suitably symbolic: it means New Son of Man.) Neo is revealed to be the chosen one. He pierces the veil of illusion, cracks the computer code of this world, and reveals 'reality' to be one big piece of software. Then there is a lot of shooting and people wearing tight leather and bending over backwards. (Not to mention two extremely bad sequels. At the end of Revelation John warns of terrible punishments if anyone adds to 'the words of this book'. John clearly understood the danger of sequels. Pity the makers of the *Matrix* trilogy didn't follow his advice.)

Apocalypse, then, is an unveiling, a disclosure, a work which draws back the curtain to show what is *really* going on. John looks out from Patmos and sees things that are happening all around him. And he sends forth the record of this exotic, unworldly journey to invite his listeners into a new way of seeing things, and a new way of living.

Of course, it would have helped if he could have been just a little bit clearer.

*

Alexandria, Egypt. About AD 247. A Thursday. Dionysius, bishop of Alexandria, is having his own problems with Revelation.

A Christian scholar of some renown, Dionysius is one of the first people to take a detailed critical approach to the text.* He admits to finding the book obscure. 'For even though I do not understand it,' he writes, 'yet I suspect that some deeper meaning underlies the words.' Dionysius shows that already there was controversy about this book:

> Some indeed of those before our time rejected and altogether impugned the book, examining it chapter by chapter and declaring it to be unintelligible and illogical and its title false. For they say that it is not John's, no, nor yet an apocalypse, since it is veiled by its great thick curtain of unintelligibility.

It is unintelligible. Illogical. It should be sued under the Trades Description Act, because, Dionysius jokes, instead of unveiling anything, it hides everything behind a 'great thick curtain of unintelligibility'. For a revelation, says Dionysius, it was not very revealing.

This is the reason why so many people react so strongly to it. As Dionysius says, some people rejected it entirely as non-scriptural. In AD 325 Eusebius listed it as theologically suspect. The Council of Laodicea – held around 360 – left it out of the canon. The church father Cyril of Jerusalem (315–86) not only evicted it from the canon, he banned all public and private reading of the book. Even as late as the ninth century, the *Stichometry* of Nicephorus of Constantinople was still listing Revelation among the disputed books of the New Testament.†

Even those who did accept its provenance were nonetheless baffled by it. Jerome, *the* Bible translator of the fourth century, wrote: 'Revelation has as many mysteries as it does words.' Augustine of Hippo – who was, let's face it, a pretty smart thinker – complained that 'though this book is called the Apocalypse, there are in it many

---

* Eusebius called Dionysius the 'great bishop of Alexandria'. He died at a great age in AD 265.

† Elsewhere it was not until the fifth century that it made its way into the Syriac versions of the New Testament, while the Armenian New Testament kept it out until the twelfth century.

obscure passages to exercise the mind of the reader, and there are few passages so plain as to assist us in the interpretation of the others, even though we take pains'. Generally, scholars avoided it. Only two commentaries on Revelation have survived from before AD 500, and one of those only exists in fragments.

Fast forward to the Reformation, and there is still deep-seated concern. Zwingli declared it to be 'not a biblical book'. It's the only New Testament book on which John Calvin didn't write a commentary. (And he was a man who liked to comment on *everything*.) Luther wanted to omit it from his translation of the New Testament altogether. 'Some have even brewed [Revelation] into many stupid things out of their own heads,' he complained.

He was right. Revelation is the ultimate theological home-brew kit. And thousands of people have made moonshine with it. But the fact is this: we cannot ignore this book. It has had more influence on popular culture than virtually any other book of the Bible. We may think of Revelation as a book which has brought us church schisms, heresies and cults. But it has also inspired armed rebellion, political upheaval, the discovery of America, great poetry and art, anthems sung at cricket matches, reggae, heavy metal, not to mention cornflakes, logarithms and communism. It has inspired some of the greatest art in the world and filled our language with memorable phrases.

As I sat in that Chipping Norton café, surrounded by Frappuccinos and Vanilla Lattés, with two women at the next table talking about a new source of organic muesli, I had a mini revelation of my own. I realised that Revelation was too important to leave to the tender mercies of the academics or the freaks. I would go where Dionysius of Alexandria feared to tread. This would be my mission. I would try to find out what this little book was all about.

And if I was going to write about this extreme book, then I would have to go to extremes. Forget Chipping Norton, I would actually go to Patmos. I would revisit Revelation. Literally. As far as possible, I would follow in John's footsteps, take a road-trip into the apocalypse, get as close as I could to the sights, sounds and smells of the Roman province of Asia in the first century. I would go to the places that John knew, the cities to which he was writing and, most importantly, the island where he saw the vision.

It would be a learning journey. A learney, if you will. Or a jearning. Or maybe not.

But anyway, that, after all, is where the word 'learn' comes from: it has roots, way back, in the proto-Germanic word *liznojan*, which means to track, to follow, to hunt.

That's it. I would follow in the footsteps of John himself. I would *liznojan* him like mad.

And all would be revealed.

11

2 Fear and Loathing in Gatwick Airport

On the train, men in suits were reading *The Times* on their iPads or preparing PowerPoint slides. A man in a Crew shirt was talking loudly on his phone in two-word sentences.

'Fantastic, Jamie. Well done. Top man. Big money.' Clearly, everyone near him had another two-word sentence in mind, one which perhaps included the words 'shut' and 'up'. Eventually someone deployed weapons-grade English politeness: 'Do you mind? This is the *quiet* carriage.'

Outside in the unquiet world, the morning was still and fresh, a beautiful sunny September day. There were farmers in the fields, tractors trudging up and down, followed by a paparazzi flock of seagulls.

The news was suitably doom and gloom. The headlines warned of increased government surveillance. Global warming was getting warmer. North Korea and Iran were developing nuclear capability. The war in Syria had produced 2 million refugees.

The Syrian situation was exercising the diehard end-timers. On one of my late-night dives into the apocalyptic internet, I discovered an article called 'The Burden of Damascus' which argued that the destruction of Damascus was all foretold in Isaiah ('See, Damascus will cease to be a city, and will become a heap of ruins', Isa. 17:1) and that this was thus a clear indicator of the end times. The writing was the usual recipe: one part out-of-context biblical prophecy, two parts clunky Lindsey-lite literalism, add a splash of American right-wing xenophobia (for example, Damascus was described as 'a veritable Disneyland for radical Islamic terrorist operations') and hey presto: The Armageddon Cocktail. And the conclusion? 'The end times battles foretold in Bible prophecy' are on their way.

This literal reading of the biblical text is the standard m.o. of the end-timers. From the moment Revelation was written people were tempted to read it as a timetable, ticking off the 'signs' as they occurred. Earthquake? Check. War? Check. Strangely thin horseman riding a green horse? Check. Assume crash positions, we're going down!

Even in fiction writers take it all literally. After Lindsey, the most popular set of writings on Revelation has been the *Left Behind* series of novels by Tim LaHaye and Jerry B. Jenkins. '*Left Behind* is the first fictional portrayal of events that are true to the literal interpretation of Bible prophecy,' said LaHaye.*

Which is the problem straight away. Because if there is one thing that Revelation is not, it is 'literally true'.

*

In the months spent planning the trip I tried to make a map. Not a map of the physical journey – that was the easy part. No, I needed a map of the text, of the book itself. I needed to discern its shape, to chart the landscape of this strange, uneven book.

It proved to be a complex task. I read and re-read the text, wandering day after day through its labyrinthine streets. My notebooks rapidly filled up with scrawled outlines and pasted-in scraps of paper. Many times I had the book summarised and bullet pointed and organised like an itinerary, but nothing seemed to work. Just when I had some kind of clarity over the structure, just when I thought I had worked out the lay of the land, it would shimmer and change. The result is that my notes from this period look more like some kind of abstract art. Ink scribbled over by pencil, red on black on blue, amendments, deletions, endless corrections and alterations.

I was not alone in this, though. Virtually every commentary I consulted – and I consulted a lot – claimed a different structure for

* Actually, this is not true. He was beaten to it by about twenty-five years by Salem Kirban, a speaker, writer and, apparently, 'blue-green algae salesman', whose two novels, *666* and *1000*, are illustrated with genuinely clever photo-montages and some rather more dubious repurposed pictures of Second World War atrocities and current events. Kirban's other books included *Countdown to Rapture*, *A Guide to Survival*, *Satan's Mark Exposed* and the no-less-apocalyptic *Unlocking Your Bowels for Better Health*.

the text. Every scholar organised the material differently. It seemed that no one could come up with an agreed outline or structure for this book.

In the end, though, I managed to break the book into ten sections. They are not neat, there are repetitions and overlaps. Characters from one section turn up later, unannounced. But this summary represents the best I could make of the wreckage of all those notes.*

The prologue: Revelation 1.1–9

This is how it begins:

The revelation of Jesus Christ, which God gave him to show his servants what must soon take place; he made it known by sending his angel to his servant John, who testified to the word of God and to the testimony of Jesus Christ, even to all that he saw. Blessed is the one who reads aloud the words of the prophecy, and blessed are those who hear and who keep what is written in it; for the time is near. (Rev. 1.1–3)

Then there is a short section in which John greets 'the seven churches that are in Asia', and quotes some early Christian sayings.

The opening scene: Revelation 1.9–20

John is on Patmos 'because of the word of God and the testimony of Jesus'. Caught up in the Spirit on the Lord's day, he hears a voice 'like a trumpet' telling him to write down what he hears and send it to the seven churches.

John turns to see who is speaking. He sees seven golden lamp-stands, in the middle of which is a figure wearing a long robe, with a sash. He has white hair, feet like burnished bronze. The figure holds seven stars and a sword is sticking out of his mouth.

---

* You can skip this section if you know the book well. Actually, you can skip this section even if you don't know the book well. It's a free world. Anyway, we pick up on p.23.

John falls down in awe. The figure is Jesus – or his angel, his messenger. He repeats the instruction to John to write down 'what you have seen, what is, and what is to take place after this'. He explains that the lampstands are the churches and the stars are the angels of the churches.

The letters to the seven churches: Revelation 2–3

Jesus passes on seven messages, each one addressed to the 'angel' of a specific church.

Ephesus: You are enduring well, but have abandoned your first love. Do the work you did at first. Whoever conquers will eat from the tree of life.

Smyrna: Do not be afraid of what you are about to suffer. Keep faithful. Whoever conquers will not be harmed by the second death.

Pergamum: You are holding fast in the midst of overwhelming pressure. But get rid of the heretics in your midst. Whoever conquers will receive hidden manna, and their name will be engraved on a white stone.

Thyatira: I recognise your love, faith, service and endurance. But get rid of Jezebel! Hold fast. Whoever conquers will be given authority and receive the morning star.

Sardis: You think you're alive, but you're dead. Wake up! Strengthen what remains! Whoever conquers will be dressed in white robes, and their name will be recorded in the book of life.

Philadelphia: I know your works. The door is open. I will protect and reward you. Keep strong. Whoever conquers will become a pillar in the temple of God. Jesus will write on them 'the name of my God' and the name of the New Jerusalem.

Laodicea: You think you are rich but you are poor. You are lukewarm water: utterly useless. I am standing and knocking: open the door! Whoever conquers will be given a place on my throne.

The Lamb and the seals: Revelation 4.1–8.1

A door opens in heaven. John hears the trumpet-voice inviting him up. Again he is caught up in the Spirit.

He sees a throne on which is seated a glittering, jewel-like figure. There are twenty-four elders in the throne room with white robes and crowns. John sees four creatures, one on each side of the throne. The creatures sing, the elders worship.

The throned figure holds a scroll in his right hand, sealed with seven seals. When John finds that no one is worthy to open it, he starts to weep. Then an elder announces that the Lion of Judah has conquered, so he can open the scroll.

Enter the Lion. Which turns out to be a Lamb, looking as though it has been slaughtered. The Lamb – which has seven horns and seven eyes – takes the scroll, and everyone starts to sing its praise.

The Lamb breaks open the seals . . .

Seal 1: Releases a rider on a white horse. The conqueror.

Seal 2: Releases a rider on a red horse. The slaughterer, the peace-taker.

Seal 3: Releases a rider on a black horse. Famine.

Seal 4: Releases a rider on a pale-green horse. Death, accompanied by Hades. This rider is given authority over 25 per cent of the earth, to kill with sword, famine, pestilence, wild animals.

Seal 5: Reveals the souls of the martyrs crying out for justice. They are given white robes and told to rest, until joined by others 'soon to be killed'.

Seal 6: Releases earthly disasters. The sky turns black, the moon turns to blood, stars fall to earth, the sky rolls up like a scroll. Everyone tries to hide.

John sees four angels holding back the four winds, delaying final disaster until the slaves of the Lord are marked. 144,000 are sealed.

A great multitude gathers before the Lord: those who have come out of the great ordeal.

When the seventh seal is opened, there is a great silence.

The seven trumpets: Revelation 8.2–11.19

John sees seven angels with seven trumpets. At an altar, an angel makes an offering of incense, which is the prayers of the saints. He then takes the 'fire' from the altar and starts to rain it onto the earth. Thunder. Lightning. An earthquake.

The angels blow their trumpets, one by one . . .

Trumpet 1: Releases hail, fire mixed with blood. It burns a third of the earth, the trees and green grass.

Trumpet 2: A fiery mountain is thrown into the sea. A third of all sea creatures die, a third of all ships are destroyed.

Trumpet 3: A star – 'wormwood' – falls from heaven. A third of all rivers and springs are poisoned.

Trumpet 4: The sun, moon and stars are struck. A third of each is darkened. Days and nights are shortened. An eagle flies out crying, 'Woe, woe, woe to the inhabitants of the earth . . .'

Trumpet 5: A star descends to earth and is given the keys to a deep pit. It opens the pit and smoke pours out, filling the sky, darkening the sun. From the smoke emerge locusts, like horses equipped for battle. The locusts attack those who do not have the seal. Their king is Abaddon or Apollyon. (This is the first woe.)

Trumpet 6: Releases the four angels bound at the Euphrates. They kill a third of mankind. They have a cavalry of 200 million troops, their lion-headed, serpent-tailed horses breathe fire and sulphur.

Despite all this, the rest of mankind still worships idols.

A mighty angel comes down with a tiny scroll. He shouts and

there is the sound of seven thunders. John moves to write what he hears but is told 'to seal up what the seven thunders have said and not to write it down'. The angel swears this mystery will only be fulfilled when the seventh trumpet is sounded.

John is told to eat the small scroll. It tastes sweet but makes his stomach bitter. He is told to prophesy again 'about many peoples and nations and languages and kings'.

Scene change: a city. John is given a measuring rod and told to measure the temple of God and those who worship there. Outside the temple courtyard is to be given to the nations who will trample the holy city for forty-two months.

Two witnesses have been authorised to prophesy during this time (they are described as two olive trees and two lampstands). But a beast from the bottomless pit will kill them in the city. The city is 'prophetically called Sodom and Egypt where their Lord was crucified'. They are killed and their unburied bodies are left in the street. But God brings them back to life and they ascend to heaven. The city is hit by an earthquake and 7,000 people are killed. (The second woe has passed . . .)

Trumpet 7: There is praise in heaven. The twenty-four elders worship the throned one. God's temple in heaven is opened, revealing the ark of the covenant. Lightning. Thunder. Earthquake. Hail.

The woman and the beasts: Revelation 12.1–14.20

A 'great portent'. A woman in heaven, standing on the moon, clothed with the sun, crowned with twelve stars. She is heavily pregnant and about to give birth.

A red dragon appears. He has seven heads (each wearing a diadem) and ten horns. His tail sweeps down a third of the stars. The dragon aims to devour the child, but immediately after the birth, the child – a son to rule the nations with a rod of iron – is whisked off to safety with God. The woman flees to the wilderness for 1,260 days.

Michael and the angels battle the dragon. The dragon, which is revealed to be Satan, is thrown down from heaven to earth, along with 'his angels'. A voice celebrates the downfall of 'the accuser of our comrades' and the sacrifice of the martyrs.

On earth, the dragon pursues the woman. She flies to safety on the wings of an eagle. The dragon tries to drown the woman with a flood from his mouth, but the water is swallowed by the earth. Thwarted, the dragon goes off to attack the woman's children, 'those who keep the commandments of God and hold the testimony of Jesus'.

Scene change: the seashore. The dragon stands there. John sees a beast rising out of the sea. The beast is like a leopard, with feet like a bear, the mouth of a lion. It has ten horns and seven heads. On the heads are 'blasphemous names'. One head had been mortally wounded, but has healed. The dragon gives the beast his power and authority.

The whole earth worships the beast – and through it, the dragon. 'Who is like the beast,' people chant, 'and who can fight against it?' The beast is allowed to rule for forty-two months. It utters blasphemies and makes war on the saints. It is worshipped by all except those whose name is in 'the book of life of the Lamb'.

A second beast rises from the earth. This has two horns 'like a lamb', but it speaks like a dragon. This exercises all authority on behalf of the first beast and makes the inhabitants of the earth worship the first beast. The second beast causes all to have a 'mark' without which they cannot buy or sell. The mark is the name of the beast or the number of its name: 666.

Scene change: Mount Zion. John sees the Lamb standing there, along with the 144,000 who have his name and that of his Father on their foreheads. A voice from heaven sings a song which can only be understood by the 144,000. They are undefiled, chaste, blameless.

An angel flies between earth and heaven bringing an eternal gospel to all on earth, calling people to fear God and worship him because the day of judgment has come.

A second angel arrives and announces the fall of Babylon.

A third angel arrives announcing punishment for those who have worshipped the beast and received his mark.

A voice from heaven proclaims blessing and rest for those who 'from now on will die in the Lord'.

John sees a white cloud with the Son of Man sitting on it. He is holding a sickle which he uses to 'reap' the earth. He is joined by an angel from the temple in heaven. The earth is reaped, crushed like grapes in a winepress.

Seven bowls: Revelation 15.1–16.21

John sees seven angels with seven plagues. He also sees all the martyrs – those who had conquered the beast. They sing a victory song.

The 'temple of the tent' is opened, and out come seven angels with seven plagues, robed in linen with sashes. They are each given a bowl of 'the wrath of God' and instructed to empty the bowls on earth.

Bowl 1: Sores afflict those who bear the mark of the beast.

Bowl 2: The sea becomes as red as blood; every living thing dies.

Bowl 3: Rivers and springs turn to blood.

Bowl 4: The sun scorches people like fire. They curse God.

Bowl 5: The kingdom of the beast is plunged into darkness. The people curse God.

Bowl 6: The Euphrates dries up, allowing the kings of the east to cross. John sees three spirits coming from the mouth of the dragon, the beast and the second beast (now identified as 'false prophets'). These call the kings of the world to assemble for battle at a place called Harmagedon.

Bowl 7: Lightning. Thunder. Earthquake. The great city splits into three. The cities of the nations fall. Babylon receives the 'wine-cup' of the fury of God's wrath. Islands sink; mountains crumble; hundred-pound hailstones fall.

The fall of Babylon and the defeat of the beasts: Revelation 17.1–20.15

One of the seven angels carries John into the wilderness. He sees a 'great whore' sitting on the seven-headed, ten-horned beast. She is clothed in luxury, richly bejewelled and holding a cup. She is drunk with the blood of the martyrs.

The angel interprets: the seven heads are seven mountains, and also seven kings. Five of the kings have fallen, one lives and one is to come. The other beast is 'an eighth but belongs to the seven'.

The ten horns represent ten kings who are yet to come. They yield authority to the beast and make war on the Lamb. The ten horns and the beast will hate the whore and will destroy her. The woman is the great city that rules over the earth.

Another angel descends, who announces the fall of Babylon. The city is ruined, the merchants weep and wail. God calls his people out of the city. A mighty angel picks up a stone and hurls it into the sea: this is the force with which Babylon will fall.

John hears a multitude in heaven praising God for punishing Babylon. They announce the marriage of the Lamb. Once again, an angel instructs John to write. John falls to the ground in worship, but is reprimanded by the angel.

Scene change: the battle. Heaven opens, revealing a rider on a white horse. From his mouth comes a sword. He is called 'faithful and true', the word of God; he will rule nations with a rod of iron, and will tread the winepress of God's wrath.

An angel summons carrion to feast on God's enemies. The beast and the kings of the earth gather to fight the rider on the white horse and his army. The beast is captured and also the 'false prophet'. They are thrown into the lake of fire and sulphur. The others are killed by the sword from the rider's mouth.

An angel descends from heaven with the key to the bottomless pit. He seizes the dragon and binds him for 1,000 years. But after 1,000 years he will be let out for a little while.

John sees figures seated on thrones, and the souls of those who have been beheaded, who refused to worship the beast, or bear its mark. They reign with Christ for 1,000 years. (After this the rest of the dead come to life.)

At the end of the 1,000 years, Satan is released. He gathers the nations – Gog and Magog – for battle. His army surrounds the saints and the holy city. But fire comes down from heaven and destroys them. The devil is thrown into the lake of fire and sulphur.

John sees a white throne and the one who sits on it. Earth and heaven flee away; the dead stand before the throne. The books are opened and the dead are judged according to the works recorded there. Death and Hades are destroyed in the lake of fire, along with anyone whose name is not found in the book.

New heaven, new earth, New Jerusalem: Revelation 21.1–22.7

John sees a new heaven and a new earth. The holy city descends from heaven as a bride. A loud voice from the throne declares that God's home is with mortals. No more tears. No more death. No more mourning, crying or pain. 'I am making all things new.'

Scene change: a high mountain. One of the seven angels takes John to a 'great high mountain' where he sees the bride of the Lamb. The holy city, Jerusalem, descends. Its twelve gates are guarded by twelve angels; the twelve foundations are inscribed with the names of the apostles of the Lamb. The city is a cube, 1,500 miles on each side. There is no temple, because the temple is God and the Lamb. The gates are never closed. The city does not need the sun or the moon: 'the glory of God is its light, and its lamp is the Lamb'. Nations walk by this light; the kings of the earth enter the city. But nothing unclean can enter it, nor anyone who does what is shameful or deceitful.

A river flows from the throne of God through the city. Trees for the healing of the nations grow either side. God's servants worship him.

The angel tells John: 'See, I am coming soon! Blessed is the one who keeps the words of the prophecy of this book.'

Epilogue: Revelation 22.8–21

John again falls to worship the angel – once again he is rebuked. He is told not to seal up the book, because the time is near. Those who wash their robes may enter the city by the gates. But outside are the dogs – fornicators, murderers, idolaters, all who love to practise deceit.

'It is I, Jesus, who sent my angel to you with this testimony for the churches.' Come. Come. Come.

No one is to add to the words of this book.

John ends: 'Amen. Come, Lord Jesus!'

*

There. I hope that's clear.

OK. If you didn't know before, by now it's obvious that this is an unusual book. But it's not *quite* as unusual as we might think, because it belongs to a genre of writing which flourished in the two centuries before and after Christ, a genre known as apocalyptic literature.

Scholars have argued for a long time over how to define apocalyptic literature. In the end, none of the definitions of this most slippery of genres ultimately succeeds. Such writings are not exclusively about the future. Although many apocalypses contain predictions of the 'end times', they are primarily about the 'now times': the times *near* to when they were written. They explain what is to come, but also what *has* happened and what *is* happening. Apocalyptic literature is an alternative history, a political commentary written in sign language.

A good modern example of this is *Animal Farm* by George Orwell, where the events of the Russian revolution, from the abdication of the Tsar to the expelling of Trotsky to the Nazi–Soviet non-aggression pact are told in the story of a farm which is taken over by the animals.

Animal Farm gives us another pointer about apocalyptic literature. Because, in the story, every animal stands for something or somebody else. Sometimes the identification is specific: Old Major is Marx, Napoleon is a mix of Lenin and Stalin, Snowball is Trotsky. Sometimes it is more general: the sheepdogs are the secret police; Squealer represents the state-controlled media; Moses the raven, the orthodox church. In its use of animals as symbols *Animal Farm* sits squarely in the apocalyptic tradition. The names and the characters of the animals speak about the nature of what they represent. Boxer, the horse, stands for the hard-working proletariat. And he shares their qualities, as Orwell saw things: he is trusting, strong, naive, ultimately betrayed.

Political cartoons often do the same thing. Animals are used to represent countries: Russia is a bear; the USA is an eagle; France is a cockerel, Spain a bull, and so on. Britain, of course, is a lion, or Britannia, or John Bull with his bulldog. The lion not only stands for Britain, it *says something* about Britain. It is leonine. It is proud, fierce, the king of the beasts. (Not to mention too idle to do much hunting, and prone to letting the females do the work.) Symbols are not just a straightforward cipher for the word itself: they express qualities about the word.

Revelation, like all apocalyptic literature, deals in symbols. Symbols are its currency, its stock-in-trade. But here's the thing, the Very, Very Important Thing which so many writers on Revelation just don't seem to grasp: SYMBOLS ARE NOT LITERALLY REAL.

You simply cannot 'read Revelation literally'. That is obvious right from the very start of the book.

One of the things that surprised me, when I started re-reading the book, is that John is actually the third in line to receive this vision. It's actually the revelation to Jesus. The opening sentences talk about the 'revelation of Jesus Christ, which God gave him . . . he made it known by sending his angel to his servant John'. So the content of the book has been revealed to Jesus and he passes it on. Yet Jesus does not appear in person, as it were. Instead, John actually gets a visit from Jesus' *angel*. Weirdly, this 'angel' figure both is, and isn't, Jesus.

The angel talks in the first person – 'I am the first and the last,' he says at that first encounter, 'the living one. I was dead, and see, I am alive forever and ever.' That certainly sounds like Jesus – but when John falls down to worship the figure, he gets a rollicking:

'You must not do that! I am a fellow servant with you and your comrades the prophets, and with those who keep the words of this book. Worship God!' (Rev. 22.8–9). No wonder that John gets confused by how he should react to this being.

So John, in fact, never talks to Jesus as such, only to his angel, his messenger. And Jesus' angel is a striking creation: he wears a robe with a long golden sash. He holds seven stars in his right hand. His head and his hair are bright white, his eyes are like fire, and there is a sword sticking out of his mouth. You'd have thought this would make it rather difficult to speak, but the angel not only speaks clearly, his voice thunders like a waterfall.

Jesus appears in various different guises through the book of Revelation, but in none of them does he in any way resemble a Jewish builder from Galilee. The white-haired figure we read about here, with the stars and the sword in the mouth, reappears later in the book, only that time he's riding a white horse. Later we see Jesus as a lamb. A dead lamb. With seven eyes and seven horns. Who then takes a scroll from God, and opens it. So, a dead, seven-eyed, seven-horned lamb with opposable thumbs.

I hope, by now, that you are starting to see why the idea of taking Revelation literally is a bit tricky. Because, as I said, these are symbols. The white-haired, sharp-tongued bloke is not just a messenger *from* Jesus, he is a message *about* Jesus. His appearance gives us information about his nature. He is glowing white because he is pure. He has a sword sticking out of his mouth because the word of Jesus Christ is powerful. And the same is true of the other symbols. That's how they work. The Roman empire makes an appearance, as a ravening bloodthirsty beast; the followers of Jesus appear as two 'witnesses' who are killed but then get up and go to heaven; Persian warriors show up, disguised as hairy locusts; Satan appears as a dragon from Greek mythology.

We cannot and should not read Revelation literally. Instead, what we are dealing with here is a kind of poetry. Not conventional poetry. It doesn't have a metre and poetic stanza structure, it doesn't rhyme. But John uses images in a poetic way: an image can mean one thing, or several things. This book has layer upon layer of imagery, drawn from myriad different sources.

This is why Revelation is such a difficult, dangerous book. Poetry is hard to control. It is imprecise, flexible, multi-faceted. Its language is challenging, difficult. (Even the Great Gonzo himself, Hunter S. Thompson, said, 'I still read the book of Revelation when I need to get cranked up about language.') And reading it requires, well, a bit of imagination. Here's Bruce Metzger: 'The book of Revelation is unique in appealing primarily to our *imagination* – not, however, a freewheeling imagination, but a disciplined imagination.'

'*Disciplined* imagination'. That's the point. This is why the book is so often misinterpreted – either it's read by people who have had an imagination bypass, and are thus unable to read things in any other way than literally, or it's seized upon by those with imaginations that thrash around like out-of-control toddlers who have been mainlining Sunny Delight.

But that raises another question. If it's poetry, if it requires a disciplined imagination for its reader to understand it, does that mean that the text itself is a creative work?

Or, to put it more simply: if it's not meant to be taken literally, aren't we really saying that John just made all this stuff up?

John makes his case right at the beginning. He was in the Spirit on the Lord's day when he saw the angel of the Lord. He saw things and heard things. You could take that either way. But there is plenty of evidence within the text itself that it is a considered, crafted piece of work. The question is, how much was craft and how much was direct, unmediated vision?

Obviously John did not just slap his vision down onto the nearest papyrus and send it off to the local churches. But in that way this is no different to any other book of the Bible. The gospel writers did not just sit down, mutter a quick prayer and get writing. They researched, compiled, collected and arranged their material. John does the same with his vision. And he was a man whose mind was already saturated with images from the Hebrew scriptures, and images from the world around him. All these he put into the text.

But behind that craft and shaping, there is a real power, a raw, visceral, passionate, visionary mind at work. John was a man who saw things that we do not see. And he wrote them down in a way which burns them into our minds.

In other words, he was a poet.

And that's why Revelation scares so many people. Because they *will* keep reading it as prose.

*

At the airport, with time on my hands, I checked the Rapture Index. It stood at 187, just one point below the all-time record high reached earlier in the year. The Rapture Index is a website which measures just how close we are to the rapture and the second coming of Christ by analysing, so it claims, over forty different factors. These include somewhat esoteric factors like 'Gog (i.e. Russia)' and 'Beast government', and also your standard signs of the end of the world: famine, plague, drought, 'liberalism', etc. It then does some complex number-of-the-beast crunching and comes up with a figure. It is a pollen count of the end times, or as it likes to term itself, a 'prophetic speedometer of end-time activity'.

The Rapture Index is, of course, an entirely fabricated measurement. If it reflects any reality, though, it is the reality of fear.

In these days of terror and uncertainty, fear is everywhere. Terror shapes our terrain. At Gatwick Airport the man on security made me take my shoes off. I have no idea why they think that me taking my shoes off poses *less* of a risk to the general public than keeping them on. By that time I'd been in hot railway carriages for hours. The foot odour must have been like Sarin. There is terror in my feet.

Fear was certainly the dominant emotion I discerned amongst people I spoke to about Revelation. Some are scared of what Revelation describes – all those monsters and beasts and fire and brimstone. Others are more worried about the book's fans. This is a book we associate with, not to put too fine a point on it, nutters.

Revelation is unavoidably associated with mad predictions of the end of the world. The latest of these had hit the headlines not long before, when the late American radio evangelist Harold Camping predicted that the end of the world would come on 21 May 2011. When that didn't happen he recalculated and predicted that it would happen six months later, on 21 October 2011. Again, nothing happened. Then there was the whole 'Year of the Mayans' thing, when, according to a bunch of websites run by people with names like 'Eden Sky' and 'Moon River', time was going to run out for us all. The Mayans had, the argument went, prophesied the end of the world, since their calendar ended in 2012. Time had already run out for the Mayans, of course; their civilisation was wiped out in the seventeenth century by the arrival of the Spanish carrying on their bodies a deadly cargo of smallpox, influenza and measles – diseases against which the Mayans had no immunity. Tragic. And they never saw it coming.

These are just a couple of recent examples from a long line of people who have made confident predictions about the end of the world – all of whom have been completely wrong.

As I retied my shoelaces in Gatwick on that autumn morning, I realised that we cannot give in to fear over this book. Revelation is too important to be left to the nutters. Or the academics. Or the nutty academics. On the contrary, John had a message for ordinary people, in ordinary cities of his day, a message which even now crackles with passion and anger and urgency. If I was to engage with that message, then it was to those cities – or what I could find of them – that I had to go first.

ASIA

'Like so many Americans, she was trying to construct a life that made sense from things she found in gift shops.'

KURT VONNEGUT

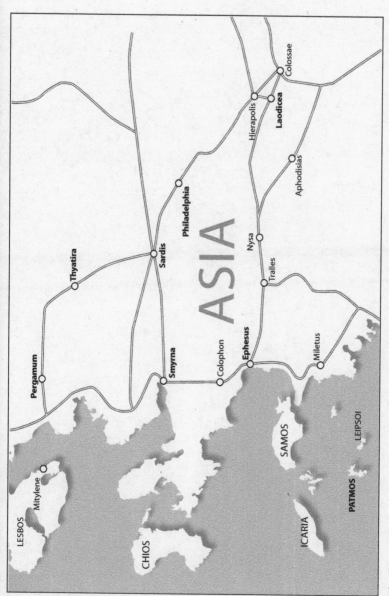

The Seven Cities of Revelation. And a few more. And some islands as well.

3 The Agora Is Right Behind the Car Park

I arrived at my hotel just as night fell. Situated on a roundabout just by Izmir's Basmane Station, my balcony was a royal box for the concert of car horns that Turks indulge in every evening. And morning. And all times in between, really. Turkish drivers sound their car horns so frequently, you begin to think it's a kind of automobile Tourette's. You rarely know what they are actually beeping the horns for. Perhaps they just want to remind the world that they still exist.

Basmane Station is an elegant building – which, frankly, makes it a bit of a rarity in modern Izmir. The station was actually built by a British company, the Smyrna–Cassaba Railway Company, which had been granted the concession to build a new railway line from Izmir (or Smyrna, to use its old name) to Turgutlu (then Cassaba) some thirty-five miles away. The architect, though, was the famous

Basmane Station. From an original design by M. Eiffel.

Frenchman, Gustave Eiffel – he of the eponymous Tower. He didn't come here, though: the station building is an off-the-peg design, if you like, an exact duplicate of Lyon Station, which Eiffel really did design, and which was built at the same time; but its architecture reminds us that Smyrna was once a cosmopolitan city, a place where Jew and Greek and Turk mixed with British, French, Americans.

I had first read about the city in H. V. Morton's *In the Steps of Saint Paul*, first published in 1936. In my battered but much-treasured copy he describes arriving at Smyrna in the 1930s, before there were such things as 'tourists' and when the whole world was still coloured sepia. Morton's impression was of 'steamship offices; of drives here, there and everywhere in a two-horse *araba* over rough cobbled roads; of cup after cup of coffee; and of a photographer who took my photograph and delivered the result in thirty minutes, thus enabling me to enrich the police records with the eight portraits demanded from departing visitors'.

My own journey from the airport on the Metro was less romantic. And, I am happy to say, a lot less tediously bureaucratic. Ancient Smyrna has been replaced by modern Izmir, and today it is one of the biggest cities in Turkey. But something has been lost. Izmir has grown enormously – mostly, one suspects, by concreting over its past.

Morton was visiting the city just a decade after the terrible night in 1922 when the city burned. For centuries Smyrna was one of the most cosmopolitan cities in Asia Minor, home to Turks, Greeks, Jews and Armenians. Its ethnically Greek population alone was twice the size of that in Athens. It was majority Christian, home to many churches in which Greeks and Armenians, Levantines and Europeans worshipped. From this place sweet, sticky figs and sultanas and apricots were shipped to the west. It was on the quayside at Smyrna that European traders first encountered coffee.

After the First World War, the victorious allies gave Smyrna to the Greeks as a colony. The Turks fought back and four years later, in the climax to the Greco–Turkish war, they recaptured the city. Four days later, a fire swept through it, destroying the Christian and Armenian quarters completely. To the Greeks it remains the *katastrophi*. Arguments still rage over how many Greeks and

Armenians lost their lives – it could be anything from 10,000 to 100,000. And in the aftermath of the war the Christian population of Asia Minor – a population which had been there for 1,900 years – fled. Families abandoned the homes and communities they had lived in since Byzantine times. Smyrna became Izmir and nineteen centuries of Christian civilisation in the heart of Asia Minor went up in smoke.

In the heady days after the First World War few people would have thought that such a disaster would be possible. Smyrna was widely known as a tolerant, cosmopolitan city. Even when the Turks entered, the presence in the harbour of no fewer than twenty-one battleships from countries such as Britain, the USA and France gave people confidence that it would be a peaceful transition.

But they were wrong. For reasons of their own, the western powers – although their foreign policies had actually precipitated this crisis – refused to intervene. In the words of Giles Milton, whose book *Paradise Lost* is a moving and powerful account of the events, these governments chose 'to abandon the refugees to their fate in order not to jeopardise the chance of striking rich deals with the newly victorious Turkish regime'.

John of Patmos could have warned them that was how the powers worked. Two thousand years before, he saw clearly the dangers of a complacent people who think that nothing bad could happen, a government which only exists to serve its own interests, and imperial powers ruled by wealth and a callous disregard for human life.

It's all there in Revelation.

*

Who was this 'John of Patmos', though? Whose footsteps was I following? The text of Revelation states his name clearly: 'I, John,' he writes, 'am the one who heard and saw these things' (Rev. 22.8). Four times in Revelation John mentions his own name.* The general assumption across history is that he was the apostle John, the son of Zebedee, the brother of James, the 'beloved disciple'.

* Revelation 1.1, 4, 9; 22.8 in case you're interested.

This idea goes back a long way. Justin Martyr, writing in Rome in the AD 160s, identified the author as John the apostle. This identification was also assumed by a man who may well have been born a few streets from where I was staying: Irenaeus of Lyons. Irenaeus came from Asia – probably from Smyrna, in fact. In his book *Against Heresy*, a sprawling catalogue of heretics, cults and theological thought-criminals that he compiled around AD 185, he says that 'John, the disciple of the Lord . . . set forth the gospel, while residing at Ephesus in Asia'. He even gives us a date, talking of 'the Church in Ephesus, founded by Paul, and having John remaining among them permanently until the times of Trajan'. Trajan reigned from AD 98 to 117; before him was Nerva (96–98) and Domitian (81–96).

But let's hop back to our friend Dionysius of Alexandria. Dionysius was a bit baffled by Revelation itself, but as a Greek-speaking man living in Egypt there was one thing that he was clear about: there was a huge difference in vocabulary and grammar between Revelation and John's gospel. He concludes that, although the author of the Apocalypse was 'holy and inspired', he was not the same writer as the one who wrote the gospel:

> *I will not gainsay the fact that [the author] was certainly called John and that this book is by one John, for I fully allow that it is the work of some holy and inspired person. But I should not readily agree that he was the apostle . . .* *

Dionysius's conclusion was echoed by Eusebius the historian, who said that the Apocalypse is 'utterly different' to the other writings: 'it has no connection, no affinity, in any way with them.' The Greek was the giveaway. The Greek of John's gospel and the epistles is good; that of Revelation is decidedly ropey. 'I will not deny that [John] had seen revelations and received knowledge and prophecy,' writes Eusebius, 'nevertheless I observe his language and his inaccurate Greek

---

* He goes on to talk of others who believed that the book was actually the work of a Gnostic teacher called Cerinthus. Dionysius does not share their view. 'For my part,' he says, 'I should not dare to reject the book, since many brethren hold it in estimation.'

usage, employing as he does barbarous idioms and in some places committing downright solecisms.'

Revelation is full of bad grammar and clumsy expressions. It is, in short, written by a man for whom Greek was very much a second language. Imagine a letter today written to a church in English but penned by an immigrant; a Pole, perhaps. It's not just that Revelation is full of weird things: it is also written in a not-quite-normal version of Greek.

The clear implication is that the writer of John's gospel – the 'beloved disciple' – and the writer of Revelation were two different people. However, they may have shared the same nationality. Because it's likely that this John – let's call him John of Patmos – was Jewish. The book is full of Aramaic expressions, Aramaic being the language spoken by Jews in Palestine. It is drenched in Old Testament allusions and imagery; over 400 such allusions, according to some writers. Revelation's John was also familiar with other Jewish apocalyptic writing, and he knows some Hebrew as well.* He may even have been a witness to the catastrophic destruction of the Temple by the Romans during the ill-fated Jewish revolt of AD 66–70. That, after all, would be enough to turn anyone apocalyptic.

Of course, he still could be *the* John. But he never describes himself as an apostle. He merely refers to himself as 'a servant' (Rev. 1.1) and 'your brother' (1.9). And no contemporary mentions the disciple John, the brother of James, being in the city. When Ignatius of Antioch writes a letter to Ephesus around AD 110, he assumes that Christians in Ephesus know about Paul, but he never says a word about John – or his Apocalypse. The same is true of Polycarp, bishop of Smyrna in the second century. He wrote to the church at Philadelphia and mentioned 'the blessed and glorified Paul' but makes no mention of the disciple John as being in the neighbourhood.

Nowadays most modern scholarship sides with Dionysius. The style and vocabulary of the Apocalypse are so different to those of the gospel, the authors must be different people.

So if it wasn't written by the author of John's gospel, then who

---

* For example, he knows the name Abaddon, and he talks of 'the place that in Hebrew is called Harmageddon'.

did write it? Well, there is a very good candidate for the position. Because there is a very early mention of just the right kind of John. Or 'Johns', to be precise. And this mention derives from somewhere very close to the region of the Apocalypse.

*

Papias was a Christian who lived in Hierapolis in the early years of the second century. His works are now lost to us, but quotes and fragments survive in the works of other writers. The historian Eusebius describes Papias as 'an ancient man, who was a hearer of John and a friend of Polycarp'. Papias took notes from those who had met the apostles. He says that if

> . . . any one who had attended on the elders came, I asked minutely after their sayings, – what Andrew or Peter said, or what was said by Philip, or by Thomas, or by James, or by John, or by Matthew, or by any other of the Lord's disciples: which things Aristion and the presbyter [elder] John, the disciples of the Lord, say. For I imagined that what was to be got from books was not so profitable to me as what came from the living and abiding voice.

The interesting thing here is that he lists two Johns: one amongst a group of the Lord's disciples, and the other whom he calls John the elder. This is interesting, as we know that the John who wrote Revelation had some kind of official status among the churches of Asia Minor – otherwise he would hardly have been in a position to send such strong messages to Ephesus and Pergamum and Smyrna and so on.

In another passage Eusebius says that Papias 'was himself an actual hearer of Aristion and John the elder. Certainly he mentions them by name frequently in his treatises and sets forth their traditions.' Eusebius's conclusion is that 'it is probable that it was the second . . . [who] saw the Revelation, which is ascribed by name to John'.

*

If this John was not the disciple, then what was his position? He is termed 'the elder', which implies some authority over the churches –

and the fact that he feels in a position to send letters to churches rebuking and encouraging them would seem to confirm that he was, at least, someone who ought to be listened to. And he was a prophet.

There are eight references to 'prophets' in Revelation.* We know from early church documents that there were itinerant prophets who would travel from congregation to congregation, bringing messages from the Lord, words of exhortation or encouragement. Paul held the role in particularly high esteem: he placed it second only to the title of apostle (1 Cor. 12.28). His letter to Corinth suggests that prophets had a special way of operating within the churches:

> *Let two or three prophets speak, and let the others weigh what is said. If a revelation is made to someone else sitting nearby, let the first person be silent. For you can all prophesy one by one, so that all may learn and all be encouraged. And the spirits of prophets are subject to the prophets, for God is a God not of disorder but of peace. (1 Cor. 14.29–33)*

Paul here uses a phrase which crops up in Revelation, too, word for word: 'the spirits of the prophets'. The Greek is πνεύματα προφητῶν (*pneumata propheton*). At the very end of the book, the angel tells John that 'I am a fellow servant with you and your comrades the prophets, and with those who keep the words of this book' (Rev. 22:9). Now, 'prophets' here could mean the historical prophets, but it more likely means the prophets of the local churches. John's 'comrades'. Put that together and you have your man. Ladies and gentlemen, I give you the author of Revelation: John the Elder. John the Elder. John the Prophet. John of Patmos.

*

So much for John. But what about the 'of Patmos' bit? One assumption which I heard time and time again about John, when I was preparing this project, was the idea that he was a prisoner on Patmos,

---

* Revelation 10.7; 11.10, 18; 16.6; 18.20, 24; 22.6, 9, if you're interested. Which I assume you are.

sent there by the Roman authorities – even by the emperor himself. John, though, never says this. The only statement about Patmos comes at the beginning of the book:

> I, John, your brother, who share with you in Jesus the persecution and the kingdom and the patient endurance, was on the island called Patmos because of the word of God and the testimony of Jesus. (Rev. 1:9)

Not untypically, it's a bit opaque. 'The word of God and the testimony of Jesus' – what does that actually mean?

The first hint of any official Roman involvement comes with Clement of Alexandria (c. 150–215) who quotes a tradition that John's stay on Patmos was ended with the death of an unnamed tyrant: 'For when, on the tyrant's death, [John] returned to Ephesus from the isle of Patmos, he went away . . . here to appoint bishops, there to set in order whole Churches, there to ordain such as were marked out by the Spirit.' However, this doesn't name said tyrant, or tell us why John had been banished in the first place (assuming he was).*

It is Tertullian who, in AD 203, makes the first explicit reference to John being exiled by the authorities. A trained lawyer, Tertullian says that John was subject to *relegatio ad insulam* – banishment to an island. However, Tertullian is not necessarily the best source here, because this bit comes in a passage where he is talking about apostles who died in the city of Rome. So, there is Peter and Paul, and then 'the Apostle John [who] was first plunged, unhurt, into boiling oil, and thence remitted to his island-exile'!

It seems to me that Tertullian has picked up on a legend, perhaps one he heard during his time in Rome, and filled in the gaps using his legal training.† But from here the story seems to snowball.

---

* Plus, the rest of the tale is an apocryphal story about John hunting down a young Christian who had become a bandit and causing him to repent.
† The deep-frying story is common in later accounts, in which the emperor Domitian has John plunged into boiling oil outside the Latin Gate in Rome. It is commemorated today by the tiny chapel of San Giovanni in Oleo –

Hippolytus, a third-century Roman writer, says that John was 'banished by Domitian the king to the isle of Patmos, in which also he wrote his Gospel and saw the apocalyptic vision; and in Trajan's time he fell asleep at Ephesus, where his remains were sought for, but could not be found'. The great Christian scholar Origen says in a passing reference that 'the emperor of the Romans – so tradition teaches – sentenced John, who testified on account of the word of truth, to the island of Patmos'.

And by the time we reach the earliest surviving Latin commentary, written by Victorinus of Pettau probably around AD 260, John is not just in exile on Patmos, but 'condemned to the labour of the mines by Caesar Domitian'. According to Victorinus, John saw his vision on Patmos, and was released on the death of Domitian: 'And John being dismissed from the mines, thus subsequently delivered the same Apocalypse which he had received from God.'

By now the story is firmly established: John was exiled by the emperor. Patmos was a prison sentence. His stay on Patmos was a kind of arrest, and Patmos was a notorious prison island, a Greek Guantanamo Bay, a Roman Robben Island.

But the problems are only too evident. First, the tradition only gets going a century after the event; second, it is getting passed around in Rome, which is some way from the action. More significantly, perhaps, there is not a shred of evidence that Patmos ever served as a penal colony. Sure, the Roman poet Juvenal claimed that the Aegean islands were 'rocks crowded with our noble exiles', but the list of exile islands in Roman records does not mention Patmos. The nearest island mentioned in the official Roman records is Samos.*

---

literally St-John-in-Oil – which stands by the Latin Gate. The event is also celebrated by a feast day on 6 May. I'm guessing everyone eats chips. The biblical scholar Jerome (c. 340–420), writing one of his fiery, outspoken tracts against an opponent, reverses this story, saying that John went first into exile on Patmos, and then was brought back to Rome where they attempted to deep fry him, only to find that he came out 'fresher and more active than when he went in'.

* The list is Amorgos, Andros, Cos, Crete, Cythnos, Delos, Donusa, Gyaros, Lesbos, Naxos, Rhodes, Samos, Seriphos. See Balsdon, 1979, p. 115. Cos, Rhodes, Lesbos and Samos were known for being 'agreeable' places to live,

Even more important than that, so important that I have to put it in capitals, is this fundamental fact:

BANISHMENT WAS A PUNISHMENT FOR POSH PEOPLE.
(I underlined it as well. So there.)

The Roman penal system was a two-tier set-up: there was one law for the rich and powerful, and another for everyone else. In sentencing, the *dignitas* or status of the criminal was always taken into account. Domitian certainly exiled his enemies. According to Eusebius, Domitian exiled his niece, Flavia Domitilla, who was 'committed by way of punishment to the island of Pontia because of her testimony for Christ'.* This certainly backs up the idea that Domitian banished people for being Christians. And it might even explain why a provincial governor felt empowered to take action against Christian leaders. But exile was a high-status punishment, an alternative to execution for people like high-born women, or those whose status or political power was such that they could not be killed.

We do know that Jews and Christians were banished from Rome *en masse* during the reign of Claudius. But mass banishment *from* somewhere is very different from individual banishment *to* a particular place. Individually, if you were from the lower classes – what Romans called the *humiliores* – you weren't banished. You were killed. Of course, you could be sentenced to hard labour – that was a useful punishment for slaves, criminals, and common or garden provincials. We know that in later times Christians were sent down the mines as punishment, but in any case there are no ancient mines or quarries on Patmos. And if John was such a prisoner, then how would he have any opportunity to be worshipping 'on the Lord's day'? You didn't get Sundays off back then anyway, let alone if you

---

for when Augustus was showing clemency.

* According to a later writer, Dion Cassius, his niece Domitilla and her husband Flavius Clemens were accused of sacrilege. The nature of this sacrilege is not named, but it is highly likely that both Clemens and Domitilla were accused of being Christians. Domitilla was exiled, and Flavius Clemens was put to death. (The cemetery of Domitilla at Rome was a Christian burial ground apparently donated by Domitilla herself.)

were doing hard labour. How would he have got his writing materials? It's unlikely that any kind of prisoner would have had the means to write a long document while he was there. At the very best John would have had to write things down on his return.*

The fact is, there is no evidence at all for Patmos being used as a place of exile, and even if it was, a nobody like John would not have qualified for such a punishment.

So – if he wasn't a prisoner, then why was he there? There is, in fact, one Roman 'sentence' which may have been applied to him. Like when Claudius banned Christians from Rome, an alternative form of *relegatio* was banishment *from* a place. This was the Roman equivalent of an exclusion order. And we know that Domitian issued these: the writer Dio Chrysostom was exiled from his homeland of Italy, but he was allowed to go anywhere else he liked. Then he was allowed back after Domitian's death.

What makes this a real possibility is that it was usually pronounced not by the emperor, but by a governor, who would declaim as follows:

'I relegate *[insert name of anti-Roman trouble-maker here]* from this province and its islands; and he must leave by *[insert date; the sooner the better]*.'

The movements of banished persons were monitored by the authorities. If they tried to re-enter forbidden territory or left their place of detention, they would be punished. Temporary relegation would become permanent. They might be put to death.

If John was exiled by the authorities, this is the most likely scenario. And the order would have had to have come from Ephesus – the seat of the local governor. So John was never a prisoner. And Patmos was never, as far as we know, a 'prison-isle'. But it's much less of a stretch to suggest that he may well have been seen as an agitator and trouble-maker and told to get out of town.

Pack your bags, son: you're on the first boat out of here.

*

* And that is if he actually could have ever returned. A later emperor, Antoninus Pius (AD 138–61), decreed that criminals might be released from hard labour after ten years if they were too old or too ill, which implies that this was not even a possibility previously.

Meanwhile, back in Smyrna, I had unpacked my own bags and was ready to explore. The area between the railway station and the port is not, perhaps, the most salubrious part of the city. Every other shop seemed to sell kebabs. (What *is* that meat? Is it from some kind of conical sheep?) Cut-price security guards sat on fold-up chairs outside closed and shuttered office blocks. I walked past dark and dingy bars in which I could see quite large women in quite small dresses. Hustlers tried to invite me in. 'English? David Beckham! Come, you have a good time!'

Down at the harbour I drank a beer and watched the waves. At the next table three lads checked their smartphones while passing round the hookah. The apple-scent of the hookah was enticing. Hawkers drifted around looking for romantic couples they could sell their red roses to. A man came by pushing a large glass case on a kind of wheelbarrow. On the side of his barrow were the words *Buzlu Badem* – iced almonds. An elderly couple bought a couple of packets and offered me some. They were cold. And almondy.

The waves lapped steadily against the concrete harbour walls. Out in the bay the lights of a large ship moved slowly through the darkness. I sat there and wondered about the lives of all these people: the waiters and the security guards and the sex workers and the club managers and the *Buzlu Badem* man and the sailors out on that ship.

What did Revelation have to say to them?

Well, in one way the book was written to people *exactly* like them. Revelation is a letter, of sorts. In the book Jesus, through John, addresses Christians at seven cities in a fairly confined geographical area in what was then the Roman province of 'Asia' – what today is western Turkey. The cities are Ephesus, Sardis, Smyrna, Philadelphia, Pergamum, Laodicea and the one I always forget. Thyatira.

That there are seven cities here is no accident. Sevens crop up a LOT in Revelation. As well as the seven cities, we will encounter seven lampstands, seven stars, a scroll with seven seals, seven bowls of plagues, seven samurai . . .* Seven is a number which, in Jewish

* Not really.

culture, symbolised perfection, wholeness, entirety. So the seven churches symbolise all the churches in the area. It is probable that these were the most significant churches among that number, but we do know of others in the region: a few miles along the valley from Laodicea was Colossae, to the church of which city the letter of Colossians was written. There was also a church at Hierapolis, one at Tralles, one at Magnesia.

The order of the messages is not random. We start at Ephesus and then progress in a semi-circle through Smyrna, Pergamum, Wossname, Sardis, Philadelphia, and end at Laodicea. This follows the direction in which a messenger would naturally progress between the cities. A boat from Patmos would most likely make land at Ephesus first. From there, it's just thirty miles north to Smyrna. And then, following this order, the average distance between each of these places is between twenty-five and fifty miles: one to three days of travelling on foot back in John's day.

These were small communities. Marginalised. When we think of the seven churches, we should not think of them in modern terms. They did not have any church buildings, they met in houses or rented rooms or workplaces. And they were few in number. In Smyrna, for example, a city of some 90,000 people, the Christian community might have numbered 50 to 100 people. It has been estimated that at the end of the first century there were only some 7,500 Christians in the entire Roman empire.

And clearly, the Christians in Smyrna were from the basement. The lower levels, as it were. John's message to them starts by acknowledging their situation: 'I know your affliction and your poverty,' he says. But then he suddenly switches everything round. Despite this, he claims that they are actually rich. Welcome to the head-spinning, upside-down world of Revelation. The letters to the seven churches show how the values of the kingdom of God are the complete opposite of the values of the world. The church of Smyrna is poor and struggling, but John says it is rich; conversely, the church at Laodicea is wealthy and established, but John says it is wretched and pitiful and poor and blind and naked.

This is one of the core messages of Revelation: the nobodies are actually the somebodies; the marginalised and ignored, the despised and outcast, are actually at the heart and soul of everything. The followers of Jesus, be they members of the elite, or the *Buzlu Badem* man, are right at the heart of the most important cosmic events.

*

All that is left of ancient Smyrna can be found just behind the multi-storey car park.

I had first visited the site with a friend seven years ago, but couldn't really take it in, mainly because I had been driving the car and he was navigating and the journey involved some incredibly narrow streets, and one particularly tight corner where the owner of a crockery shop had decided to pile a load of plates out on the narrow pavement. It was a slapstick moment waiting to happen, but fortunately the car just missed them.

This time was more relaxing. I was on foot, I had more time, and the crockery shop was nowhere to be seen. I arrived early – so early, in fact, that the man at the ticket office looked shocked that anyone should want to visit at that hour. He was sitting at a table with a friend, drinking coffee, stretched out like a cat, warming up gently in the early sunshine.

'Ticket?' he asked in surprise, putting down his cup.

'Yes please.'

'OK,' he replied, in a tone which in English would have been accompanied with a shrug and the statement, 'it's up to you . . .'

I had the place to myself.

The 'Agora Park' in Smyrna is not, I grant you, the most impressive of archaeological sites. In an open space of emerald-green grass interspersed with grey gravel, the remains of ancient Smyrna – columns, plinths, arches, capitals – have been laid out neatly, like a skeleton in an anatomy class. The corpses of buildings dissected, laid out for an autopsy. Inscribed tablets stacked together. Filed. Catalogued.

Beyond this space the modern city spreads out; on the left stands the stark, white, brutalist multi-storey car park. But despite the unpromising surroundings, it was possible to appreciate the beauty of Smyrna's location. Beyond the city, in the bright, sharp morning sun, the mountains were brown and green and the sky was a brilliant glaze of blue.

George Bean, writing in the 1960s, said: 'Smyrna is among the most pleasant places of the earth.' Recent expansion has rather changed all that – Izmir is now the third largest city in Turkey and has all the housing, smog and traffic congestion that you'd expect. But gazing out over the Agora with the mountains behind it, you could see what a fine location this must once have been.

The remains of the Agora. And the car park.

The situation of the city gave it huge natural advantages. It lies at the south-eastern end of the boot-shaped gulf of Smyrna (almost exactly the same shape as Italy, only the other way round), making it a natural port. To the landward side, the city was sheltered by the hill known as Mount Pagus, which the Turks called, with characteristic poetry, *Kadife Kale* – the velvet castle. Ancient Smyrna was beautiful, and knew it: it proudly declared on its coinage *Smurnaion proton Asias . . . kallei kai megthi* – 'Smyrna, first in Asia . . . in beauty and in size'. The city claimed to be the birthplace of Homer and a shrine in the city – the *Homereion* – contained the poet's statue. While I was there, the only picture of Homer I saw was the one out of the Simpsons.

One legend tells how the city was founded by the Amazons – not the booksellers, but female warriors. Others connect it with Tantalus, the legendary king of Phrygia. Tantalus is most famous today for his mythical punishment: in Tartarus, the lowest layer of hell, he stands in a pool of water beneath a fruit tree with low branches. When he reaches for the fruit it moves away from his grasp; when he stoops to take a drink from the water, it flows away from him. His particular torment gives us the word 'tantalising'.*

The original inhabitants of the city were Aeolian Greeks – one of the four major Greek tribes (the others were the Achaeans, Dorians and Ionians). During a war with the Dorians, the Aeolians fled across the Aegean to Asia Minor. Herodotus tells us that some Ionian refugees who had been expelled from the town of Colophon came and found refuge in Smyrna, then promptly seized the city while the inhabitants were celebrating a festival. You can see why they were kicked out of Colophon. Later, the city was refounded by Alexander the Great (it had been in ruins for three centuries). Or that's the story, at any rate. Death and rebirth, destruction and renewal feature heavily in the history of Smyrna. *Smyrna* is in fact the Greek word for myrrh, a fragrance most commonly associated with death and burial.

The Smyrnaeans were big fans of Rome. Early adopters, if you like. In 195 BC – before Rome had even reached the peak of its power – Smyrna was the first city in the world to establish a temple to the worship of Roma, goddess of Rome. In wars, they sent naval forces to help the Romans. Their admiration for Rome was so great that, at one point, when their senate heard that the army of Sulla was endangered by the severity of the winter, they stripped off their clothes and sent them off to the beleaguered army.

Their fidelity – or foresight – was rewarded and when the Romans took over the region Smyrna was granted the status of a 'free city'. Many years later they showed their loyalty to Rome in a different way when, in AD 27, they became the second city in the region to build a temple to an emperor. The magnificent building was dedicated to the emperor Tiberius.

* His name is linked with infanticide and human sacrifice. Not to mention cannibalism. A favourite of the gods, he invited them all round for a banquet. Perhaps to test their powers of perception – not to mention their sense of taste – or to honour them in a bizarre way, he served up his infant son, Pelops, who had been cut into pieces and boiled. Zeus brought the boy back to life, and Tantalus was punished for his crime. Pelops later on crossed the Aegean back to Greece, where the region of the Peloponnese is named after him.

The Smyrnaean underworld.

Wandering around these ruins, I found the solitude of that moment strangely moving. The Agora, the central square, must have been impressive once, vibrant and bustling with life. To one side, there had originally been a huge basilica – today only the basement survives. A metal stairway took me down to the lower levels, my footsteps clanging eerily in the quiet, a cat looking at me sleepily. Here, below the basilica, was a warren of tunnels and storage spaces where the slaves and the tradesmen scuttled about, fetching food and wine for the people above. The world of the elite must have been forever present to them, yet forever out of reach. Tantalising, indeed.

*

The letter to the Christians at Smyrna is short and to the point. They seem to be poor and afflicted but no, they are rich. They are being slandered by some Jews in the city. And – here John drops a bombshell – bad times are coming. Prison. Possibly even death.

The Romans viewed Jews as an ancient, if eccentric, race who nonetheless made a substantial contribution to the empire. Accordingly, Jews were well established in the cities of Asia Minor.

They served on city councils and held privileged municipal and imperial positions. They amassed wealth. They paid for public buildings. At Miletus they had a special row of reserved seats in the theatre. They did not lose their identity as Jews, but neither did they shy away from Roman life. They were a thriving and integrated part of their society.

But if Jews in the diaspora were content under Roman rule, the same could not be said for those in their homeland. In AD 66, after years of simmering unrest, the Jews in Judea rose in revolt against the Romans, ousted the Roman garrison from Jerusalem and reclaimed the city. A Roman expeditionary force which was sent to recapture Jerusalem failed to do so and was slaughtered as it retreated north. The Romans eventually sent in a much bigger army, which quickly reconquered the rest of Judea and Galilee, laid siege to Jerusalem and recaptured it in AD 70. The revolt was crushed, the Temple was destroyed and many thousands of Jewish prisoners of war were taken into slavery.

This placed the Jews dispersed around the empire in a difficult position. They do not seem to have supported the revolt – why would they, living in the heart of the empire, as they did? The rebellion in Judea must have come as a terrible and even unwelcome shock to them. As it turns out, they do not seem to have been unduly punished for the actions of those in their ancestral homeland. But it must have made these Jews spread around the empire more nervous about being associated with radical movements – especially messianic radical movements. Messianic radical movements whose 'messiah' had been executed. By the Romans. Whichever way you looked at it, it didn't look good. Perhaps some Jews, anxious to assure the Romans of their good citizenship, reported the Christians to the authorities – this seems the likeliest explanation of the 'slander' accusation.

Or maybe there were more specific issues. In two cities – Smyrna and Philadelphia – Revelation talks about conflict between the Christians and the Jews; but it does not seem to have been a big issue in the other cities. As Christianity grew, though, so the split between Jews and Christians grew wider, and in some places Christians were not welcomed in, or were even expelled from, the synagogues. The book of Acts shows tension between the two kindred communities. In Corinth it is the Jews who drag Paul before the Consul. (To be fair, 'starting arguments in synagogues' was Paul's specialist subject. He was frankly brilliant at it.) In Rome the conflict between the two sides was such that at one point the emperor Claudius expelled all the Jewish Christians. So perhaps the issue was more over doctrine than politics.

Whatever the cause, John describes these Jews pretty harshly, as 'those who say that they are Jews and are not, but are a synagogue of Satan'. Whatever John's attitude springs from, though, it is not anti-Semitism. To accuse John – who was a Jew, we should remember – of anti-Semitism, in the way we understand it, is completely anachronistic. In the first century it was not at all unusual for deep and bitter hatred and conflict to break out among and between different Jewish groups. The Dead Sea community, for example, use the same kind of rhetoric in their writing: a hymn found among the Dead Sea Scrolls, written by a Jew, labels the rest of Israel the 'congregation of Belial', which is just another way of saying 'synagogue of Satan'.

So, the conflict with the Jews is causing problems. That's business as usual. But then John drops a big, big surprise. 'You are about to suffer,' he says. 'And some of you will be thrown into prison.' And he tells the poor-but-rich Smyrnaean Christians that they must be prepared to suffer to the point of death.

Let's be clear. Revelation was not written to Christians who were being persecuted and killed. For years, the assumption has been that it was indeed written to such Christians. In fact, there's no evidence for widespread persecution in Asia Minor at the time that the letters were written. And there's not much evidence of persecution in the text itself. Certainly, during the time of Nero, Christians had been brutally persecuted in Rome, made scapegoats for the fire that destroyed so much of the city. But there is no evidence that this persecution was taken up anywhere else in the empire.

This is something we need to get into our heads about this book. From John's perspective, the big problem with most of the seven churches is not that they are being attacked by Rome, but that they are colluding with it. In Laodicea and Sardis and Ephesus, things are going fine. They are perfectly at home in the Roman empire.

John says all this is going to change. Revelation is a great big slap in the face of complacency. In Smyrna, John says, they will be thrown into jail. 'Do not fear what you are about to suffer,' says Jesus through John. 'Be faithful until death, and I will give you the crown of life' (Rev. 2.10). The word used for 'crown' here is *stephanos*, which means the crown of victors (as opposed to *diadema*, which means a royal crown). This is the crown which was placed on the heads of those who won races at the games. This kind of crown was a common symbol in Smyrna: crowns appear on every known pre-imperial coin from the city – sometimes three times on the same coin. And the priestly magistrates of the city were known as the *stephanephoroi* – 'crown wearers'. Once again, John is reversing the normal way of seeing things. The powerful, the winners, the elite will not get to wear the crowns: instead, those whom Roman society considers losers will wear them. No, says John, forget that lot up in the basilica, dishing out the honours and trusting in Rome to keep them safe and wealthy. They will lose everything. But you – you will win the race.

Revelation, then, does not take place against a background of violent persecution, but against one of insidious assimilation. John's churches are suffering not from violent trauma, but from sleeping sickness. In that sense, this letter is not comforting, but deeply discomforting. Revelation is not written to console those going through trouble: it is written to make trouble.

John is a trouble-maker. He wants to stir things up, to shake the boat. He wants these people to stand up for what they believe.

Some Christians, at least, heeded his call. There was a stadium in Smyrna once. Its remains were visible, apparently, in the nineteenth century, but it has disappeared now, its stones plundered to build houses. In AD 156 Polycarp, the aged bishop of Smyrna – who, according to Tertullian and Irenaeus, had been appointed by John himself – was dragged into this arena and executed. He was offered the chance to save himself. All he had to do was perform the required sacrifice to the emperor and his life would be saved. He refused. On 22 February he was burned at the stake. As he was dragged to his death, the crowd shouted out their accusation: 'This is the teacher of Asia, the father of the Christians, and the overthrower of our gods, he who has been teaching many not to sacrifice or to worship the gods.' The ancient account of his death describes how he 'was now crowned with the crown of immortality and had won a prize that no one could challenge'.

*

When I rose, early the next morning, Izmir had an ethereal, ghostly quality. The sunlight was almost white. There was a pale mist on the hills. The buildings looked like they were made of porcelain: everything seemed delicate and fragile.

I breakfasted on the Turkish version of eggy bread, some terrible coffee and saffron-coloured cakes with raisins and the scent of sesame. By the time I made it down to the street, the car horns and the diesel fumes had chased any delicacy far away. The crowded bus wound through impossibly narrow, labyrinthine streets before arriving at the *otogar* – the bus station – at the edge of town.

I was going to explore just why Polycarp was killed. Why John predicted that trouble was bound to come.

I was going on a day trip to Satan's throne.

4 And the Winner Is . . . Pergamum!

The bus headed north from Izmir, through a wide plain between the mountains and the sea. At Menemen the bus stopped briefly and the young conductor leapt off, returning with cakes for everyone. Buses in Turkey are a pretty civilised way to get around. For the princely sum of 12 TL (about £4) you not only get taken to Bergama, but you are also provided with free hand freshener, glasses of water, orange juice, tea or coffee and cake, not to mention a rather jolly Turkish romcom on the TV in which a fat man lost his trousers regularly but somehow still ended up with the pretty girl.

It was a modern way to follow an ancient route. The route we were travelling – along the E87 – is pretty much the same as that followed by travellers in John's day. The same can't be said for the coastline, which has silted up over the centuries. In John's day the gulf was wider, and the coastline therefore ran further to the north. In fact the town of Menemen, now about fifteen miles from the sea, was shown as being on the coast in a map from as recently as 1717. But those who carried John's message to the churches would have travelled this route. It can still be traced in ancient itineraries.

Some 1,800 years before me, for example, a man called Aelius Aristides (AD 117–81) made the same journey. His career as a Greek orator had been interrupted by ill health and he was travelling to Pergamum to seek a cure. The journey from his residence in Smyrna took him north on the road beside the sea which led to where Menemen is now. The description of the journey lists the towns where he stayed: Larisa (where the inn rooms were 'intolerably disgusting'), Cyme, Myrina, Gryneum (where he made a sacrifice to Apollo at the temple which, according to Pausanias, stood in 'a beautiful grove of fruit trees and other wild trees'),

Elaea and then to Pergamum. This is the ancient equivalent of the E87. Gryneum is south of Yenişakran; Cyme is on the Nemrut Limani – the Bay of Nimrod – just to the north of the town of Aliaga; Elaea – which was famous for its thyme-scented honey – lies on the coast. At one point the minibus turned off down a rough track to deliver a load of students to a kind of small, rather forlorn-looking resort. I looked out for any ruins, but there were just some scattered olive groves. Then again, Elaea does mean 'olive'.

North of Menemen we rejoined the coast briefly, the sea spreading out to the west, lined by a number of windswept and rather unappealing beaches. Then the bus ducked back inland until we arrived in the cramped centre of Bergama, ten miles inland from the Aegean coast, the town that now sits under the ancient granite citadel-hill of Pergamum.

*

The ancient cities of Asia were connected by a network of roads which made travel, trade and communication easy. The Romans specialised in road-building, because roads enabled them to do more of the two things they were really good at: trade, and war. One of the most important things to remember about Revelation (and, indeed, the whole of the New Testament) is that it was written by and to people living under occupation. John was working, worshipping and writing in Asia, a region which had been conquered by the Roman empire.

Well, I say 'conquered'. Actually, the area had not so much been conquered as donated. Or bequeathed.

In the fourth century BC, Pergamum was the greatest city of the region, and home to the regional ruler, King Attalus I of Pergamum. He adopted the rather biblical-sounding title of 'King and Saviour' and for a bit he was the most powerful monarch in the east. Then the Romans came along. They were a new power, on the rise. Attalus could see which way the wind was blowing, and he became their enthusiastic ally and supporter. His heirs continued this approach, so much so that when his grandson, Attalus III, died in 133 BC, after a short reign of only five years, it was discovered with some surprise that he had left the entire kingdom to Rome. And so it was that Asia Minor became part of the Roman empire without ever putting up a fight.*

Pergamum, then, was the Romans' first foothold in Asia Minor. And the Pergamenes were wholehearted in their enthusiasm for all things Roman. In fact the citizens of Asia Minor generally became some of the most devoted fans the Roman empire ever had. Cities competed for honours from the Roman administration. They particularly coveted the rights to house the provincial assembly – an assembly of over 100 delegates from the region, which decided local policy and then asked the Romans for permission to put it into practice. The assembly met at Pergamum at first, but moved to Smyrna sixty years later. And then it went to Ephesus, Sardis, and Laodicea. It was a matter of prestige. (Not unlike today when the European Parliament is in Brussels, but once a month moves, at enormous expense, to meet in Strasbourg.)

However, this region went way beyond mere admiration of the Romans. They went in for full-on adoration. They literally worshipped their rulers.

In 29 BC, the emperor Augustus permitted the erection of two temples at key places in Asia. One was in Nicomedia, in the northwest of Turkey. And the other was in Pergamum. And what was significant about these temples was that they were the first temples to worship Augustus himself as a god.

This was the beginning of Rome's greatest PR triumph: the cult of emperor worship. The temple in Pergamum is lost now – its exact location unknown. But it appears on many coins from the city, and its influence was clearly immense. The imperial cult spread from there throughout the region and for fifty years Pergamum basked in the glory of being the centre of emperor worship in the region. The emperors themselves were initially slightly reluctant to be worshipped as gods, but they were canny enough to realise that it could be made

---

* Not officially, anyway. There was a resistance, led by an illegitimate nephew of Attalus III, but in 130 BC this was quelled by the Romans, who were keen to take control of their unexpected legacy. Then there was another bout of resistance between 88 and 86 BC, but this too was crushed by Rome.

into a test of political loyalty. And it became an institution which dominated life in Asia Minor.

Having said that, a city could not just decide to bung up an imperial temple: permission to build one had to be granted by the emperor himself. The Roman imperial machinery decided which cities should have the honour of worshipping at its shrine. Just as with their original occupation, Rome hadn't imposed emperor worship here: the locals had begged for the privilege. These people loved the emperor – adored him – and they took every opportunity to tell him so.

Perhaps the best – or worst – example of this came in 9 BC, when the assembly promised a golden crown to the person who could devise the best way to honour the emperor. The winner was Paulus Fabius Maximus – who, by sheer coincidence, just happened to be the proconsul, the man sent from Rome to take charge of Asia. His winning idea was that the province should reorganise the entire calendar around the emperor's birthday. The edict containing his proposal is buttock-clenchingly over the top:

> He [Augustus] gave a new appearance to the whole world, which would gladly have accepted its own destruction had not Caesar been born for the common good fortune of all. Thus a person could justly consider this to be the beginning of life and existence . . .

The council thought this idea was terrific and issued a decree which thanked providence for

> sending to us and to those after us a saviour who put an end to war and brought order to all things . . . the birth of the god was the beginning of good tidings [Greek: euangellion] to the world through him.

And so the Asian calendar was duly changed. New Year, previously celebrated at the autumnal equinox, now began on Augustus's birthday, 23 September. (Not forgetting the institution of mini-celebrations of his birthday every month.) Some of the names of the months were also changed, acquiring imperial names such as 'Kaiseros' or 'Tiberios'.

Pergamum was the first city to have a temple to the emperor. But others muscled in on the imperial cult. Augustus granted Ephesus the right to dedicate a sacred precinct to Rome and Caesar. Of the seven cities directly addressed in Revelation, all but Thyatira eventually had imperial temples. Having a temple became a badge of honour. Cities personified themselves as *neokoros* – wardens of provincial imperial temples.

Having a temple was an all-round Good Thing: it brought visitors to your city, to attend festivals and Very Important Meetings. The visitors included not just official dignitaries, governors and the like, but also tinkers, salesmen, artisans and prostitutes. Tax breaks were given to craftsmen selling their goods during the holidays. The sanctuaries would be decorated with flowers, and animals would be sacrificed at altars throughout the city – at the gymnasium, the council house, temples of other deities, theatres, in the main square. Processions toured the city carrying pictures and symbols of the emperor. The whole thing became a city-wide celebration. Pergamum had an imperial cult choir which sang specially composed hymns for the occasion. Incense was burnt. Animals were slaughtered. It was a happy time for everyone. Except the animals.

The divinity of the emperors was celebrated on coins and in temples, in inscriptions, in ceremonies and banquets, at the games, the theatre, the festivals. The imperial cult became the way in which ordinary people encountered the emperor. No one saw him in real life. No emperor visited Asia Minor through the whole of the first century. People just saw him in idealised statues or on coins. Yet to live and breathe in Asia Minor was to be part of this idea-system. And emperor worship was more than 'a nice idea to show your support of Rome'. It became a test of loyalty. Inevitably, if you wanted to be part of society, if you wanted to show that you were a fine upstanding citizen, you had to demonstrate your loyalty to the emperor.

They were not worshipping the emperor in an ironic fashion, or with a wink and a nod, just because it was good for business. For the ancient people of this region – a region which had once been very powerful – emperor worship gave them a way of coming to terms with new and unpleasant realities, particularly the recognition of their own relative powerlessness. They were under new rule. Far easier to be reconciled to this new rule if your rulers were super-human. Because they had never fought against Rome, it was easier for them to assume that you *could not* fight against Rome. What would be the point? The emperors were gods.

What is striking about this – what is striking about virtually all of the ways in which Augustus and his successors were described – is that it is exactly the kind of language which the new Christians used to describe Christ. Augustus was the saviour, the bringer of peace, the lord; his birth was the start of the *euangellion*, the good news. Christians talked of their saviour – a Jewish peasant from Palestine who was executed as a criminal – in exactly the same way. And the book of Revelation spends a huge amount of time mocking, insulting and generally subverting the pretensions of empire.

For example, Revelation chapter 4 begins a section set in heaven, where John sees the throne room of God. It is full of references to Old Testament prophets like Ezekiel, with its weird visions of strange creatures whirring around the throne. But John's description is also a parody of imperial court ceremonial. One of the main tasks of the emperor and his local representatives was to dispense justice, to read written petitions, hear cases and receive emissaries from the cities of the empire. In the provinces this was delegated to the procon-suls and the governors, assisted by their friends and advisors and other public servants. Rulers of various ranks were surrounded by lictors who carried the fasces, the rods with which criminals were beaten. These lictors acted as bodyguards and announced the approach of the magistrates. How many lictors you got depended on your rank: consuls were permitted twelve. Domitian surrounded himself with twenty-four.

All this kind of thing feeds into the depiction of God in Revelation, where he sits on a throne in a cosmic throne room, surrounded by twenty-four elders on thrones, a number of strange living creatures, hosts of angels, etc. He hears the cries for justice from the citizens of his kingdom. He dispenses justice, punishes breaches of the law and rewards his faithful servants.

'Around the throne,' writes John, 'is a rainbow that looks like an emerald.' It's slightly difficult to see how a rainbow can be coloured green, but we won't worry about that; what's interesting is that the rainbow image can be seen to come from two very different sources. A rainbow is a sign of God's covenant, as expressed to Noah in Genesis. But also, coins of the day – issued in Ephesus – show the imperial throne with a rainbow behind it.

And all the time the elders chant, 'You are worthy, our Lord and God, to receive glory and honour and power.' They wear crowns, which they cast before God. We know that priests of the imperial cult in Antioch in Pisidia wore golden crowns bearing the picture of Caesar.* So here we have the *real* priesthood wearing *real* crowns – a depiction not only of where the real power lies and who is truly worthy of honour, but also a deliberate mockery of the theatrical shows of emperors on earth.

*

This is the big issue which drives Revelation. The imperial cult claimed that the emperor was divine and must be worshipped. John knew that that was a lie. He knew that there was only one real throne room, only one divine being. And he knew that in Asia, the home-land of emperor worship, the Christians were going to pay the price for refusing to bow down.

Over subsequent decades the pressure on Christians to engage in emperor worship was to become ever more intense. Tertullian, writing in the second century, scornfully rejected the practice. Christians, he wrote, 'as men believing in true religion prefer to celebrate the Emperor's birthday with a good conscience instead of riotous behav-iour'. And he mocked the 'feasting from street to street, to turn the city into one great tavern, to make mud with wine, to rush about in groups to acts of violence, to deeds of shamelessness, to the incitements of lust'. Meanwhile, the *Acta Sanctorum*, an account

---

* In the second-century work of Christian romantic fiction known as *The Acts of Paul and Thecla*, the heroine, at one point, tears the crown from the head of Alexander, imperial priest of Pisidian Antioch. To be fair, he was assaulting her at the time.

of martyrs, has a dialogue between Phocas and Africanus, allegedly an early second-century governor of Pontus:

> Africanus the governor said, 'Is this the Phocas who denies the existence of the gods and that the emperor Trajan is a god? Come now, has not every bellicose race been destroyed by his hands? Who then can he be but god?' But Phocas remained silent . . .
>
> Africanus said, 'Are then the emperors not gods?' Phocas said, 'Is it not enough for Trajan to be called King, without you also giving him that incomparable name?'

'Is it not enough?' Nope. Not for imperial Rome.

Those who worship the beast chant the same kind of slogans used of the emperors: 'Who is like the beast, and who can fight against it?' The inevitable victory of Rome was one of the empire's favourite themes. The myths of empire had to be powerful in order to drown out rumours that there might be an alternative. The Roman empire broadcast its myths through its coins, inscriptions and statues. Their coins – the nearest thing the Roman world had to mass media – feature images of military victories or promote what you might call the advertising slogans of the empire: 'Imperial Security'; 'Eternal Harmony'; 'Glory of the empire'. The portrayal of the goddess victory on coins is particularly frequent; she has a right foot on the globe and carries a shield inscribed with the name of the victory which has just been won.

John has new information. He knows that there is a different way. So he takes those images and inverts them. Through the lens of Revelation, Rome the city becomes cruel, oppressive Babylon; the goddess Roma becomes a bloodthirsty, blinged-up call girl; the Roman empire is the beast from the sea, working on behalf of Satan; the imperial cult and the apparatus of regional government, meanwhile, are the second beast, the beast from the land, who 'exercises all the authority of the first beast on its behalf, and makes the earth and its inhabitants worship the first beast'.

In Revelation, the picture of Rome and the empire is unremittingly negative. For John the empire is a land of vice and depravity, a land

61

of murder and illusion and idolatry. The big issue behind Revelation is the question, 'How can you obey Christ and the Roman empire?' John's answer is clear: you can't.

And it is this which really drives the book. Revelation is not, first and foremost, a prophecy about end times: it is an act of resistance and a summons to civil disobedience. Not violent resistance, though. John counsels patience and endurance. He and his contemporaries had seen what violent resistance had led to in Judea and Galilee: whole towns slaughtered, families enslaved, thousands of people crucified by the Roman forces. In Revelation it is God, not man, who brings about the fall of Babylon, and it is the word of Jesus which will defeat the armies of evil.

*

Emperor worship might seem a hard thing for us to understand today, although it persists in many places around the world. In the strange, warped regime of North Korea the 'dear leaders' of the Kim family are worshipped, and every house has a shrine – a picture of the dear leader on the wall. It was only relatively recently – and after the Revelation-style nuclear bombs of the Second World War – that the Japanese emperor renounced his claims to divinity, but he is still worshipped by some today. Tyrants have always claimed a kind of divinity: the worse their behaviour, the more godlike they claim to be.

Closer to home, do we not bid in exactly the same way to build the temples of our gods? While I was in Turkey, the host city for the 2020 Summer Olympics was announced. Istanbul lost. Tokyo won. Cities throughout the world crave permission to host these events. As I write this, there are riots and protests in Brazil, where the world cup is costing the country nearly $11 billion. So far six workers have lost their lives in building the stadia. The country has a crumbling infrastructure, inadequate sanitation and nowhere near enough schools. All hail FIFA!

Governments routinely offer tax breaks and incentives to multi-national companies to lure them to their cities. We are constantly told that if we dare to make demands of the gods of international banking, then they will take their temples to money elsewhere. The

City of London will no longer be *neokoros*. It happens all over the world. According to the charity Action Aid, developing-world countries give out over $2 billion every week in the form of tax incentives, supposedly to encourage the big global companies to invest. In 2011, the Rwandan government showed that tax incentives cost it over US$234 million – that's a quarter of its potential tax revenue.

The gods may have changed, but the lies remain the same. Worship is a political act. Who or what we worship reflects our values and our deepest beliefs. Revelation urges Christians in the heartlands of the imperial cult to reject the lies and the false worship. The reality is that they are not poor, but rich; they are not weak, but strong; they are not lower-class plebs, but victors with crowns. But they must keep the faith.

5 The Postman of the Apocalypse

The best thing that happened to me at Pergamum was that I got a lift from the postman.

'Acropolis?' said the conductor, when we pulled into the Bergama *otogar*. He gestured up the street. 'One kilometre.'

Yes, one kilometre. The trouble was, it was one kilometre vertically.

The only way was up, to coin a phrase. *Acropolis* is Greek for 'Why the hell did we build it up here?' Actually, it's not. It means 'summit city', from the Greek words *akron* ('summit') and *polis* ('city'). But having walked it, I prefer my meaning.

The letter to Pergamum contains the only mention of a named martyr in Revelation: 'I know where you are living, where Satan's throne is,' it begins. 'Yet you are holding fast to my name, and you did not deny your faith in me even in the days of Antipas my witness, my faithful one, who was killed among you, where Satan lives.'

We don't know the circumstances of Antipas's death. The event had clearly been a cause of massive trauma for the church. Was he a test case? Was it an isolated incident of mob violence? An attack in the night? Or a quasi-judicial killing? The word John uses to describe Antipas is *martus*, which literally translates as 'witness', but is the word from which we get the word 'martyr'.

So – the Christians in the city are standing firm. But there is a problem. John, reusing an Old Testament image, accuses them of holding to 'the teaching of Balaam, who taught Balak to put a stumbling block before the people of Israel, so that they would eat food sacrificed to idols and practise fornication. So you also have some who hold to the teaching of the Nicolaitans. Repent then. If not, I will come to you soon and make war against them with the sword of my mouth' (Rev. 2.14–17).

We know nothing about the Nicolaitans. Presumably they were a sect led by a man called Nicolaus. That anyone with such a fabulous name could be a heretic baffles me, but there you go. They also turn up in the message to Ephesus, although the Ephesians are praised because they 'hate the works of the Nicolaitans'.

What had the Nicolaitans done to earn such disapproval? The hot issue in Pergamum – and probably the issue over which the Nicolaitans and John were in dispute – was how far Christians could go in paying homage to the other gods. Balaam was a Moabite prophet in the Old Testament who lured Israel into worshipping idols. And for a Christian living in first-century Asia Minor, idols were *everywhere*.

As I emerged from the cramped, curious back streets of Pergamum's old town, I reached a gap in the buildings where I could see across to the strange, brutalist building that is known as the Red Hall. It is the remains of a huge temple dedicated to the god Serapis. From a distance, it rather reminded me of Battersea Power Station.

The Red Hall was built after John's day, during the boom years of the ancient city, under the emperors Trajan and Hadrian, a time when the population of the city was perhaps as high as 150,000. It gets its name from the red brickwork of the building, but to the inhabitants of the time it would have been more of a White Hall: originally it was faced with white marble, some fragments of which still cling on to the upper parts. On each side it is flanked by two circular tower-temples and together the whole thing formed a worship complex dedicated to Egyptian gods. It's not known for sure which gods got the tower-temples: it could have been Isis, Osiris, Horus, Anubis. But the main building was probably the temple of Serapis.

Serapis, by the way, was an entirely manufactured god. He was devised by Ptolemy I of Egypt – who ruled after the death of Alexander the Great – as a way of unifying the Greeks and Egyptians in his country. Opinions on Serapis's origins vary, but they seem to have taken the Egyptian bull-god Apes and given him a makeover to make him look more like a male, Greek god. He went on to achieve great popularity elsewhere: there were temples to Serapis in many major cities throughout the Roman empire. He was a god created by a marketing agency.

Inside the Red Hall was a huge podium, on which stood a statue estimated to have been over thirty feet tall. The base of the statue is still there, and it contains a hole – a secret trapdoor which led to a tunnel system connected with the towers. The implication is that the statue was hollow, and priests could climb up into it from below and deliver messages to the people – straight from the god's mouth. In the fifth century the statue went silent. The Red Hall was converted into a church, dedicated – of course – to John the Apostle. Nowadays one of the temple-towers serves as the minaret of a mosque.

The Red Hall, in all its redness. It was originally faced in white marble, traces of which can still be seen on the upper pillars.

The temple to Serapis, for example, was only one of many in Pergamum: there were temples to Athena, Zeus, Hera, Dionysus,

Demeter, and a major healing centre dedicated to the medicine-god Asclepius. The gods dominated the lives of the people. And as the creation of Serapis demonstrates, the gods formed a kind of glue to hold society together. Virtually all engagement in civic life involved the gods. Education was based around the stories of the gods. A show at the theatre would begin with a sacrifice to Dionysus at an altar in front of the stage. Athletic contests, horse races and the games in the arena were dedicated to various deities and all public meetings began by invoking the relevant god.

The gods affected every level of society. Slaves, of course, had no option but to be involved in the religion of the household; Christian wives would have to follow their husband, if he were not a Christian, in honouring the family gods and ancestors. For craft-workers, their livelihoods might depend on being involved in the trade associations, where worshipping the appropriate god was the unquestioned norm.

Walk the streets and you'd see the gods. Festivals honoured the local deities. Statues of Artemis, Athena or Dionysus would be paraded through the town. Animals would trudge behind, adorned with ribbons and garlands, eyes wide in fear at the noise of the crowds and, perhaps, some sense of what awaited them at the end of the journey. The parade wound its way through the town to the relevant temple or place of sacrifice, where the animals would be killed. Sacrificing to the gods was ubiquitous. Altars were everywhere. Some were enormous, like the Altar of Zeus in Pergamum, but most were simple affairs, little more than blocks of stone which served to mark the place where the sacrifice should happen. The animal was killed near the spot and some of the blood – and there was a *lot* of blood – was poured onto the stone.

The animals would have their throats cut and their blood drained. Then they would be butchered. The gods got the inedible bits: head, spinal column, tail – these were burned. The rest was barbecued for priests or worshippers, or sold to the meat markets, while the hides of the animals were sold to tanners. The gods got a nice smell, the traders got meat to sell, you and I got some lunch. Everyone won. But to Christians it meant that even ordinary food might be tainted by association.

The sacrifice was not always meat. Poseidon liked tuna, appropriately enough for the god of the sea. And the sacrifice was not always edible: in Sparta the correct sacrifice to Ares was puppies. Libations of wine were also common, poured out onto the altar from a *phiale*, a bowl of oriental lotus-petal design. This is the image behind the seven 'bowls' which are poured out in Revelation 15.*

Along with these big public occasions, there was also a vast array of private dining clubs and associations in which it was advantageous for a citizen to be involved. These meals might celebrate historic occasions, such as military victories. They might be banquets of various guilds or trade associations. They might be religious festivals. They might even be small, private parties held in a temple setting. You could hire the temple, much like hiring McDonald's for your child's party, or taking over a restaurant for a twenty-first. But at each meal the food would be dedicated to the gods first.

Sometimes the invite even came from the god himself. A fragment of papyrus from Egypt runs: 'The god calls you to a banquet being held in the Thoereion [i.e. the temple of Artemis Thoeris] tomorrow from the ninth hour.' Actually, the god doing the inviting here is our friend Serapis; he's just holding his party at Artemis's house. It's symbolic of the syncretistic nature of Roman religion. Every god was welcome.

---

* It may be that, typically, Revelation deliberately and provocatively parodies pagan ritual. For example, there was a ceremony called the Taurobolium of Cybele, which involved cutting the throat of a bull on a raised platform and allowing the blood to gush down all over a linen-clad priest standing underneath. It was some kind of identification ritual: through immersion in the blood of the bull, it was as if the priest himself had somehow been sacrificed to the gods and so was purified and consecrated. The centre of this cult was in Rome in the Temple of Cybele on the Vatican Hill, where St Peter's Basilica now stands. Cybele was a popular goddess in Asia Minor and we know that the Taurobolium was performed in the region, although the first recorded instance dates from AD 105, ten years after Revelation was written. But it's likely something similar had been performed in earlier times, and this certainly would help make sense of images like that in Revelation 7, where the martyrs have somehow washed their robes and made them white in the blood of the Lamb.

The issue of eating meat sacrificed in the temples was a hot potato for Christians. (Not literally, obviously.) Several decades before, delegations of apostles at Jerusalem had discussed the issue of how far, exactly, Gentile followers of Jesus were to adopt Jewish ritual and practice. The conclusion of the meeting was clear:

> *it has seemed good to the Holy Spirit and to us to impose on you no further burden than these essentials: that you abstain from what has been sacrificed to idols and from blood and from what is strangled and from fornication. If you keep yourselves from these, you will do well. (Acts 15.28–29)*

But a few years after that, Paul was less hardline. He was prepared to allow those who knew that 'no idol in the world really exists' to eat meat sacrificed to idols – but they should abstain if it was going to cause a problem to other, less confident Christians (1 Cor. 8.4–13).

There was a cultural and social expectation that if a friend, a patron or the god himself sent you an invite, you should put on your best toga and attend. This presented a real dilemma for Christians. Should they remain 'pure' and take a stand, thus heightening the tension between themselves and their community? Or should they maintain social and business connections, even at the risk of being involved with idolatry?

Paul understood the difficulties. Other writers were more hardline, calling on Christians to turn their backs on the social norms, causing misunderstanding and even hostility. As 1 Peter says, 'They are surprised that you no longer join them in the same excesses of dissipation, and so they blaspheme' (1 Pet. 4.4).

John, training his eye to the east from his rocky perch on Patmos, is uncompromising. Writing about this issue to the church in Thyatira, he even seems to quote the Jerusalem declaration: 'I do not lay on you any other burden . . .' he writes. There seem to have been some elements in the churches who wanted to do away with this burden altogether. John gives them Old Testament code names – Balaam in Pergamum, Jezebel in Thyatira – but they represent that part of the Christian community who have made an unacceptable 'arrangement' with the civic religious powers, with the gods and their representatives. John refers to such behaviour as 'fornication': he's using the Old Testament image of idolatry being adulterous behaviour towards God. Adultery. Fornication. It's sin. There is no compromise.

*

I emerged from the old town and onto the main road. Above me, rising steadily, was the steep rubble-strewn slope up to the ancient acropolis of Pergamum. Where the official entrance was, I wasn't sure. There was a gate at the bottom. It was shut, but there was a hole in the fence right by it. I could easily nip through there . . . But then I remembered I was English. It was my duty to do the right thing and join a proper queue if I could find one. I mean, I was young(-ish), fit(-ish) and had time on my hands. It couldn't be that long a walk.

> *There will now be a Public Service Announcement:*
> (1) *It is a very long, hard walk along the main road to the entrance.*
> (2) *There's a cable car to the top, which I had somehow managed to miss.*

After what seemed an eternity, the road still seemed no nearer ending. Each bend around the mountain brought not an entrance, just more road. After a while the certainty that I was going the right way was replaced by the certainty that I would soon have an aneurism.

And then a white van pulled up. The driver leaned across.

'Acropolis?' he said.

'Yes,' I gasped.

'I take you.'

A small man in a light-blue uniform. No, an *angel*.

I hopped in and we set off. He introduced himself.

'I am postman of the acropolis.'

There could hardly have been a more appropriate way for me to arrive at the site. Somewhere around AD 92 an envoy had trudged along the road north from Smyrna, following the line of the coast, with an important letter. One of John's fellow prophets, perhaps. And I, too, was now arriving with the post.

The road twisted and turned, revealing vistas of astonishing grandeur.

'Very beautiful,' I said, looking down.

'Yes,' he replied, softly. 'Very beautiful.'

I thanked him heartily at the top.

'You know this man?' said another standing near as I climbed out of the van. He was smartly dressed, slick black hair, neat blue shirt.

'No,' I said. 'But he came to my rescue.'

'Ah. Very good. Very good. I do the same.' And he proceeded to tell me the best way down from the acropolis, on foot. 'There is gate at the bottom,' he said. 'Very stupid – sometimes they close it. But you can leave there. Even if it locked, you can go through the fence.' He laughed. 'Next time is easier to enter there, no?'

I smiled, wanly. He told me the name of a carpet shop that he recommended. If it wasn't a flying carpet, frankly I wasn't interested.

*

The old gods dominated the civic, cultural and religious life of Asia Minor. And they dominated physically. You could not walk anywhere in the ancient world without encountering the gods. Their statues would be raised on high, their temples built on elevated platforms which dominated the cityscape. The high points of any city were reserved for the most special buildings and the richest people. In Jerusalem the Temple was built at the highest point in the city. In Rome, the Capitoline Hill, the highest of its seven hills, was the religious and political centre of the city.

I have been to these places. But of all the ancient high places I have visited, I haven't been anywhere where the high point is as high as Pergamum. Pergamum is astonishing. Towering some 1,300 feet above the plain of the River Caicus, the acropolis dominates the land for miles around. Flights of shallow wooden steps move you from one amazing vista to another. Turn one corner and a kingfisher-blue lake appears beneath, like an uncut jewel embedded in the landscape. Turn the other way and the caramel-coloured plain stretches out for miles and miles.

The theatre on the Pergamum Acropolis. At least there was a good view if the play was boring.

The citadel itself was built on a series of artificially constructed terraces. At the top is the temple of Athena and the famous library of Pergamum. Athena was the goddess of learning, so having the library nearby was an obvious choice. The rulers of Pergamum at the time were keen on books. So keen that they acquired a reputation for collecting them in a rather aggressive manner. When the custodians of the famous library of Aristotle in Scepsis heard that the king's representatives were coming, they hid the library underground (where, sadly, it suffered damage from damp). At its height Pergamum's library was home to 200,000 scrolls. It was a rival to the famous library at Alexandria. The story goes that Ptolemy, King of Egypt, was so jealous that he banned the export of papyrus, which could only be made from reeds grown in Egypt. So the Pergamenes started writing on the hides of animals instead. (The animals were dead at the time. It made writing much easier.) The hides were scraped thin and polished to provide a smooth writing surface: the resulting material was called 'parchment' – derived from 'Pergamum'. Alexandria won in the end. The library of Pergamum was given away by Mark Antony (who didn't actually own it) to Cleopatra (who couldn't be bothered to read it).

Descending from the temple of Athena, you come to the theatre. Clambering down over the seats, I stood and looked down at the greatest backdrop in the world. Behind the stage the hill drops away and you are left looking out over the vast plain. One can only imagine what effect those performances had on the spectators, sitting watching the actors in their masks with the backdrop of miles and miles of Asia rolling away into the distance. Not a bad piece of scenery.

But my real goal lay further down still. Go halfway down from the theatre and a small path leads you out to the side. There, on a terrace, there is a rectangle of stones on a raised plinth, marked by two trees.

This was the throne of Satan.

Well, possibly. It was the Altar of Zeus, anyway. It's been suggested that the structure, with an altar raised on massive columns, resembled an enormous throne. And it was an altar dedicated to Zeus Soter – Zeus the Saviour. And its pillars were decorated with snakes. So it is possible that this famous monument, with its serpent motif

The site of the altar of Zeus at Pergamum.

and its blasphemous claim, was what was in John's mind when he described the city. Certainly the three-fold celebration of Zeus was commonplace: 'Zeus was, Zeus is, and Zeus will be,' chanted the worshippers.

There is not much there now.* A raised pavement. Some shady trees. But in its day, this building and its location must have been stunning.

I scrambled down through the city, past building after building, from terrace to terrace, until I reached the gate I had passed hours earlier. It was not locked, only pulled to. The man at the top was right. It would have been much easier.

*

I was not quite done with Pergamum. I wanted to follow the serpent trail.

The lady at the tourist information office told me that it would take twenty minutes to walk to the Asclepion. I got there in ten. Either she walks very slowly or I have an unusually large stride. Or maybe she was on commission with the local taxi company. Anyway, the walk takes you out of the modern city and past a military barracks festooned with signs and pictures showing a camera with a big red line drawn across it. A bored-looking sentry sat on some sandbags and watched me trudge past. Out of town the landscape was arid and dry. There were warnings of fire risk everywhere, and as I walked I was passed by a red vehicle with 'Warden' written on it. Nearby some boys were throwing stones at a thin, ragged horse. I gave them my best English disapproving stare. It didn't work as well as the stream of abuse in Turkish which emerged from one of the houses beyond when their mother saw what they were doing.

By now my feet were sore and my head was sunburnt. I was in need of medical attention. So it was just as well that I was heading to one of the major medical centres of the ancient world: the Asclepion at Pergamum, a temple to Asclepius, the god of healing. His symbol

---

* Most of the remains of the ancient city were removed by the Germans in the nineteenth century and can now be seen in the Pergamum Museum in Berlin.

was a snake, and, originally, the temple was home to a number of apparently free-range sacred snakes which slithered around the sanctuary. People came to the temple from miles around, to lie in one of the first-century hospital wards attached to the temple in the hopes that one of the sacred snakes would touch them and heal them.

The sanctuary of Asclepius stands out among the landscape, green, almost lush. An avenue of trees leads you towards the main area. Asclepius wasn't always a god. He appears in Homer's *Iliad* as an ordinary doctor whose sons, Podaleirius and Machaon, followed in his footsteps and served as army medics in the Trojan war. But some time in the fourth or fifth century BC, he had become a god, and, eventually, hundreds of sanctuaries around the world bore his name.

Asclepius and his snake.

75

But the sanctuary at Pergamum was the most famous. Pergamum was so associated with Asclepius that, even in Rome, he was known as *Pergameus deus* – Pergamum's god. The city had a real reputation for medicine. The most famous physician of Roman times, Galen, was born in Pergamum and worked in the Asclepion, which only added to its fame. There is a statue of Galen in the town square. He lounges rather nonchalantly against a pillar, holding an open book. Around the top of the statue there is coiled a bright-green snake.

Asclepius was on night duty. Consultations with the god were a matter of getting a good night's sleep and hoping he'd make a house call. The sick would sleep in the sanctuary and, while they slept, Asclepius would visit them in their dreams and either cure them, or tell them how they could be cured. I suppose it was a kind of dream-therapy. These dreams, if not obvious, would then be interpreted by the priests. The rest of the treatment involved diet, hot and cold baths and exercise. It was an ancient health spa. First-century rehab.

Our friend Aelius Aristides, whose route I had followed to the city, was a regular visitor. On one of his visits (he was a bit of a hypochondriac) the god appeared to him in his dream and told him to smear himself with mud and run three times round the temples, finishing by washing the mud off at the sacred fountain. He took his medicine, even though the winter night was bitterly cold. Two companions offered to accompany him, but the night was so cold that one of them gave up immediately, while the other one started to spasm and had to be carried to the baths to thaw out.

In fact, Aristides was often prescribed freezing-cold baths and the like. In one of his dreams, Asclepius told him to go and plunge into an icy river. You get the feeling that either the god didn't like Aristides much, or it was a kind of aversion therapy.*

* On another occasion Aristides was informed in a dream that if he wished to save his whole body he should cut a part of it off and sacrifice it to the god. Thankfully, the priest interpreted this more leniently, and Aristides was allowed to just take one of his rings off and give that instead. So the sanctuary gained a piece of jewellery, and Aristides kept his finger. Win–win.

The Asclepion. Where the ancient world went for rehab.

The day was, I am glad to say, a lot warmer when I went to visit. And despite having a nice snooze under one of the tamarisk trees that dot the sanctuary, I was not visited by any dreams. Still, I did wash in the sacred fountain, which was deliciously cool. I didn't drink the water, though. It didn't look very healthy.

*

The final stop in Bergama was the museum. They had a model of what the Altar of Zeus would have looked like. It was a big building, but quite low. It looked a bit like a garage. Painted bright white. Marble. Lots of columns.

In the message to Pergamum, Jesus promises a reward to those Christians who 'conquer':

> *To everyone who conquers I will give some of the hidden manna, and I will give a white stone, and on the white stone is written a new name that no one knows except the one who receives it. (Rev. 2.17)*

There has been a lot of debate as to what these white stones mean.

Some suggest that it refers to ancient trials, where jurors signified the guilt or innocence of those on trial by putting a black or white stone respectively into an urn. Others propose that it refers to white stones used as amulets, engraved with the name of a deity, or even to stones used to mark membership in a special group. Or it may be a reference to the *tessera* – a stone or token used as a kind of admission ticket or receipt. The *tessera hospitalis* was used in contracts and agreements; each party broke the stone in half and kept one half as a pledge. However, there's no evidence that these stones were normally white.

The scholar Colin Hemer – author of the best book on the seven cities – made an intriguing suggestion based on the physical appearance of Pergamum itself. The dominant stone at the acropolis is a dark, grey-brown granite. But in the museum, all the inscriptions and the carvings were in a white marble. Scattered among the ruins of the acropolis I saw many fragments: pillars and marble blocks, courses of white marble slabs on top of the darker, greyer stone. All of the most important buildings of the city were also built or clad in marble. Set against the dark stone of the acropolis, these stand out from a long way off: all those bright columns of the temple of Zeus must have been visible for miles.

Every day the Christians at Pergamum must have gazed up at those decorated columns on the hill. Every day they must have passed inscriptions engraved with the names of the great and the good who had made their mark in the city. Perhaps they yearned to join that elite – perhaps they were even prepared to join them at the banquets in their pagan temples. But John says if you stand strong, you will get your own engraving. Your own white stone.

Well, perhaps. Perhaps it means all of these things at the same time. That's the thing about poetry. Words have layers of meaning. Words can mean different things at the same time. Revelation is poetry, not puzzle. It doesn't always have to have a neat solution.

The same is true when we consider why Pergamum is 'Satan's throne'. This may refer to the temple of Zeus on the hillside. Or it may be because Pergamum was the place where the imperial cult first found root. Among all those white stones in the museum, though, there was one that particularly caught my attention. It came from the Upper Gymnasium and was a plaque in honour of Gaius Julius. He is described as a *neokoros* – temple warden – of 'the goddess Roma and of the god Augustus Caesar'. It sounds like a caretaker role, but in fact he was the chairman of the board – chief trustee, head of the management team for the imperial cult centre in Pergamum. He was 'priest of Tiberius Claudius Nero'. The plaque was a thank you to one of our sponsors: Gaius had, at his own expense, provided all the oil used during a festival organised by the whole province in honour of Rome and Augustus.

Perhaps the throne of Satan that Jesus was referring to was not Zeus's throne, but the emperor's.

*

The journey back was longer. More stops. But at least we still had free drinks and cake.

Then on the final leg from the Izmir *otogar* back to Basmane Station, the rather large bus I was on tried to drive down a particularly narrow street. There was a tearing, ripping noise as its wing mirror tore down a shop's awning. We all alighted and stood outside the shop while an extremely angry shop owner argued with an extremely calm, even cheerful bus driver. For all the intervening years, the streets in some cities in this part of the world are still as crowded and difficult to navigate as they were in Roman times.

I talked to a man next to me and we debated whether to wait for the next bus. He decided he would. We compared maps on our phones. I tried to figure out an alternative route; the bus driver continued to argue with the store owner. At the end of a long day, I was thirsty and tired and impatient, and even though my feet ached from all that walking I yearned to be on the move. So I bade farewell to my new-found friend and set out for the nearest metro station. Ten minutes of increasingly painful walking brought me to Stadyum metro station, from where I took the Izban to Basmane.

And then one of those strange, eerie coincidences. Twenty minutes later, as I crossed the street from Basmane to where I was staying, a bus drove by, and in it was the man I had been talking to. We stared at each other. Waved a greeting.

Maybe he was another angel, checking I had got back safely.

6 Hard Times in the Burning Land

Finding the remains of ancient Philadelphia is tricky. Mainly because there aren't any – not really. Nothing visible, at least. Today the site is covered by the modern town of Alaşehir around halfway between Laodicea and Sardis. The route to Alaşehir takes you along a wide river valley – the River Cogamus, as it was known in John's day – through a broad expanse of green fields between two ranges of brown mountains.

Alaşehir lies to the south of the main highway, at the foot of what was once called Mount Tmolus. At a small, wooden-fronted café, I bought chewing gum and bottled water and drank a small glass of hot, sweet apple tea and asked the owner whether she knew anything about a place called 'acropolis'. We pored over the map together to no real purpose. There was some shrugging. A bit of pointing. But in the end there was nothing for it but to head on up.

I *think* I stood on the acropolis. It didn't look much like one, admittedly. Not compared, say, to Pergamum. No marble columns

The acropolis at Philadelphia. Unless it isn't.

here. No scattered remains, even. Just a flat, coffee-coloured patch of ploughed field above the town. Beyond some ancient, withered olive trees, the red roofs of low houses spread out before me, sheds and outbuildings and, beyond them, Alaşehir, shrouded in a kind of mist. The acropolis is one of three hills at Alaşehir which jut out from the mountains like the bridge of a ship. I was definitely on one of them.

So that must have been the acropolis.

Unless it was one of the other hills.

*

Frankly, the place was always fugitive. Always in danger of disappearing. Philadelphia stood on shaky ground, both figuratively and literally, because this part of Asia Minor was earthquake central. In his *Geography*, Strabo describes how the city was 'ever subject to earthquakes. Incessantly the walls of the houses are cracked, different parts of the city being thus affected at different times.'*

In this place, unlike most at that time in history, it was definitely safer to live *outside* the city. Strabo says most people were farmers, 'since they have a fertile soil'. Beyond Philadelphia was the 'Catacecaumene country' – the burnt land – a volcanic region of dark soil, 'black, as though from conflagration'. There were no trees there, but, Strabo said, many vines which produced excellent wine. Today vineyards surround the city and line the highway along the river valley.

In AD 92, Domitian ordered that the vineyards in the provinces be reduced by at least 50 per cent. Evidently there was a surplus of wine in the empire and Domitian was attempting to protect the wine industry in Italy. Or he may have been trying to persuade people to plant corn for food instead. Either way, it was bitterly resented in

---

* Strabo (*c*. 64 BC–AD 25) was a Greek geographer, historian and traveller. He was born in Amaseia in Pontus (modern Amasya, north Turkey). He travelled widely not only in Asia Minor and Greece, but to Egypt and as far south as Ethiopia. His most famous work, the *Geography*, was probably updated many times throughout his life, but the final version dates from AD 24. He died in AD 25, making further updating tricky.

places like Philadelphia, where it caused real hardship. In the region to the west there was famine, and steep inflation. The outcry was such that, according to Suetonius, Domitian in the end 'did not persist in carrying out the measure'.

And it is this event which seems to be referenced in the famous Revelation passage about the four horsemen of the apocalypse. In Revelation 6.5–6, the opening of the third seal releases a rider on a black horse, holding a pair of scales. John hears a voice crying: 'A quart of wheat for a day's pay, and three quarts of barley for a day's pay, but do not damage the olive oil and the wine!' This is a deeply satirical sideswipe at Domitian's disastrous policies. People are starving, inflation is rampant, food is running low, but Italy's wine and olive oil production must be defended at all costs.

For Philadelphia this would have been particularly hard. It was a wine-producing city. Dionysius was its patron deity. There on the border of the burning lands, grapes were one crop which thrived. Hard times at the edge of the burning land.

*

Church-wise, Philadelphia is one of the good guys. 'I know that you have but little power,' the message runs, 'and yet you have kept my word and have not denied my name' (Rev. 3.8–9). As in Smyrna, the opposition is coming from the Jews and for the second time we get a 'synagogue of Satan' reference. The message reassures the Philadelphians that their opponents will 'come and bow down before your feet, and they will learn that I have loved you'. This is an adaptation of one of the common memes of Jewish apocalyptic literature: the idea that one day the Gentiles would bow down before the people of Israel. Isaiah writes: 'The descendants of those who oppressed you shall come bending low to you, and all who despised you shall bow down at your feet; they shall call you the City of the Lord, the Zion of the Holy One of Israel' (Isa. 60.14). However, Revelation reverses this here: it is the Jews who will bow down to the followers of Jesus.

We don't know what the argument was about, but there may be a hint in some letters, written about fifteen years after Revelation, by a Christian leader called Ignatius of Antioch, who was being taken under armed guard to be killed in Rome. In his letter to Philadelphia, Ignatius includes a curious line: 'But if any man preach unto you Judaism, hearken not unto him; for it is better to hear Christianity from one circumcised, than Judaism from one uncircumcised.' This seems to indicate that things had got rather mixed up: there were circumcised people (i.e. ethnic Jews) preaching Christianity and uncircumcised people (i.e. Gentiles) preaching Judaism. So are the latter those 'who say they are Jews but are not'?

We don't know what the conflict was, really. But the Philadelphians are the only group among John's correspondents who are going to be kept safe during the time of trial, and at the end of the message, Jesus promises: 'If you conquer, I will make you a pillar in the temple of my God; you will never go out of it. I will write on you the name of my God, and the name of the city of my God, the new Jerusalem that comes down from my God out of heaven, and my own new name' (Rev. 3.12).

This is the first mention in Revelation of one of the most powerful images in the whole book: the New Jerusalem. In John's vision the city descends 'prepared as a bride adorned for her husband' (21.2). This is the final destination for followers of Jesus. They will live in the perfect city, and their God will live with them.

The 'source code' for this idea is found in Isaiah 65, which pictures the creation of a new heaven and a new earth. In two of the most beautiful verses of the Old Testament God describes the perfection of life in this place:

I will rejoice in Jerusalem, and delight in my people;
no more shall the sound of weeping be heard in it,
or the cry of distress.
No more shall there be in it an infant that lives but a few days,
or an old person who does not live out a lifetime;
for one who dies at a hundred years will be considered a youth,
and one who falls short of a hundred will be considered accursed.
(Isa. 65.19–20)

The image of the ideal city, the perfect dwelling place – paradise on earth – persisted. And some seventy years later and thirty miles to the west of Philadelphia, some people were going to take up that idea in a way which would change Revelation's reputation forever.

*

In 2001 a group of archaeologists finally located the city of Pepuza, a city which had been lost for 1,500 years. Now, you may have missed this in the news. It didn't make big headlines. And, frankly, it doesn't look much these days. There is a kind of cave monastery, carved into the cliff face, above a ravine. There are the fragmented remains of a necropolis – a graveyard, a city of the dead. The rest of the site lies broken and shattered beneath a wide, sweeping bowl of land filled with fields and vineyards in central Turkey, in the area known as Phrygia.*

But for apocalypse addicts, Pepuza is fascinating. Because it was what happened at Pepuza, sometime around AD 160, that really got the alarm bells ringing about John's Apocalypse.

It starts with a Christian called Montanus. He had once been a pagan priest – probably in the mystery cult of Cybele – but he had become a Christian, and one day, in a small village in Phrygia called Ardoban, he fell into a trance and began to speak in tongues.† God, he decided, had made him an instrument of a new outpouring of the Holy Spirit – a true prophet. His teaching soon attracted two female followers – Priscilla and Maximilla – who deserted their husbands to join him. Along with others, they relocated to the town of Pepuza, where they started to write down some of the messages they received during these trances and even started to treat them as scripture.

It was not all trances and tongues, though. They were what are

---

* The site was discovered thanks to a large inscribed marble slab which was brought to the Usak archaeological museum by a local villager, whose grandfather had been using it as a front-door step since 1975. He had dug it up in a field.

† Jerome described Montanus as a 'castrated half-man', which may indicate that he was a priest of Cybele, the Phrygian mother-goddess. Or it may simply have been Jerome being, as usual, fabulously rude. Another source claims that Montanus was a priest of Apollo.

known as rigorists: they obeyed a strict moral code. Perhaps motivated by their belief that they were living in the end times, they discouraged remarriage of widows or widowers, or even the bearing of children by married couples. They fasted for long periods and practised a simple, austere lifestyle. Their movement gathered many followers, who called it the New Prophecy (the name 'Montanism' was first coined by Cyril of Jerusalem some 200 years later). Contemporary opponents called them Cataphrygians or Phrygians or Pepuzites, or sometimes Priscillianists, after the prophetess Priscilla. To many who encountered it, the New Prophecy seemed to have rediscovered the raw, visceral, radical power of the early days of the church.

According to a writer called Epiphanius (and we should be aware that most of the writing about the Montanists comes from their opponents), it was Montanus himself who 'named Pepuza and Tymion Jerusalem, in his desire to draw to them people from everywhere'.* Later, one of their prophetesses – either Priscilla or a fourth-century Montanist prophetess called Quintilla – prophesied that the New Jerusalem would descend there. 'Appearing as a woman clothed in a shining robe, Christ came to me; he put wisdom into me and revealed to me that this place is sacred and that here Jerusalem will come down from heaven.' Whoever thought of it, the adherents of the New Prophecy flocked to Pepuza and organised themselves into a functioning society.

And not long after, the big red emergency telephone started buzzing in the local bishop's office.

---

* Epiphanius of Salamis (*c.* AD 315–404) was a fourth-century cleric, best known for his work the *Panarion* or 'medicine chest'. It's a catalogue of heresies (hence its other name, *Against Heresies*) presented in the form of a book of antidotes for anyone bitten by the serpent of heresy. It was written around AD 375. In his wonderful, labyrinthine *Dictionary of Christian Biography*, the Victorian historian Henry Wace describes Epiphanius as 'an honest, but credulous and narrow-minded, zealot for church orthodoxy' who 'often frames long narratives out of very meagre hints'. Nevertheless, in his time he was hugely popular and crowds used to queue for hours to hear him preach. Probably because he was a friend of Jerome and just as fabulously rude.

The bishops of Asia Minor declared this New Prophecy to be the work of demons. A local synod in Hierapolis around 190 denounced it. Their decision was upheld by the bishops of Rome, Carthage and elsewhere in North Africa. The leaders of the increasingly institutionalised church were baffled as to why, if he wanted to speak to people, God hadn't chosen to use the proper channels (i.e. them).

But the odd thing about it is that there is nothing heretical in any of the Montanist teaching that has been passed down. The Montanists were orthodox. Perhaps that was part of the problem: perhaps they were a bit *too* orthodox, too enthusiastic, too serious. (The official, established church has always feared enthusiasm. It makes the rest of the church look so lukewarm. And Revelation has something to say about that . . .)

Pepuza is not far from Philadelphia, and from early on Philadelphia seems to have been associated with prophecy. In the passage condemning Montanism in Eusebius's *Ecclesiastical History*, he mentions a prophetess called Ammia in Philadelphia. She was one of the figures to whom the first Montanist prophets appealed as a kind of 'line of descent'. So we can faintly discern a possible line from John to Philadelphia, through the local prophets and then to the Montanists.

Certainly, the Montanists had a Revelation view of life. For a start, they removed themselves from all the official structures and went, as it were, into the wilderness. But there is also in their teaching an emphasis on the visionary experience, and a church order which placed prophets in high authority. And two of the sixteen surviving oracles deal with one of Revelation's core themes: the need to endure, and not fear persecution.

The Montanists' emphasis on personal revelation was just one reason why the 'proper church' found the whole thing distasteful. Another was their disrespect for the established order. By now the bishops had become the acknowledged leaders of the church. But in the leadership structures set up in Pepuza, bishops were not mentioned at all. Instead, the Montanists gave authority to prophets. Worse, *female* prophets. *Prophetesses*. Montanism gave a status to women. Priscilla and Maximilla became noted leaders (later they even had Montanist churches named after them). And they weren't the only ones. Epiphanius complained that 'Among them women are Bishops and women are elders and the like; as there is no difference, they say, "In Christ Jesus there is neither male nor female".'

Despite official condemnation, the New Prophecy spread. It made its way to Rome, where it was tolerated until the AD 190s. It became especially popular in North Africa, where the theologian Tertullian became a Montanist.* It even survived in Constantinople. In the fourth century, Constantine ordered Montanist books to be collected up and burned. Theodosius, the first emperor to make heresy officially a crime, decreed that Montanists should be executed. Eventually, in AD 550, the emperor Justinian sent the boys in. The shrine of Montanus at Pepuza was destroyed, along with the tombs of Maximilla and Priscilla. Montanist buildings were confiscated and handed over for 'orthodox' use. Their relics were burnt. Montanist meetings were prohibited. The private property of Montanists was confiscated and fines were levied on the followers of the New Prophecy. The movement's leaders were exiled or even executed. As for the town itself, there was still a monastery there in the eighth century and a bishop of Pepuza was present at a synod in Constantinople in 879. But a series of earthquakes reduced it in scale and importance, and eventually it disappeared from history.

Montanism's dependence on its imagery made the book of Revelation guilty by association. This movement's rise is the first instance of Revelation being used to question and challenge the authority of the church. Montanism's 'heresy' consisted of giving a voice to those outside the official hierarchy, and it really started a trend: ever since, Revelation has been the text of choice for freelance prophets, visionaries, radicals and revolutionaries. And the New Jerusalem has been one of their most potent images.

*

* Admittedly, he was more what you might call a conservative Montanist, as he was deeply opposed to the ministry of women. This may have a lot to do with the culture of North Africa, where Tertullian lived. Or it may have to do with the fact that he was deeply opposed to a lot of things. He was a fabulously Grumpy Old Theologian.

It is an image that has found a strong foothold in western culture too.

One of the most curious conjunctions of Revelation and the modern world came in 2011, during the marriage service of Prince William and Kate Middleton. At this Royal occasion the crème de la crème of the British establishment, not to mention assorted creaminess from elsewhere in the world, all stood up in Westminster Abbey and belted out 'Jerusalem' – which people think is a hymn, but which is actually a poem about revolution, written by a republican who loathed the established church.

But the English do have a good, long history of disarming radicals and welcoming them into the establishment. Today that song by William Blake has become the unofficial English national anthem, sung at rugby and cricket matches and Royal weddings and state occasions, often accompanied by the whirring sound of William Blake spinning furiously in his grave.

Blake, like John, was a visionary poet. Walking the muddy streets and the dark alleyways of London, he glimpsed eternity. When he was a boy of eight or ten, he saw a tree full of angels, their wings 'bespangling every bough like stars'. When he told his parents what he had seen, he was beaten for telling fibs. You don't get trees full of angels in Peckham Rye. When he was four, according to a story told by his wife, he saw God. Given the beating he got later for seeing angels, it was probably best that he kept that one to himself.

Blake saw in Revelation the vocabulary he needed to describe his visions. Confusingly, though, the song we call 'Jerusalem' wasn't called that by Blake. It's actually the preface to his poem 'Milton'. He did write a poem called *Jerusalem*, just not this one. Well, I say 'poem'; really it's a vast, mystifying epic myth. In fact, it's an apocalypse: an unveiling. Blake sees beyond the grimy streets of London to glimpse 'into Eternity':

> *I see London, blind & age bent, begging thro' the Streets*
> *Of Babylon, led by a child; his tears run down his beard . . .*
> *The Corner of Broad Street weeps; Poland Street languishes;*
> *To Great Queen Street & Lincoln's Inn, all is distress & woe.*
> *The night falls thick.*

'Fallen, fallen is Babylon the great!' Blake saw the churches of London as John's 'synagogues of Satan' and called the alliance of church and state 'the Beast and the Whore'. This sprawling poem is drenched in imagery from Revelation. Jerusalem, the bride of Christ,

> . . .*walks upon our meadows green,*
> *The Lamb of God walks by her side,*
> *And every English Child is seen*
> *Children of Jesus & his Bride.*
> *Forgiving trespasses and sins*
> *Lest Babylon with cruel Og*
> *With moral & Self-righteous Law*
> *Should crucify in Satan's Synagogue!*

Blake, of course, was a painter as well as a poet, a dealer in words and images. His painting of *The Four and Twenty Elders Casting their Crowns before the Divine Throne* depicts God holding the seven-sealed scroll – although it has to be said it looks a bit more like a musical instrument. The first time I saw it I thought the Ancient of Days was about to give a sax solo. *The Angel of Revelation* shows John sitting at a kind of rocky desk on a promontory, dwarfed by an enormous figure behind whom various horses are riding forth.

But it's his Great Red Dragon pictures which I find most startling. He depicts the dragon from Revelation chapter 12 as very much a human figure, angelic even, with a muscular, finely defined body. This is a beast who works out. But when he turns his back he is huge, spiny, his sinewed, leathery wings full of flame and fire.*

*

* Blake's paintings have featured in fiction about serial killers. *Red Dragon* is the title of a thriller by Thomas Harris, where a serial killer known as the 'Tooth Fairy' is obsessed with Blake's painting. Blake's paintings also feature in the TV series *The Mentalist*, where the main character, Patrick Jane, hunts Red John. Although I only mention that because it's my eldest daughter's favourite TV programme.

Blake was a supporter of revolution. And if we needed any reminding of his anti-establishment credentials, in his drawing of the seven-headed beast the heads of the beast suggest establishment figures: judge, soldier, pope, king, bishop and priest. But when Blake was writing, he wasn't making waves so much as riding a wave that had already been surging upwards and inspiring radical, even revolutionary movements for over a century.

In the seventeenth and eighteenth centuries in England, Revelation served as a fount of anti-establishment theology, philosophy and politics. The English Civil War – the English revolutionary war – was a conflict with a distinctly apocalyptic feel. The king was beheaded and the war killed a higher proportion of the population than any other British war, before or since. Apocalyptic fever spanned both sides of the political divide. Cromwell's porter went mad with apocalyptic fever and was locked up. He spent his time preaching from the windows of his cell to the crowd that gathered below. A royalist writer declared that the words 'Rex Oliver Lord Protector' were a code which added up to 666 (although only if you dropped the 'L' from 'Lord'). Sometimes you had to remember what the official apocalyptic line was. In 1641 a clergyman was arrested in England for declaring that the Pope was *not* the antichrist. Twenty years later, in Restoration England, speculation about the second coming was a criminal offence.

The example of Revelation also inspired a series of radical groups: the Levellers, the Ranters, the Diggers, all of whom took direct inspiration from the Bible. But of all the groups which rose and fell during this time, none were more apocalyptically minded than the Fifth Monarchists. In the book of Daniel, the prophet had foreseen four empires. The fifth monarchy, they believed, would be the rule of Christ. Given that the end was obviously extremely nigh, they aimed to reform Parliament and the government in time for Christ's second coming. The movement was split over how this would happen. There were Fifth Monarchist congregations who believed that the new kingdom would be established through prayer and preaching. And there were other splinter groups who believed in more direct action. In fact, the Fifth Monarchists were the only group to try to overthrow both Oliver Cromwell and Charles II. They were anti-everyone, it seems.

The ringleader was a cooper and preacher called Thomas Venner, who led a congregation of mainly ex-Army men which met in a room above a pub. Sounds like a great place for a church, actually. Anyway, their plot to overthrow Cromwell was discovered and Venner was imprisoned. Then Cromwell died and the monarchy returned in the shape of Charles II. In 1661, Venner led a group of Fifth Monarchists in an attempted coup, attacking the City of London with the somewhat contradictory cry of 'King Jesus and the heads upon the Gates'. The coup lasted four days before collapsing. The leaders were captured, and executed two weeks later. During his trial Venner claimed that 'if they had been deceived, the Lord himself was their deceiver'.

Venner was executed. Hung, drawn and quartered, and his body put on display outside the congregation he led. Strangely enough, Venner's granddaughter, Elizabeth, married a linen draper's son named John Potter who went on to become Archbishop of Canterbury. Somehow, I don't think her grandfather would have been proud.

Apocalyptic speculation did not go away. The American and French revolutions gave new impetus to apocalyptic speculation. Joseph Priestley, the discoverer of oxygen, ammonia, carbon monoxide and other smelly substances, wrote a book, *The present state of Europe compared with ancient prophecies*, in which he claimed opponents of the French Revolution were followers of the beast. As well as being a scientist, Priestley was a theologian and radical political thinker and saw the French Revolution as a harbinger of the second coming of Christ. He moved to America to wait for the end. 'It cannot, I think, be more than twenty years,' he wrote.

And, as the country was swept by new uncertainty in the form of the Industrial Revolution, the book of Revelation continued to both inspire and inflame. One of the strangest outbursts was centred around Joanna Southcott, a devout Methodist from Devon who started to receive visions, revelations of Satan's downfall and the arrival of the millennium. She identified herself with the woman clothed with the sun and also the bride of the Lamb, and in 1802 she began to hand out seals to selected followers whom she believed to have been saved. In 1814, when she was sixty-four, it was revealed that she was pregnant. Twenty-one doctors examined her; seventeen agreed that she was expecting. Her followers – and even one of the doctors who examined her – were convinced that this was a supernatural birth. If she was the woman clothed with the sun, then this must be the child in Revelation 12:5, who would 'rule nations with a rod of iron'. He would be called Shiloh. Sadly, she died two days after Christmas, before she could give birth. Not that there was a child, anyway. An autopsy revealed that she was not, and never had been, pregnant. Her followers held her body for four days, confidently expecting that she would be resurrected in order to give birth, but nothing happened. Her prophecies were written down and sealed, in the manner approved by all the best apocalyptic writers.

But her followers were still filled with revolutionary zeal. One of them, a Liverpool textile worker called Peter Morrison, was arrested for prophesying that 'there would be no hedge, nor even a brick standing . . . the clergy would be lost forever and would be like dung – for they were dumb dogs that did not bark – and all the property belonging to the rich would be taken away and given to the sealed people'.

'Jerusalem' – undeniably Blake's biggest hit – is a work born in a time of revolution and social upheaval. And it became an anthem of the early socialist movement, which took up enthusiastically his vow to build the new city of heaven 'in England's green & pleasant land'.* As the Industrial Revolution spread its 'dark Satanic mills' across Britain, Revelation's vision of a perfect heavenly city gave people hope that a city could be something other than a place of oppression and suffering and unremitting toil. Many were not content to wait for God's New Jerusalem, though: if it was slow in arriving, they would build it for themselves.

One of the greatest of the New Jerusalemites was Robert Owen, a utopian socialist who founded an enlightened industrial community at New Lanark in Scotland, and bankrolled New Harmony in Indiana, USA. He inspired both trade unionism and the cooperative movement. In the words of Engels, 'every real advance in England on behalf of the workers, links itself to the name of Robert Owen'. Much of Owen's political language comes straight out of the Apocalypse. He described socialism as 'the millennium in practice';

---

* Sic. Blake was a big fan of the ampersand.

his periodical *The New Moral World* was subtitled 'Gazette of the millennium'.*

Etienne Cabet, a radical French pacifist and reformist politician, was deeply influenced by Owen. He was later exiled to Angleterre for his political beliefs, where he wrote a book called *The Voyage to Icaria*, a utopian novel which described the reign of God on earth and included the memorable phrase 'from each according to his capacities, to each according to his needs'. He turned out to be influential in other ways, too. In 1839, Cabet returned to France and tried to set up a movement to realise the vision of his book – the Icarians. The movement was heavily communitarian and so Cabet called the guiding principle *communisme*. Cabet and his followers later moved to America, to try to found a new kind of society in the new world. The movement collapsed, but his book and the idea of *communisme* inspired a hairy German bloke called Karl Marx.

Ernst Bloch once said: 'It would be difficult to make a revolution without the Bible.' That goes double for Revelation. In 1848, when revolution broke out across Europe, a workers' paper of January 1849 confidently declared that 'the times of a new heaven and a new earth are near'.

This final book of the Bible, and its compelling, inspiring image of the New Jerusalem, still inspires radicals and revolutionaries today. It is no coincidence that Revelation is one of the key texts for the liberation theologians working among the favelas and the shanty towns of South America. To Christians crushed by cruel political and economic forces, the image of the government as a beast is an entirely appropriate metaphor. Revelation reminds the discontented and the dispossessed that the world does not have to be this way, that beasts can be defeated and, most importantly, that God hears their prayers.

Vive la Revelation!

---

* His son David Dale Owen invented the US Geological Survey. I don't know what that proves but I thought I'd mention it.

7 The Land of Gold and Myths

The day was overcast. Cool. Thunder grumbled far in the distance. Above the temple, the remains of the old acropolis stood stark against the sky, jagged, decayed like a broken tooth. Some traditions had it that Zeus was born in the Tmolus Mountains. It felt like the old, stony, thunder god was still there, reliving past glories, wondering why no one had called, complaining to his agent, *'I'm ready for my close-up . . .'*

In a green valley, dotted with tamarisk and olive trees, lie the ruins of the once great temple of Artemis at Sardis.* This was one of the biggest temples in the world and is the seventh largest of all the Greek temples that have been discovered. Begun around 300 BC, work stopped before it was completed. Either they ran out of money, or the plans were too ambitious, or, more likely, the thing kept getting hit by earthquakes. When John wrote to the city the temple was still awaiting repairs from the earthquake of AD 17. It was not fully completed until the second century AD, by which time new gods had taken over the sponsorship role. With Roman money funding the renovations, the emperors wanted a slice of the action, so the temple became a centre for the imperial cult. They partitioned the place. A wall was built which divided the interior into two rooms, one for the boys – Zeus and Antoninus Pius (emperor from AD 138 to 161), the other for the girls – Artemis and Faustina, Antoninus Pius's wife. The temple was abandoned in the fourth century and a small church built at one end. That too was abandoned in time.

Now the temple's ruins squat in the valley, grey granite blocks, gloomy columns, and above them craggy, broken cliffs that make it

* According to local inscriptions, not to mention the discovery of a large head of Zeus, the temple was dedicated to both Artemis and Zeus.

The temple of Artemis at Sardis. In the far distance, the remains of the once impregnable acropolis.

look like the site of some ancient giant quarry. I sat there for some time, nursing tired feet and reading Herodotus. The father of history, he is called, although it has to be said that a lot of his history consists of him passing on suspiciously tall tales and then saying, 'Might be true. Who knows?' It makes him the most entertaining of the ancient historians by far. He'd have been great on TV.

Sardis is a place rich with legend. And rich with legends about riches. It sat on the Pactolus River, a tributary of the Hermus (today the river is called the Gediz). The stories said that Midas, the legendary king whose touch turned everything to gold, bathed himself in the Pactolus to rid himself of the curse. This not only made the Pactolus one of the only known cures for irony, it also had the effect of filling the river with the gold that he rinsed off from his skin. And all that gold flowed downstream, making the Lydian kingdom, whose rulers lived in Sardis, fabulously wealthy.

According to Herodotus, the Lydians were 'the first people we know of to use a gold and silver coinage'. He also credits them with the invention of shopping and records that: 'They also claim to have invented the games which are now commonly played both by themselves and by the Greeks.' Such games were only invented to distract the people from a terrible famine: every other day they would spend all day gaming, to take their minds off not eating. So the Lydians give us (a) cash, (b) shopping and (c) distracting yourself from reality with games. For an ancient place it sounds terribly modern. Or maybe, deep down, we are still terribly ancient.

The earliest Lydian rulers belonged to the Heraclid dynasty, but they were succeeded by the rather unpronounceable Mermnad dynasty. The first king in this line was Gyges (c. 680–652 BC), a powerful ruler who appears in Assyrian inscriptions with the rather twee-sounding name of Gugu. But he's also in the Bible, it is generally agreed, as Gog, the mythical ruler taken as a symbol of evil tyranny in Ezekiel 38. Much later, Gog became a Jewish apocalyptic shorthand for the forces of evil which will rise up in the last days. He pops up, of course, in Revelation, where he is tricked by Satan into gathering against the saints for the (or a) final battle. Fire comes down and consumes them all and the devil is thrown into eternal torment (Rev. 20.7–10).

Gyges is famous anyway, as the first king to gain the throne through stalking. The Heraclid king Candaules was infatuated with his wife, whom he declared to be the most beautiful woman on earth. He was so convinced of her beauty that he told Gyges, his favourite bodyguard, to hide in his wife's room while she was undressing and see her in all her glory, as it were. Gyges was shocked by this suggestion, but the king insisted. However, the queen spotted him as he fled the room, and she gave him an ultimatum: he had seen her in the buff, so he would have to either (a) kill himself, or (b) kill Candaules and marry her. So that's either 'Kill yourself' or 'Kill the king, take his place and marry the most beautiful woman in the world'. Tricky . . . Gyges went with Plan B, naturally: he killed the boastful Candaules and took over the kingdom.

It's one of several stories which associate Sardis with hubris – pride before a fall. Take the most proverbially famous king of Lydia – Croesus, as in 'as rich as . . .'. Croesus ruled in the sixth century BC (c. 561–547). Legend has it that he was the richest man in the world. Remains of Croesus' gold refineries have been found at the base of the mountains. Such wealth attracted enemies. But Sardis was OK. It had the ancient world's equivalent of Fort Knox: its acropolis.

'Sardis' is really a mistranslation. The name is plural, so it's more correct to talk about Sardises. Or Sardi. Anyway, there were two cities here. Most people lived in what you might call Lower Sardis: down the valley, by the Pactolus, handy for the shops, etc. But when danger loomed, they retreated to the acropolis, an ancient fortress perched high on the precipitous mountain top, some 1,500 feet above the 'new' town. The acropolis was one of the most easily defended places in the ancient world: surrounded by precipices on three sides, the only entrance from a narrow ridge path which leads onto the slopes of Mount Tmolus.

In 547 BC, Croesus was threatened by the rising power of Cyrus – the Persian king who had defeated the Babylonians (freeing the Judean Jews from exile along the way). So Croesus went to consult the oracle at Delphi, who gave him a reassuring message: If Croesus crossed the Halys River (the frontier of his kingdom) he would destroy a great empire.

Comforted by this, Croesus launched a pre-emptive strike. He crossed the river and provoked the Persians into a war. The first battle was a stalemate, with neither side coming out on top. In the second battle Croesus' cavalry was destroyed, the horses apparently scared by the unfamiliar scent of the Persians' camels. And if you've ever smelt a camel you'll understand why the horses were scared. So Croesus returned to Sardis, to work out why the Delphic oracle was apparently malfunctioning. He was confident that he would win in the end. After all, he had something that Cyrus could never defeat, camels or no camels: the hill-top fortress at Sardis. That was unconquerable.

Cyrus duly laid siege and promised a handsome reward to any soldier who could find a way in. Nothing worked until, one day, a watching Persian saw one of the Lydian troops accidentally drop his helmet over the battlements. Thinking that he was unobserved, the Lydian climbed over the wall, retrieved the helmet, and climbed back in again. No one was guarding this part of the wall, since it was over a precipice that was assumed to be completely inaccessible.

That night the Persian soldier led a group of comrades up to the place where the Lydian soldier had come over the wall, and climbed into the city. The rest, as Herodotus would say, was history (probably). The impregnable fortress had held out for a massive two weeks. The oracle was right. An empire was defeated. Not the Persian empire, but the Lydian one.

Another tale from Herodotus tells of Croesus watching the Persian soldiers moving through the conquered city.

'What are your men doing?' he asked Cyrus.

'They are plundering your city and carrying off your treasures,' Cyrus replied.

'I think you'll find that nothing there belongs to me any more,' Croesus pointed out, drily. 'It's *you* they are robbing.'*

Later, the city was controlled by the Seleucid king Antiochus III. During his reign a rival briefly took control of the city. Antiochus recaptured the acropolis by secretly entering an unguarded section, just as Cyrus's troops had done some 350 years earlier. Some fortresses never learn. But despite this, 'capturing the citadel of Sardis' became a phrase meaning 'to do the impossible'.

Sardis is a place always associated with over-reaching, with pride and then a fall. I thought briefly about trying to make it up to what remains of the citadel, but I lacked the energy. There is nothing there now, after all. The once impregnable fortress has been shattered by an enemy more relentless than the Persians. Earthquakes and erosion have swept away the summit, taking the acropolis with it. Today the mountain looks as if it has been quarried by an enormous digger.

*

Following the earthquake, the Lower City was rebuilt, helped by a large cash injection from the emperor Tiberius. And during New Testament times the population was as high as 100,000. The impressive

---

* Croesus was sentenced to be burnt to death, but on his funeral pyre he told Cyrus about the prophecy of the Delphic oracle. Cyrus, reflecting, perhaps, on the two-faced nature of the gods, decided to spare Croesus, who spent the rest of his days as an adviser to Cyrus. Presumably, advising the king never to trust an oracle.

remains of the Lower City have also been renovated. The façade of the huge gymnasium is intact – which struck me as an almost miraculous survival, until I realised it had actually been largely rebuilt. It is too clean, too complete. Two German boys had climbed up to the first storey and were sitting there with their legs dangling down with what one can only describe as an almost complete disregard for (a) respect for historic monuments and (b) health and safety.

The gymnasium at Sardis. Here shown without dangling Germans.

Next door to the gymnasium was another impressive building: the largest ancient synagogue ever found outside Palestine, big enough to hold 1,000 worshippers. Although this building dates from after John's time, it shows how well established the Jewish community was, and how confident they were in their social position. The Jews added benches, and then, in the fourth century, went even more lavish, with a colonnaded forecourt, a fountain, a marble table, decorated mosaic flooring and an elevated throne. You don't build such an ornate building if you are worried you're going to be kicked out any moment.

It also contains some very un-Jewish items. There is a table in the shape of an eagle; there are two statues of lions. These were reclamation jobs: statues obtained from other buildings or shrines in the city and repurposed for the synagogue. The eagle was a symbol of the Roman empire. The lions were antiques: they have been identified as sixth-century BC sculptures, probably from a temple to the goddess Cybele.

Cybele was big in Sardis. A local Phrygian fertility goddess, she was linked with the nearby Tmolus Mountains. She was their mountain goddess, protector of ores and metals. The goldsmiths of Sardis, understandably, were devoted to her, and an altar to the goddess sat in a precinct in the gold-refining district. But the goddess Cybele was adopted throughout the empire. The Romans called her *Magna Mater*, 'Great Mother'. Or 'Big Momma' to you and me.

Given traditional Jewish teachings against graven images, the presence of the lions shows that the Jews in Sardis were quite relaxed about such things. And there is no evidence at the site of there having been a balcony, which would be the usual place for women. Which either meant that no women were allowed in the synagogue, or that they were allowed to worship alongside the men. Certainly the Jews here were part of the political and social fabric. Many inscriptions from the site tell of gifts given in the fulfilment of vows. And the donors' names are often followed by the title 'citizen of Sardis'. Eight of the donors who gave money for the beautification of the synagogue were members of the city council (*bouleutes*), a position which required a considerable amount of personal wealth.

Sardis was a wealthy place. I walked up the street running alongside the synagogue to the south. It was essentially a shopping mall, originally paved with marble and lined with columns. The shops date from the fourth to the seventh century AD. And working from items and inscriptions found in the shops, archaeologists can tell the religion of some of the owners. Six have been identified as Jewish shops or residences. There were two restaurants, some houses. Three of the units were owned by a man called Jacob who ran a cloth-dyeing business. There was a hardware store, a glassware shop, and a paint shop owned by a man called 'Jacob the elder'.

When John was writing to Sardis, Jews had been established there for over 500 years. Again, we have a link to the Old Testament, because in Obadiah 20, the prophet refers to 'the exiles of Jerusalem who are in Sepharad'. This is close to the Aramaic form of the name Sardis found from around the mid fifth century BC. Similarly, Jews read the land of Lud, mentioned in Genesis, as referring to Lydia. According to Josephus, Antiochus III transported 2,000 loyal Jewish families from Babylon and settled them in Phrygia and Lydia, where they benefited from tax breaks and were allowed to follow their own customs. Some of these surely ended up in Sardis.

Sardis was in fact the most important Jewish community in Lydia. Josephus records that Lucius Antonius, a governor of Asia, confirmed the rights of Jews in the city in a letter to the city council. They were to be allowed to have 'an association of their own in accordance with their native laws and a place of their own, in which they decide their affairs and controversies with one another'. Jews were allowed to assemble and to have their own meeting house, 'clean' food was on sale in the marketplace and they could decide their own legal issues.

The shops in Sardis. The retail experience loses a bit nowadays.

The Christians, then, were very much the newcomers here. And yet there does not seem to have been any enmity between the groups. John's message to Sardis doesn't mention conflict or tension with the Jews – unlike his messages to Philadelphia and Smyrna. Instead, it emphasises images which would have been familiar to residents of Sardis from their knowledge of the city's history. A city with a great history is told that it is living on reputation alone: 'you have a name of being alive, but you are dead'. A city whose fortress has collapsed in an earthquake is urged to 'Wake up, and strengthen what remains and is on the point of death'. A city which was defeated by a surprise night-time attack is warned that Jesus 'will come like a thief, and you will not know at what hour I will come to you.' The problem in Sardis is not persecution or opposition, but love of reputation. Dwelling on past glories, perhaps. Or proud of appearance. But no longer alive. A zombie congregation: the church of the living dead.

*

'If you conquer,' promises Jesus, 'you will be clothed . . . in white robes, and I will not blot your name out of the book of life.' This is another Revelation image with roots in the Old Testament, where Moses pleads with God to forgive the sin of the Israelites. 'But if not,' he says, 'blot me out of the book that you have written' (Exod. 32:32). We know that, in subsequent centuries, registers were kept of Israelite citizens. So by extension, this idea becomes applied to those who were allowed entry into the heavenly kingdom. In Daniel, the register concept is specifically related to the day of judgment when, during 'a time of anguish . . . your people shall be delivered, everyone who is found written in the book. Many of those who sleep in the dust of the earth shall awake, some to everlasting life, and some to shame and everlasting contempt' (Dan. 12:1–2). This is in fact the only explicit statement in the Old Testament of bodily resurrection.

The same idea was appropriated by the Christians. Paul asks the Philippian church to help Euodia, Syntyche, Clement and 'the rest of my co-workers, whose names are in the book of life' (Phil. 4.3). The writer of Hebrews describes 'the assembly of the firstborn who are enrolled in heaven' (Heb. 12:23).

Some Jews, on the other hand, began specifically excluding Christians from their registers. Around the end of the first century – the time when Revelation was being written – the prayers in the synagogues began including specifically anti-Christian phrases. They are known as the curse of the Minim: 'May the Nazarenes and the Minim suddenly perish and may they be blotted out of the book of Life and not enrolled along with the righteous.'

But it was a recognisable concept for Gentiles as well. There were registers of citizens across the Græco-Roman world. The cities of Asia Minor had their record offices, and throughout Greece it was common for those condemned to have their names erased from the official records.

John uses the phrase 'book of life' five times in Revelation.* Anyone whose name is not found in that book will end in destruction; in John's phrase, they will be 'thrown into the lake of fire' (Rev. 20.15). It became one of the standard images associated with the idea of final judgment. So much so that, when William the Conqueror decided to list all his newly conquered territory in a book, many of the conquered Anglo-Saxons believed that this was the end of the world. Hence the name they gave to the book – the *Domesday Book*: the book of the day of judgment.

For all the glories of the lower site, there was something eerie about Sardis. Maybe it was just the gloom of the day. A little way along the road from the main site, a track takes you up through some vines to the site of the hippodrome. Its outline can be traced among the vines: the slopes of the seating area, the curves of the track. It seemed to me that in the distant thunder I could hear the beats of the horses' hooves, the thunder of the chariot wheels, the roar of the crowd. But no. All gone now. I was the only person in that place: a ghost place, a shadow land, lines of walls and banks of seating traced in grass and earth.

I saw the German boys again as I was driving away. One of them was limping.

Hubris.

* Revelation 3:5; 13:8; 17:8; 20:12, 15; 21:27, since you ask.

8 The Plateau and the Pit

As you drive east along the Maeander valley, the ground turns pale, grey-white, dry and dusty. The modern road follows the ancient trade route, from Ephesus through the heart of ancient Christian Asia. Follow this road far enough and it would take you right through Phrygia, into the depths of Cappadocia, over the Taurus Mountains, across the sands of Persia, all the way to the Euphrates. That morning I sat in the café at the hotel, following the 'Eastern Trade Route' on the map that came with my 1908 copy of Ramsay's *The Church in the Roman Empire*. (No one can accuse me of not using the latest, cutting-edge research. Also, some previous owner had helpfully highlighted the route in bright pink.) One day, maybe I would set out and just keep going. But not today.

My route ran alongside the coiling, serpentine Maeander to Aydin, the site of ancient Tralles, whose bishop Polybius visited the captive Ignatius at Smyrna and whose most famous son, Anthemius, designed the world's most beautiful building, the church of Hagia Sophia in Constantinople. Beyond Tralles, in John's day, was what Strabo called 'a modest town': Antioch-by-the-Maeander, where the ancient road crossed the river via a bridge. In the third century a slave scratched a picture of the bridge on the wall of a house on Delos, along with an inscription saying, 'This is the land of Antioch, rich in figs and water; saviour Maeander, save me and give me water.' Clearly he was both thirsty and homesick. Further down the valley, the Maeander divides. The northern branch becomes the Hippourios River, but the road – and my route – followed the southern branch, the River Lycus. And there you find, just north of the main highway, the remains of Laodicea – Laodicea-on-the-Lycus.

The first thing that strikes you is the size: this was a *big* city.

There is no acropolis here – the whole thing is an acropolis: a huge, raised, diamond-shaped plateau, shaped not unlike the Isle of Wight (which in many ways seems like it has got stuck in the same era). The site was covered in savannah-high grass. It seemed less like an archaeological site, more like a nature reserve for old masonry. An arch emerged from the undergrowth, like a strange rock formation out at sea. Pillars, like the trunks of stone trees, the theatre – one of the theatres, actually, since there were two – like a huge bowl of ruined masonry. Occasionally you stumble across old tombs, their covers discarded and their incumbents long gone. Like old abandoned cars: a scrapyard of funerary monuments.

The remains of Laodicea rise from the foliage.

Although excavation work continues, most of ancient Laodicea remains submerged. At the west of the city, the top of the triple-arched Ephesus Gate emerges from the ground, like the humps of some sea monster. Ramsay's mysterious, romantic trade route from the Mediterranean came through here, drilling straight through the heart of the city, emerging on the other side at the so-called Syrian Gate. From there it took you east towards Colossae, and on to central

Anatolia. In John's time the Syrian Gate was new, built by Tiberius Claudius Tryphon, a freedman of the emperor Claudius. An ex-slave made good, he dedicated his gate to the emperor Domitian sometime around AD 84–5.

A messenger arrives in the city, footsore and tired, bringing news from John on far-off Patmos. He crosses the bridge over the small Asopus River (its columns can still be seen, rising above the surrounding vineyards). He is walking in the way of many other Christians, who sent letters along the roads in their own social network. Epaphras crossed this bridge in AD 60, bearing greetings from Paul imprisoned in far-off Rome. Thirty years later, here comes one of John's prophet-postmen.

And not a welcome message, at that.

Looking around on that day, Laodicea seemed sunken, submerged. As though the ground had, for a moment, become molten, and swallowed the city whole.

Which, in a way, it had.

*

Its position on the main trade route made Laodicea one of the wealthiest and most important commercial cities of Asia Minor. Although there were earlier settlements on the site, Laodicea as a city was really established by the Seleucid ruler Antiochus II (261–246 BC), who named the city after his wife, Laodice. Thank heavens she wasn't called Brenda. (Mind you, he divorced her in 253 BC, so clearly they didn't stay together for the sake of the city. As a love-gift goes, a bunch of flowers might have been cheaper.)

Still, Laodicea prospered, even if Antiochus's relationship with Laodice didn't. It minted its own currency – the coins featured Zeus, Asclepius, Apollo, plus various emperors, of course – and offered extensive banking facilities. (Cicero cashed a cheque here in 51 BC.) The region was known for its wool, and Laodicea traded in a unique black wool from the local area. Nearby Colossae also traded in wool, but theirs was cyclamen pink.

Laodicea boasted a major medical school, which was governed by Alexander Philalethes, whose pupil, Demosthenes, specialised in

The main street of Laodicea. Follow this road and it would take you far to the east, all the way to the Euphrates.

eye-care (I suppose being a 'pupil' helped). The region was known for its highly effective eye-salve, its recipe a closely guarded secret, but which probably used alum from the springs at nearby Hierapolis.

Christianity had established itself fairly early in the city, building on the presence of a large Jewish community. These Jews were wealthy enough to send considerable sums to the Temple: Cicero records a charge that twenty pounds of gold intended for Jerusalem was seized by the Roman authorities at one point. By the time Paul was writing to the city – in a letter which is now lost – there was a church in Laodicea under the leadership of a woman called Nympha (Col. 4.15).

Laodicea's location made it wealthy. But it faced problems. The biggest problem was water. That slave on parched, dry Delos, yearning for the water and figs of the Maeander, would have had the same problem just fifty miles down the valley in Laodicea. In summer the grass withers to brown straw, the yellow-white dust gets everywhere and, more significantly, the Lycus River dries up. Although there are nearby streams, they are not enough to supply a major city like Laodicea.

So water had to be imported. The Laodiceans built an aqueduct from a few miles away near Denizli. But instead of carrying the aqueduct on across the valley, as the water neared the city it was fed into two pressurised pipelines which plummeted into the valley and then up onto the plateau. The water pressure was good. The water *quality* was appalling.

I went in search of plumbing.

No, I don't mean I needed the bathroom. I genuinely was in search of ancient waterworks. (Actually, that *really* sounds like a euphemism.) Anyway, the road skirts the site of Laodicea to the south. I parked the car by some rather run-down houses and climbed up a slope into a field. Two small boys were there, playing football. They looked at me curiously, wondering, presumably, what a middle-aged, balding Englishman was doing clambering through a field. I passed a goat, chewing thoughtfully. He looked at me curiously as well, although in his case he was probably simply trying to work out if I was something that tasted any better than dry grass.

But there, in the field, I found what I was looking for: a terracotta pipe. Ancient plumbing. And that, my friends, is the thrill of international travel.

You know those TV commercials that warn you of the catastrophe awaiting your washing machine if you don't use their product to treat it for limescale? Well, the Laodiceans could have done with that stuff. The ancient pipe sticking out from the hillside showed a thick layer of calcium on the inside. The problem was that the water from the area was full of calcium carbonate: the same geology that created the white cliffs of Hierapolis also made the water supply to Laodicea taste simply horrible. This was a city with badly clogged arteries.

Strabo wrote that 'the changing of water into stone is said also to be the case with the rivers in Laodicea'. He did say the water was drinkable, but there's a world of difference between being drinkable and being good to drink. You can drink blood. You can drink urine, just about. You can even, at an absolute pinch, drink non-alcoholic lager. But you wouldn't want to.

Calcium-clogged pipes at Laodicea.

And that is why the message to the Laodiceans in Revelation begins as it does, with a reference to their water supply:

I know your works; you are neither cold nor hot. I wish that you were either cold or hot. So, because you are lukewarm, and neither cold nor hot, I am about to spit you out of my mouth. (Rev. 3.15–16)

Every Sunday, in some church around the world, a preacher will stand up and declare that the Laodiceans were 'lukewarm' about their faith. They were neither heavily pro (hot) nor heavily anti (cold). They were just ho hum. Or as my kids say, 'meh'. But this is not what John is saying. The word 'lukewarm' was not a metaphor for 'ambivalent' at the time. What he says is that they're neither the cold, drinkable fresh water of Colossae, nor the hot, medicinal water of Hierapolis. Both of those are useful. The Laodiceans aren't lukewarm, they're useless. Undrinkable. So the opening of the letter has an unmistakably local metaphor. And it continues in the same vein.

The message continues: 'You say, "I am rich, I have prospered, and I need nothing." You do not realise that you are wretched, pitiable, poor, blind, and naked' (Rev. 3.17). The Laodiceans, who had pulled themselves up by their own bootstraps after the earthquake, who were proud of their wealth and independence, were really nothings and nobodies. The letter recommends that instead of focusing on worldly wealth and privilege, they should 'buy from me gold refined by fire so that you may be rich; and white robes to clothe you and to keep the shame of your nakedness from being seen; and salve to anoint your eyes so that you may see' (Rev. 3:18).

Again, these words had a strong local resonance. Never mind the gold in the banks, what about spiritual gold? Never mind the black woollen cloth that brings such trade, choose white garments instead. And you know that eye treatment you all swear by? It's time to *really* open your eyes.

The letter to the Laodiceans is one of the parts of Revelation which is really opened up by knowledge of the place and its history. What we don't know, of course, is how the Laodiceans received it. Did they have ears to hear? Or did they send John's messenger packing, straight back out through the Ephesus Gate?

The message to Laodicea illustrates perfectly how the Christians for whom John felt responsible were facing very different challenges. In Laodicea's case, the problem was their luxury and wealth. They were rich people in a rich city, enjoying banquets at which their wealth was at its most conspicuous: fine clothing (locally sourced, don't you know), servants waiting at table, opulent furnishings, the best food and wine. John turns all this on its head. The Christian 'banquet' in Laodicea offered its guests neither a cold, thirst-quenching drink, nor a hot, medicinal one. Jesus says that he wants to come and eat with them, but only if they make changes to the menu.

Laodicea's Christians were simply sinking into their surroundings, and John wanted them to wake up. For the Christians in Laodicea, John wasn't solving a problem, because they didn't know they had one. He was causing a crisis, not solving one. The message to Laodicea must have landed like a bombshell into the smug, self-congratulatory world of the Laodicean Christians.

One of the best modern interpreters of Revelation, Harry O. Maier, speculates on what it's like to read Revelation like a Laodicean: not as someone who is persecuted, but one who is quite contented with the world, happy with a system that doesn't mind most people living in poverty as long as we can live in wealth. As I left the plumbing and the boys and the goat behind me, I reflected on how Laodicean our world is. We live in luxury, we revel in our designer labels and our 'high-ticket' branded goods. How would I feel, I wondered, if one day Jesus told me that really I was naked, wretched, pitiable, blind? If I heard him hammering at the door, or yelling through the letterbox, would I be pleased to see him? Would I even invite him in?

*

So the water supply was Laodicea's first major problem. The second was that, like Philadelphia and Sardis, Laodicea was earthquake central. In AD 60, some thirty years before John was writing, the city was completely destroyed in an earthquake. But again, Laodicea's wealth came to the fore. It refused any state handouts from the emperor and in a show of independent civic pride, paid for its own rebuilding. Laodicea was a proud, self-sufficient city. Various inscriptions attest to this spirit of independence. The enormous 900-foot-long stadium, with its state-of-the-art 360-degree seating and a subterranean tunnel through which horses and athletes could enter, was built by Nicostratus – who completed it, he boasted, 'on his own'. This was the Nicostratus Stadium, much like the Emirates or the O2 arena.

Revelation, though, is full of stories of the proud being flattened by events beyond their control. Earthquakes, volcanoes, scorched earth and fire in the sky: the Apocalypse is very much Catacecaumene country, the burnt land. The opening of the sixth seal brings about 'a great earthquake, the sun became as black as sackcloth, the full moon became like blood, and the stars of the sky fell to earth as the fig tree drops its winter fruit when shaken by a gale'. In the face of this, all of society – the kings, the generals, the courtiers and men of high status, slave and free – run to the rocks and hide, perhaps in the ornate cave-tombs, little houses for the dead, that were carved into the soft rock of the Lydian cliffs. There is another earthquake in chapter 8, when the angel throws incense down on the earth; two more in chapter 11, one of which kills thousands in Jerusalem, and the other when John's sight of the temple in heaven is accompanied by 'flashes of lightning, rumblings, peals of thunder, and earthquake, and heavy hail'. Or the British Summer Bank Holiday, as it's better known. The final earthquake comes during the emptying of the seventh bowl: 'a violent earthquake, such as had not occurred since people were upon the earth' (Rev. 16:18).

Why so many?

Mainly because people remembered such things. The earthquake of AD 17 destroyed or damaged up to fifteen towns and cities in the region. Sardis and Philadelphia suffered the worst: both were so devastated that their tribute money – the tax they paid the Romans for the privilege of, er, being Roman – was remitted for five years. Laodicea, as we've seen, was wrecked in AD 60. And a decade or so before John went to Patmos, news of the eruption of Vesuvius – a devastation which engulfed the town of Pompeii and even destroyed ships far out into the bay of Naples – had spread throughout the empire. So when John writes of mountains being shaken and when, with the blowing of the second trumpet, he writes that 'something like a great mountain, burning with fire, was thrown into the sea' (Rev. 8:8), many of his listeners would already have seen such events for themselves – or small-scale versions of them, at any rate. And those who had not witnessed them would have heard the stories.

Earthquakes feature so frequently in other apocalypses that scholars have a term for them: the eschatological earthquake. The idea is of a cataclysmic event, which collapses creation, steamrollers it, resets it to its original shapeless, formless state. It's the ultimate leveller. For example, 1 Enoch opens with a whole lot of shaking going on:

> *And the high mountains shall be shaken,*
> *And the high hills shall be made low,*
> *And shall melt like wax before the flame*
> *And the earth shall be wholly rent in sunder,*
> *And all that is upon the earth shall perish,*
> *And there shall be a judgment upon all (men).*
> *(1 Enoch 1:4–7)*

It's the language of cosmic trauma. These events are a kind of shorthand, symbols for an event which resets creation. They are (in a first-century context) undeniably from God – no human agency could perform such deeds. They strike at political and civic structures, because earthquakes destroy cities.

Laodicea had been rebuilt. But it was still on shaky ground.

*

Laodicea was one of several cities in the region where we know of churches. A few miles to the south-east was Colossae. And directly north was Hierapolis, or Pammukale, as it is known today. Pammukale means 'cotton castle' in Turkish – the name refers to the white calcium carbonate which has been deposited over thousands of years by the hot springs. From Laodicea you can see these white cliffs quite clearly, bright Tippex-white in the sunshine, turning shades of pink as dusk descends.

There was something else in Hierapolis which also feeds into the imagery of Revelation – an ancient tourist attraction which brought visitors from miles around. Nowadays people go to the site for the springs. (And they did in John's day – 'The city is full of natural baths,' said Strabo.)

But Hierapolis had another ancient claim to fame. It was, quite literally, a hole in the ground. Strabo describes it as a crack of 'only moderate size, large enough to admit a man' but which 'reaches a considerable depth'. From the depths came a dense, misty vapour, so thick that you could scarcely see your feet. The crack was enclosed

The main western entrance to Hierapolis.

by 'a quadrilateral handrail, about half a plethrum [about fifty feet] in circumference'. This was ancient health and safety. Outside the rail you could breathe, but 'any animal that passes inside meets instant death. At any rate,' says Strabo, 'bulls that are led into it fall and are dragged out dead; and I threw in sparrows and they immediately breathed their last.'

This was the Plutonium – named after Pluto, god of the underworld and friend of Mickey Mouse. It was, people believed, the gateway to hell. The only people who could survive the gas were the *Galli* – the priests of Cybele – although even they apparently emerged looking as though they had been half-suffocated. The *Galli* were eunuchs and Strabo was unsure as to whether their ability to withstand the vapours came from the divine protection of the goddess, or from their lack of accoutrements, as it were.

A recent Italian excavation has found the remains of the gateway itself, plus the remains of a thermal bath, a statue of Cerberus, the three-headed guard dog of the underworld, and a carving of a coiled serpent, symbol of the underworld.

'We could see the cave's lethal properties during the excavation,' said the lead archaeologist, in the accompanying press release. 'Several birds died as they tried to get close to the warm opening, instantly killed by the carbon dioxide fumes.' As evidence he posted a picture of some very small, very dead birds. Although, frankly, without the post-mortem results we don't know what caused the death. Could have been old age. Could have been a heart attack. Or the Italians might have fancied them for lunch.

The Plutonium was still in use in the fourth century AD. The temple by the entrance was destroyed 200 years later by Christians; the entrance to the pit was eventually closed up by earthquakes.

Today, most of those heading for the underworld use the more conventional approach.

*

The pit or the abyss is an image which often crops up in Revelation. John, perhaps with places like the Plutonium in mind, describes a deep pit from which the ultimate forces of darkness arise. Out of the pit emerge all the truly terrifying things in Revelation. In chapter 9, the blast of the fifth trumpet reveals a star which falls to earth where he – this star is a being of some sort – is 'given the key to the shaft of the bottomless pit'. The key turns. The shaft opens. Smoke rises like the smoke of a great furnace . . .

This fallen star is the 'king' of the abyss – the angel of the bottomless pit. That he 'falls' from heaven to earth needn't necessarily mean that he is fallen morally; it could just be that he has descended. In fact he seems to be carrying out God's orders. His name is given as Abaddon in Hebrew, Apollyon in Greek. The Hebrew word means 'place of destruction'. The Greek word means 'destroyer'. Out of the pit come the bearded locusts, representative of relentless, terrorising warfare. Out of the pit come the worst fears, the darkest horrors. Out of the bottomless pit will come the beast.

'Abaddon' appears elsewhere in the Bible, too – as the subterranean land of the dead in the book of Job, and as a place of destruction in Psalms and Proverbs. It becomes then like the Greek realm Hades: at once a place and a person. Apollyon is related to the Greek word for 'destroy', but John may be having a jibe here at

Apollo, the archer god, one of whose emblems was a locust. (His others were a mouse and a lizard, though. Not what you'd call fearsome.) Domitian had portrayed himself as Apollo, as had Nero.*

The idea of the abyss has some history in Christian teaching as well. When Jesus casts Legion out of the possessed man, the demons beg him 'not to order them to go back into the abyss' (Luke 8.31). Paul, writing his letter to the Romans, uses the abyss to mean the abode of the dead (Rom. 10.7).

At his second appearance in the book, in chapter 20, the angel of the bottomless pit is very clearly on the side of good and seizes the dragon, 'that ancient serpent, who is the Devil and Satan', and throws him into the pit for a thousand years. It is all these images – the pit and the devil and the smoke and the fire – that have been jumbled together with other biblical passages to inform our ideas of hell.

In the Bible, Satan – or *the* Satan, as he is generally referred to – is not just the embodiment of all evil. In the Old Testament, he actually has a job to do. He appears to have access to heaven, and he acts as a kind of witness for the prosecution. His name is really his job title: the word *satan* means 'adversary'. In the centuries between the end of the Old Testament and the beginning of the New, though, his job description expanded and he became the primary force for evil. He gained new names: Beelzebub, or lord of the flies. Or simply the evil one. A rebel against God, he appears as a malignant tempter of Jesus, or an evil force capable of entering humans and tempting them to do evil. In Greek he becomes *diabolos* – the slanderer. Other names were also attached to him: Beliar, Beelzebul, Abaddon, Apollyon, Lucifer, Sammael, Semihazeh, Asael. In Revelation he appears under several of these aliases. He is the great dragon, that ancient serpent, the devil, Satan, the deceiver of the whole world (Rev. 12.9).

---

* Like the beast, various historical figures have also been identified with Abaddon. The radical Franciscan Arnold of Villanova thought it was Thomas Aquinas, whose star fell, Arnold felt, from lofty theology and divine truth to dark, earthly ignorance. Others identified Abaddon with Luther, and the abyss with Lutheranism.

His attacks are tests and trials – trace memories of his origin. He is still the accuser, the tester. Although he now seems to have fallen much further, he still carries out this task with God's permission. His imprisonment in the pit for a thousand years is the origin of the famous (some might say notorious) idea of the millennium, the thousand-year rule of Christ, during which Satan is bound. At the end of this, Satan is released from his prison, and he deceives the nations into making war against 'the camp of the saints and the beloved city'.

Why this strange release? Well, maybe it goes back to his original job description. He is given one last opportunity to go out into the world and test people. It seems that, at the end, even God has a kind of faith in the accuser. He may overreach his rightful role, but it is still his to do. It's a final sorting out of the enemies and the faithful.

This image – Satan in the pit – is certainly one which has seared itself into the collective consciousness of the western world. And there is no greater reflection of that than his appearance in that most reliable of cultural indicators, *Doctor Who*, which did its own version of Revelation in an episode called 'The Satan Pit'. A mysterious beastly force has been possessing members of a spaceship. The beast terrorises each member of the crew, preying on their fears and weaknesses. The Doctor abseils down an enormous pit. At the bottom he finds – well, a Satan. A beast, with huge, red, curled horns. Straight out of the medieval doom paintings. It's a trap, or 'a road test for the final judgment', the Doctor muses. Rose eventually sends the human possessed by the beast into a black hole. 'Go to hell,' she says.

In Revelation no one has a forked tail and horns, though. The Satan is a serpent, a dragon. But this pop culture reference does reflect Revelation's depiction of the abyss not as the Satan's home, but as his prison. And he only gets out when God says so.

Before I left Pammukale I went to the springs and paddled around barefoot – rather painfully, actually, since the calcium is like sandpaper. It was too late to explore properly. The nearby Pammukale museum was closing and, regretfully, I had missed the opportunity to explore the intriguingly named 'Museum of Small Findings'. And

The calcium deposits at Pammukale.

I knew that beyond that building, up the hill, out in the ruins of Hierapolis there was Christian history. According to Christian tradition, somewhere out there Philip the evangelist and his daughters were buried. There had been a Christian community in Hierapolis from very early on. And if John knew Laodicea, then it was highly likely that he had come here as well.

But I had run out of time.

I stepped out of the springs, dried my feet and moved on.

9 The City That Time Forgot

There is nothing there.

No. Really.

Well, I mean, there's a modern town there, Akhisar, where life is lived and people are born, grow up, get married, and die and all that. But of ancient Thyatira, nothing. Just some chunks of old columns, a tomb in the grounds of the hospital and the remains of some sort of civic building dating from the fifth or sixth century AD. The rest of ancient Thyatira has gone. Disappeared. The past has been resurfaced.

Even in John's day, Thyatira was a nondescript kind of city. The other cities the angel wrote to were visually striking: Pergamum high on the hill, Ephesus with its famous temple and harbour, Laodicea on that plateau. But Thyatira was just a town, on level ground in the middle of a wide, unremarkable valley. No hill or mountain provided it with an acropolis or even a defensive citadel. Which probably explains why, whenever Thyatira receives one of its rare mentions in ancient literature, it's mainly because some ancient force or another has simply rolled right over it.

But Thyatira did have one thing going for it: trade. It may have had an unremarkable, unspectacular situation, but it was perfectly positioned for a manufacturing and trading city – even during those times when what was getting traded was itself. Founded in the third century BC, when the *Pax Romana* came along the city flourished. There were three gymnasiums, and a long, colonnaded portico lined with 100 columns. There were shops and shrines. Think new town. Think growing town. A town on the up. Yes, Thyatira is the ancient world's equivalent of Milton Keynes.

The city is connected with trade elsewhere in the New Testament. Lydia, the seller or manufacturer of purple cloth, came from Thyatira. There was a *bapseis* guild in the city – a guild of dyers. And this guild is mentioned more in the inscriptions of the city than any other.

Trade guilds were common in the cities of Asia. Pergamum and Laodicea had dyers. Smyrna, silversmiths and goldsmiths. Ephesus, bakers. Thyatira and Philadelphia, wool-workers. Sardis, builders. In Thyatira, along with the dyers, there were guilds of wool-workers, linen-workers and leather-workers. There were 'makers of outer garments', tanners, potters, and bakers. There was a guild of slave dealers; we know that there were thriving slave markets at Ephesus and Sardis and Thyatira. The Rotary Club, eat your heart out.

The guilds shared some of the tasks of our modern trades unions, protecting the rights of workers, engaging in collective bargaining, and even, occasionally, going on strike. At Miletus some builders consulted the oracle over whether they should abandon the job they were on and move to another one. The world turns, civilisations rise and fall, but one thing remains constant: builders never turn up when you expect them to. But guild membership also had a deeply religious aspect. Banquets for members of the guild often took place within a pagan temple shrine; animals were sacrificed to the gods and then eaten by the guilds.

The patron deity of the guilds in Thyatira was Apollo Tyrimnaeus, a god associated with the power of the sun. This version of Apollo was a mashup, specifically developed to meet local needs. Tyrimnos was a military hero from the early days of the city, depicted on their coins holding a battle-axe, riding a horse, and entirely naked, except for a cloak. (Let's hope he was careful with the axe.) By John's day, the coins showed the god Apollo, the son of Zeus, but in the style of Tyrimnos. Wearing his clothes, as it were. Or lack thereof. It was a blend of traditions: an older, Phrygian god mixed with the Greek Apollo. And for good measure he is often shown shaking hands with those other famous gods, the Roman emperors. This god is an admixture. A blend. An alloy. It also might be why the message to Thyatira contains the only overt use in Revelation of the title 'the Son of God'.* Apollo was the son of Zeus, after all.

It also might explain why the figure of Jesus we meet early on in the book of Revelation, rather curiously, has metal feet.

---

* Although it's clearly implied elsewhere (e.g. Rev. 1.6; 2.27; 3.5, 21; 14.1).

In Daniel 10.6 we read that 'one like a son of man' has 'arms and legs like the gleam of burnished bronze'. In the first century, bronze feet and arms were common on what are called chalcolithic statues – where the body was made of wood and the limbs and head were made of metal. There was a famously huge statue of Nero in Rome which had feet of bronze. Bare feet were also a sign of divinity. The famous statue of Augustus known as the *Prima Porta* depicted the emperor barefoot. Sort of like Paul McCartney on the *Abbey Road* cover. Reliefs found at Ravenna show four deceased members of the imperial family with bare feet, as does a statue of Claudius as Jupiter in the Vatican.

The Greek word that John uses in talking about Jesus' feet here (Rev. 2.18; 1.15) is *chalkolibanos*, a word unique to Revelation. John uses it twice but it is not found in any other ancient text. It's a compound word describing, probably, a compound metal. Most translations opt for either burnished bronze, or fine brass. The first part, *chalkos*, is usually used of copper and its alloys brass (copper and zinc) and bronze (copper and tin). Bronze was also called *oreichalkos*, most commonly when making imperial coins. But the second part of the word is strange: *libanos* means frankincense, either the tree from which the incense was derived or the incense itself. So *chalkolibanos* could mean brass-like or brass-coloured frankincense – i.e. yellow frankincense. More likely, though, is that this was some kind of special metal produced in Thyatira.* There was certainly a guild of specialised metal-workers in Thyatira known as the *chalkeis*.

Perhaps there was a statue of their patron Apollo in the town, its feet embellished with this special metal? Whatever the case, Revelation's depiction of Jesus builds on Old Testament imagery, but also squarely positions him up against the statues of the gods in the cities of the empire. Apollo may be the son of Zeus; Jesus is the Son of the real thing.

*

* Colin Hemer suggested that the metal is zinc, although there aren't many examples of zinc being used in the ancient world. (Brass was made using zinc compounds, rather than the metal itself.)

The letter to Thyatira is the longest message of the seven, well over twice as long as the shortest message, to Smyrna. The reason for that is that John here wants to address a very specific problem: a false prophetess whom he calls Jezebel. The Thyatira church is praised at first; their 'last works are greater than the first'. In other words, they are showing steady improvement. But they tolerate the presence of this woman 'who calls herself a prophet and is teaching and beguiling my servants to practise fornication and to eat food sacrificed to idols'.

In the Old Testament, Jezebel was the name of King Ahab's Phoenician wife, who brought the prophets of Baal into the court of Israel and tried to wipe out the true prophets. The implication is that, as a prophetess, this new Jezebel is stating that it's fine to be a fully paid-up member of the guilds, to go to the feasts, to eat meat sacrificed to idols. She leads a faction within the Christian community who see no conflict between following Jesus and being involved in civic life and the ritual that goes with it. It's just, you know, good business.

False leadership was, from early on, a big problem for the church. Ancient culture was an aural culture: for the most part news and teaching was spoken, heard, learnt and remembered. So the good news about Jesus was taken out through the Roman empire by a steady stream of travelling apostles, teachers and prophets, telling their stories, passing on what they had learned and serving the church.

Lucian of Samosata was a satirist who wrote in the mid to late second century. His story about a charlatan philosopher called Peregrinus is one of the earliest pagan accounts of Christians. On the run after murdering his father, Peregrinus ends up in Palestine, where he tricks a group of Christians into making him their leader:

> He was prophet, cult-leader, head of the synagogue, and every-thing, all by himself. He interpreted and explained some of their books and even composed many, and they revered him as a god, made use of him as a lawgiver, and set him down as a protector, next after that other, to be sure, whom they still worship, the man who was crucified in Palestine because he introduced this new cult into the world.

Peregrinus was thrown into prison, but continued to be supported by the church. Indeed, his fame spread further afield:

> Indeed, people came even from the cities in Asia, sent by the Christians at their common expense, to succour and defend and encourage the hero. They show incredible speed whenever any such public action is taken; for in no time they lavish their all. So it was then in the case of Peregrinus; much money came to him from them by reason of his imprisonment, and he procured not a little revenue from it. The poor wretches have convinced themselves, first and foremost, that they are going to be immortal and live for all time, in consequence of which they despise death and even willingly give themselves into custody; most of them.

Lucian goes on to say that Christians are guilty of 'denying the Greek gods' and 'worshipping that crucified sophist himself and living under his laws'. Now Lucian is a satirist, not an historian. But the work shows us what pagans like Lucian believed of Christians. The faith he describes is inescapably Jewish; Lucian uses terms like 'synagogues' and 'priests' and 'scribes'. The community includes widows and orphans, holds goods in common, supports its members in prison, is ready to suffer for its beliefs and has a network of communication which brings other Christian leaders to offer support. Most of all, they deny the Greek gods and worship Jesus.

It's a picture which could have come straight out of Revelation. But it also pokes at a vulnerability within the system. Peregrinus is a con artist who is able to exploit the Christian community for his own ends. In this letter, though, the issue is slightly different. There is no indication that Codename Jezebel and Codename Balaam are profiting from their teaching. The problem is that – as John sees it – their teaching is pulling the Christian communities away from the true path.

This was a problem which had been spotted much earlier by Paul, whose letters often deal with problems of leadership, or situations where one faction is set against another. In Acts, he has a meeting in Miletus, just south of Ephesus, where he warns the Ephesian leaders that there is trouble coming, that 'savage wolves' will descend on the flock, 'distorting the truth in order to entice the disciples to follow them' (Acts 20:29). In Thyatira we see one of these wolves in action; encouraging compromise and integration, denying the cost of discipleship. The issue for the Christians in Thyatira was that they were too enmeshed in the life of the city itself. The upwardly mobile city had caught them up along with it.

Thyatira reached the height of its commercial success in the next two centuries. The emperor Hadrian apparently visited the city around AD 124, the emperor Caracalla in 214.

Which is more, frankly, than I did.

I *meant* to go, but you know, sometimes arrangements don't go right, plans go awry.

Oh, all right. I didn't even make any plans or any arrangements. I wasn't going to go all that way to look at a few pillars in a park.

I had to get to Ephesus.

10 Missing Temple, Missing Man

The train from Izmir to Selçuk. Orange and blue livery. Grey sheds. Small wayside stations with painted cast-iron pillars. A plain filled with olives and fig and apple trees. Mountains in the distance, tan-coloured, speckled with greenery. Grey rocks studding the landscape. And above it all, the brilliant blue Aegean sky. A salesman weaves through the carriages, bearing a towering ziggurat of *simit* – Turkish bread-rings covered in sesame seeds – on a tray. Part salesman, part circus act.

My travelling companions for the journey are: three Danish men, in Turkey for a friend's wedding; two Chinese girls carefully studying their guidebooks; a Turkish woman and her daughter; and a dead Englishman called John Turtle Wood.

OK, so the latter was more there in spirit. I was reading the account he made of his excavations in Ephesus 150 years earlier, when he took the same train journey.

The magnificently named John Turtle Wood was one of the great amateur archaeologists of the Victorian era. He was an architect and originally came to Turkey to design railway stations on the line from Smyrna (Izmir) to Denizli (Laodicea). But he conceived a passion for archaeology and, particularly, for discovering the site of the Artemision at Ephesus – the temple of Artemis, the greatest of the seven wonders of the world.

The site of the city of Ephesus itself was not lost, although *Murray's Handbook to Asia Minor* – the Rough Guide of its day – recorded that 'a visit to Ephesus will often be productive of disappointment'. Even in the 1930s H. V. Morton could write: 'Few people ever visit. The Turkish lads who herd the goats of Seljuk sometimes wander through its marble streets, but they are not too fond of doing so. Ephesus has a weird, haunted look.'

Ephesus was a city crammed with magnificent buildings and monuments. But the most important monument, the one which brought visitors to Ephesus from all around the Græco-Roman world, was the Artemision. The original temple had burned to the ground in 356 BC, on the night of Alexander the Great's death. It was rebuilt about five years later, a magnificent building of unsurpassed splendour. It measured 140 yards by 75 (four times the size of the Parthenon in Athens) and was adorned with 128 pillars, each 60 feet high.

The statue of the goddess stood on a plinth at the western end. She was depicted as a multi-breasted woman, a fertility symbol, wearing a crown of city walls. Like her chest, her fame was enormous. The Greek traveller Pausanias wrote: 'All cities worship Artemis of the Ephesians and individuals hold her in honour above all the gods.'* He puts her fame down to 'the antiquity of the sanctuary', the size of the temple and the 'eminent' status of Ephesus. The magnificence of her temple, and the cult surrounding it, made Ephesus a pilgrimage city, and its traders and silversmiths made their money selling statues of the goddess.

When Wood arrived at the site the temple was long gone. No one had set eyes on it for 500 years. The British Museum gave him a barely adequate amount of money (in return for which they had the rights to anything he might find) and for six years he dug, defying malaria, bandits, Turkish bureaucracy, poverty and being attacked in the streets of Smyrna by a 'lunatic Turk'. He fended off the assailant with his walking stick, but was stabbed in the chest and nearly died.

Despite finding a considerable number of fragments (most of which ended up in Room 82 of the British Museum), after six years of searching Wood had still not managed to find the Artemision. Then he struck lucky. In February 1866 he began excavating the great theatre. In the southern entrance he found an inscription describing

* Pausanias (c. AD 110–80) was the author of the first known guidebook, the *Description of Greece*. It took him ten years of travelling to research. He was probably from Lydia, the area which includes the cities of Revelation. As well as travelling through Greece, he went to Syria, Egypt and Palestine. His book is eye-wateringly detailed, and so reliable that modern archaeologists later used it to help them discover ancient ruins.

Artemis of the Ephesians. Getting a dress to fit must have been murder.

how, on Artemis's birthday (it's 25 May, in case you want to send a card), statues of the goddess would be carried from the Artemision, arrive at the Magnesian Gate, be taken to the theatre and then returned to the temple by the Coressian Gate.

Now all he had to do was find those gates, then the roads from those gates, and by triangulating the two he could find the site of the Artemision. It took him another three years, during which time he nearly died falling off a wall, had all his furniture stolen by burglars, was stricken by malaria and had all his workmen detained for questioning in a murder investigation.

Finally, in May 1869, with the British Museum threatening to cease funding this 'apparently hopeless enterprise', he found what he had been searching for: the wall of the temple. And over the next few years he unearthed what little of the original remained. It was a remarkable piece of detective work, not least because there was no sign of the temple remains at the surface. Over the centuries, streams flowing down from the mountains had buried it beneath a twenty-foot layer of silt.

Wood was a pioneer, one of the true legends of Victorian excavation. He carried on working at the site for another six years before finally returning to England. He was granted a pension of £200 by the government. He died among another ancient people: the inhabitants of Worthing, Sussex. The book he wrote about his experiences is a wonderful read and a testimony to his enduring love for the area. 'I never became weary of the scenery by which I was surrounded,' he wrote, 'for the mountains on which my eyes daily rested changed from hour to hour as the sun travelled its course, and the desolation of the place was fully compensated by its constant and never-ceasing loveliness.'

'Never-ceasing loveliness' is not a phrase you would use of the Artemision today. The route from the town of Selçuk takes you along a path that is little more than the verge on the side of the main highway, through a small public exercise area – little used, it seems – across a patch of public land cluttered with litter and old cans and dog's mess. A pair of rusty gates leads you to a half-empty car park, where three or four listless hawkers will try to flog you postcards, hats, fridge magnets and plastic statuettes of Artemis. One man – the most prominent salesman – had spread his goods out all over his tiny red car.

'Look,' said one of the hawkers, 'here is 3D picture book. See it as it used to be. Bring back to life.' Good luck with that. It would take more than a 3D book to bring this place back to life.

The Artemision is a drab and desolate place. The remains, such as they are, lie in a wide, swampy depression. At one end is a green, stagnant pool from which a frog occasionally croaks in a slightly depressed manner. At the other end stands a rickety pillar on the top of which a crane had built a nest, making it look as though the pillar was wearing a toupee. This place is more grotty than grotto, and a lot more shabby than sacred.

You get the feeling that the hawkers here would rather be making their pitch at the more impressive site that is Ephesus proper, but they too are the also-rans.

The discovery of the Artemision was a marvellous act of treasure hunting, but the treasure itself had long gone.

*

The Artemision today. In the background the medieval citadel and the remains of the Basilica of St John.

Ephesus has deep Christian roots. At one time or another many apostles and well-known church figures ended up in the city. There was Paul, of course – irascible, excited, passionate, never giving an inch – who stayed in the city for two years between AD 53 and 55. In Ephesus, according to his own words, he 'fought with beasts' and was forced to leave the city to save his own life in the aftermath of the silversmith's riot. There were Priscilla and Aquila, who founded the church in the city; and Apollos, a Christian from Alexandria, the great grain-capital of the ancient world.

But perhaps the city's most famous inhabitant is someone who is, in a way, harder to pin down. He can still be traced there, even in the name of the pleasant modern town of Selçuk. Its original name was Ayasoluk, itself a corruption of *Agios Theologos* – Holy Theologian – the Greek term for John. Church tradition says that John lived in Ephesus, taught there, worshipped there. From Ephesus, according to church tradition, he was sent into exile on

Patmos. And, returning to the city, he made it his home for the rest of his life.

And he was buried just behind my hotel.

*

The remains of the Basilica of St John stand on the side of a hill overlooking the ancient site of the Artemision. Today these extensive ruins are no longer a place of worship. As I walked up the hill towards the entrance, a call to prayer shivered through the air from the mosque on the street below. Turkey is now, of course, an Islamic country. But at one time – for many centuries, in fact – this region was the heartland of Christianity.

Ephesus was one of the major Christian cities of the world. At the beginning of the second century, the bishop of Ephesus was one Onesimus, who may well be the same person who is mentioned in Paul's letter to Philemon.*

In the heyday of the Byzantine empire, Ephesus was resplendent with magnificent churches, the meeting place of important church councils, its status enhanced by the tradition that Mary, mother of Jesus, spent her last years in the city. And the biggest and most important building of all was one of the greatest churches in the Byzantine empire – the huge, sixth-century Church of St John the Theologian.†

In its day it was one of the biggest churches in the world. Among the ruins there is a sign claiming that if it were intact today it would still be the seventh largest cathedral in the world. Actually, I noticed that the sign had the curious heading: 'Proposed Sign for erection at the Basilica of St John'. This was rather confusing since the sign

---

* Among his 'team' are Burrhus, a deacon, and Crocus, Euplous, and Fronto (Ignatius, Eph. 2.1), who I rather thought was a character in *The Lord of the Rings*.

† The Eastern Orthodox Church only grants the title 'theologian' to three people: John, Gregory of Nazianzus and a monk called Symeon, whom it terms the 'New Theologian'. It is using the word not in its modern sense of academic discussion – theology – but in the sense of someone who had a personal, intense vision of God. A direct encounter.

The Basilica of St John as it looks now and (below) as it was in its glory days.

ST JEAN IN MEZARI
THE TOMB OF
ST JOHN

actually had been erected. I couldn't work out if this was the finished sign or whether it was a sign of things to come. Anyway, nearby a wonderful model shows the church in its heyday, a huge six-domed basilica, a glorious mountain of domes and colonnades. A multitude of white marble pillars, contrasting with deep-scarlet brick, arched windows in their hundreds. To the north stood the octagonal baptistry, with its tiled roof. The entrance was topped with five cupolas and beyond that the main dome of the church soared majestically over the high altar. I took a little video of the model and for a moment I was a helicopter flying over the Byzantine empire, all sweeping fly-past shots and overhead views: what a journey that would have been.

All gone, of course. Now there are only ruins, where the swifts and the swallows dart. I wandered. Some of the Byzantine brick walls have been restored with courses of slim, almost tile-like Roman brickwork. A couple of elegant arches were graceful reminders of the grandeur. At one point a coachload of Japanese tourists arrived, and the site was full of the buzz of noise and the whirring of camera shutters. And then, as soon as they had come they had gone. And it was just me. Alone in an avenue of sun-bleached columns, staring at a small plaque on the ground: ST JEAN IN MEZARI, 'The Tomb of St John'.

*

As we've seen, the traditions linking John with Ephesus go way back, to Irenaeus of Lyons in the late second century. A man called Polycrates, writing to Victor, bishop of Rome, also records the tradition that John 'has fallen asleep at Ephesus'.

Out of these tiny threads of tradition, later writers and storytellers wove a huge tapestry of wild, apocryphal stories. They read more like fairy stories than anything else. The earliest examples are found in *The Acts of Saint John*, a late second-century text full of marvellously bonkers events. It tells how the apostle John arrives in Ephesus, raises various people from the dead, preaches and heals people in the theatre, and prays so powerfully outside the Artemision that the altar of Artemis shatters into many pieces and 'half the temple fell down', killing a young priest, whom John later restores to life. (Maybe it is John's fault that the temple was so comprehensively ruined?) *The Acts* claims that John spent four years in Ephesus and then went to Smyrna and Laodicea. His journey includes many more wonders, including a miraculous expulsion of bed bugs from a mattress at an inn. (The bed bugs wait patiently at the door while John sleeps, before returning to their mattress in the morning.)

Curiously, the earliest copies of these apostolic adventures contain no reference to Patmos at all. But they do contain bits which seem to have been added by more esoteric, probably Gnostic, writers. The most famous of these is an episode where John, describing the last supper, tells how Jesus organised everyone into a circle and they all had a dance, while singing a distinctly mystical hymn:

> The number eight singeth praise with us. Amen.
> The number twelve danceth on high. Amen.
> The whole on high hath part in our dancing. Amen.
> Whoso danceth not, knoweth not what cometh to pass. Amen.
> [Oh, oh, the hokey cokey, etc.]

Not so much the last supper, more the last waltz. Obviously much of this is nothing more than pious fiction, but it does display a basic assumption: that John lived and died at Ephesus. Generally, the stories also assume that there was just one John, who wrote the gospel, the letters and Revelation. But the early church historian Eusebius records the claim that 'two persons in Asia have borne the same name, and that there were two tombs at Ephesus, each of which is still to this day said to be John's.' It's quite possible that the author of the gospel – the Beloved Disciple – came to Ephesus. It was that kind of place: everyone seemed to end up there at some point. But given his association with Ephesus, I think we can be sure that John the Elder was definitely there. Perhaps he even died there.

Perhaps he was buried nearby.

Perhaps.

I sat for a long time by the grave that afternoon.

There are apocryphal accounts of John's death in various books. In *The Acts of John*, he ordered his friends to dig him a grave, a trench where, after giving thanks and preparing himself, he lay down.

His friends covered him in a linen cloth and went home. They came back the next day 'and found not his body'. Another version says they found only his sandals, but that the earth moved as if he was breathing underneath.

Another work, called *The Story of John, Son of Zebedee*, dating from the fifth or sixth century, describes how John lived in Ephesus until the age of 120, where 'he sat in that hut winter and summer, until a hundred and twenty years had gone over him. Then his Lord hid him in that place as He hid Moses in the mountain of Moab.'

Later, on Patmos, a monk told me yet another version in which, close to death, John ordered his friends to dig him a grave. They dug it deep enough to cover only the bottom half of his body, and he ordered them to bury him completely. Pointing out that he was still alive, they refused to do this. So in the end he lay down in the grave and they covered him with a cloth. Later, his faithful secretary Prochorus, who was not present for this partial burial, went to see his old master, but all he found was a bit of cloth and a hole in the ground.

All stories.

But all with disappearances. Clearly people found the idea that John might have been whisked up to heaven like Elijah attractive, especially when we consider the fact that he had made some day trips there during his time on Patmos. But interestingly, no church, as far as I can tell, has ever claimed to hold the relics of John. This is odd, because, after Constantine made Christianity official, there was a godly rush for saints' remains and they started miraculously turning up all over the place. Mark's remains were at Alexandria (before the Venetians stole him). Peter and Paul are at Rome. Matthew has been claimed by Salerno and Luke is supposed to be at Padua, with other bits at Prague and Thebes.

The body of John went awol. 'Legend states,' claims the meta-sign in the church, 'that when the tomb was opened in later centuries it was found to contain only dust which quickly dissipated in the air.'

That's John for you. You can't see him for sacred dust.

When Dean Stanley visited Ephesus in the early twentieth century, accompanying the then Prince of Wales, the site was in a parlous state. 'There is nothing to recall St. John,' he wrote, 'except the rock-hewn tomb, called by his name near the summit of the deserted hill; the grave of the greatest of all the apostles, if we may measure greatness by the divine excellence of the works which bear his name, lies overgrown with brushwood, and only marked by the broken offerings of a few Greek peasants.'

I was feeling a bit broken by this point, certainly. I had a blister on my foot the size of, well, my foot. And after a long day travelling I could give the average Greek peasant a run for his money in the hygiene stakes as well. But I had no offering to make. I just sat there, thinking how nice it would be if the remains of John of Patmos were actually there. Or near, at least. It would be nice to think that, after his exile, he did make it home.

11 The Coin and the Harbour

I was given a lift to Ephesus by the hotel owner, a rather jolly, friendly man, who the night before had sat watching the football, between serving me fresh sea-bass, followed by an enormous heap of cold, plump grapes. Business was not good. A hotelier in the town for many years, he was bemoaning the fact that tourist numbers were down.

'It's Syria,' he said. 'Everyone thinks that Turkey is near Syria.'

Well, bits of Turkey are near Syria, of course, but those bits are a long, long way from Ephesus. But then there had been protests earlier in the year from Turks who are fearful of a pro-Islamic agenda in the government. Young Turks – particularly young women – look at what life is like for their contemporaries in the rest of the Islamic world and see a world of burkas and religious oppression. And they don't want it. But the unrest put visitors off, even though, that too, was a long way away.

'People who don't come,' he said. 'They don't realise what they are missing.'

Well, that's true.

Ephesus is fantastic. An inscription found in the city boasts of Ephesus being the 'most illustrious city', and nothing on the site would make you dispute that boast. He dropped me at the Magnesian Gate, one of the two gates discovered by Wood, from which he worked out the location of the Artemision.

Entering through the Magnesian Gate would bring the traveller to the wide expanse of the State Agora, the administrative district of Ephesus. Lined by colonnades and full of temples and shrines, the large square was a celebration of the apparatus of state. It was full of reminders of who was actually in charge. On the north side a judicial and administrative centre was dedicated not only to Artemis – understandable in Ephesus – but also to two emperors: Augustus and Tiberius. And more or less smack in the middle of the Agora is a low, square-shaped wall. In the middle of the square a solitary fir tree rises up. This was the site of a small temple, built some time around 25 BC and dedicated to the 'divine' Julius Caesar and to Roma, the goddess of Rome.

Along with Artemis, of whom there were many statues in the city, Ephesus had plenty of other gods on display too. There were statues of Aphrodite in abundance, sometimes draped, sometimes coyly nude, wisps of material just about covering her modesty. There was Eros, Athena, and an abundance of foreign gods such as Isis and Serapis. Male gods were less evident; this was, after all, a city dominated by a goddess. There were a few statues of Zeus, and of Apollo who, according to myth, had first suggested the site of the city to the founders and whose sanctuary stood at the harbour. Asclepius stood in the baths, of course. At the Triodos, the crossroads in the centre of town, stood Hecate, goddess of crossroads. (An inscription on the South Gate, in the Lower Agora, calls on Hecate to take revenge on anyone urinating there.)

In John's day, then, Ephesus was a city of many gods. Some were the old deities, ancient, as deep-rooted as mountains; others had been added to the pantheon within living memory. In fact, the newest temple in the city belonged to the newest of the gods. And these were very new indeed. . .

*

Leave the beaten track. Head off at right angles to the tour groups. Off-piste. On the less-visited south side of the State Agora, there is a marble-paved street, lined with fallen pillars. Go to the west end of the street. From there the dedicated – not to say slightly obsessed – explorer can scramble up a bank of brush and dirt to reach a wide plateau-like terrace.

Nobody comes up here. Why would they? There is nothing to see here; it's just sun-dried grass and brown scrub and the odd bird. A few cylinders from long-toppled columns stand in the vegetation like discarded oil drums. But cross the plateau and the view suddenly opens out and the whole city unfolds in front of you. To your right the expanse of the State Agora, straight ahead the slopes of Mount

Pion, to your left the curving sweep of Curetes Street, as it descends to the Lower Agora and then on to the harbour.* Today the view is obscured by trees and the hillside is home to nothing but scrub and brown dirt. Silt has overcome the once great harbour and the sea is a long way out of sight. But in John's day there were houses on the slopes and a constant flow of trade clattering up and down the stone streets. What a view this must have been.

Apart from the view, though, there is little to mark this mound out as special. But this may well be one of the most influential places in the book of Revelation. This is no normal mound. Beneath the dry earth and the scorched brown grass are arches and tunnels, stone walls, windows. This is a man-made terrace, and on it once stood the most impressive temple in the city: the Temple of the Flavian Sebastoi – the 'august Flavians'. They were the imperial family: Vespasian, his sons Titus and Domitian, the latest top dogs in the Roman empire.

The proper entrance to the temple was on the northern side. From the Upper Agora, a road known simply as *Kathodos* – 'the way down' – led you to a spacious courtyard which today is known as Domitian Square. Visitors to the temple would then pass through a triple gateway, across the square and up a double stairway to the top of the terrace, where the temple stood behind a row of columns.

The dedication of the temple took place in AD 89 or 90, and it was a massive occasion for the area. Cities throughout Asia sent gifts: statues which were installed in the temple precincts proclaiming their 'reverence to the *Sebastoi* and . . . goodwill towards the *neokorate* city of the Ephesians, [because of] Asia's common Temple of the *Sebastoi* in Ephesus'.

---

* In John's day, one of the most important buildings in Ephesus was the Prytaneion, the temple of the sacred flame of Hestia – the flame in the temple was kept burning continuously. The goddess Hestia's name means 'home and hearth': she was the original domestic goddess. Her temple was manned by priests known as Curetes. Their names are inscribed on columns lining the main street which heads down towards the lower city and the theatre. For that reason the main street in Ephesus has become known as Curetes Street.

The site of the once magnificent Temple of the Flavian Sebastoi. Below:
The entrance from 'Domitian Square'.

Ephesus had a shiny new temple to the emperor. The Temple of the Sebastoi in Ephesus was the third provincial temple of the imperial cult in Asia. At that time no province had more than one. Asia was blazing a trail. It was the empire's new BFF. And everyone knew how important it was to show your loyalty.

Having the imperial temple gave Ephesus a higher status than other cities. And serving in the imperial temple gave individuals increased status as well. Those who served as high priests for the Temple of the Sebastoi were members of the elite strata of society. The imperial cult was a way for both city and citizens to acquire status. It gave them access to the circles of the elite and powerful. It was a good chance to meet those with cash and influence. This is why in Asia Minor the imperial cult was popular among trade associations of the area. It was like the Freemasons, with togas.

*

Let's go downstairs for a moment. In the ruined substructure of the Temple of the Sebastoi, in the vaults, archaeologists found the remains of an enormous statue. All that was left was a huge head and the left arm, but at one time it stood twenty-five feet tall. It was what is known as an acrolithic statue – the torso was made of wood and the head, hands and feet were made of stone. Its left hand held a spear. Acrolithic statues were dressed like mannequins – draped with cloth covering the wooden frame and leaving only the stone head and the extremities visible. This statue probably stood against a wall (we know that because the back of the head was left unpainted).

The head is huge. It stands today in the museum at Ephesus, a massive carved boulder of stone. There are arguments as to whether it represents Titus or Domitian – but whichever brother it was, you could not miss the message: the emperor was not like normal men. He was a giant, a creature of unyielding and unstoppable power. He was a god. And it is that idea, expressed in these statues and in these temples, that Revelation reframes. Because in the warped mirror-world of Revelation the emperor appears, not as a mighty, godlike warrior, but as a beast, a beast so powerful that his supporters chant: 'Who can oppose him?'

*

Head of an emperor. Domitian or Titus? Whoever he was, he was big.

As we've seen, Ephesus was one of the most important and influential centres of Christianity. And this sense of importance is reflected in the message Jesus delivers to the church in Revelation. It begins with the church being commended for 'your works, your toil and your patient endurance'. The church is 'enduring patiently and bearing up for the sake of my name' and has 'not grown weary'. But there is bad news: 'you have abandoned the love you had at first. Remember then from what you have fallen; repent, and do the works you did at first' (Rev. 2.2–7).

141

So we see a picture of a once mighty church, still powerful, still enduring, still working, but which has lost touch with its glory days. This is a church which has hit the heights, but which now has fallen back from its previous achievements. This is a church which, spiritually, is in danger of silting up.

The opening to the letter is intriguing. Jesus describes himself as one 'who holds the seven stars in his right hand'. This obviously refers to his appearance at the beginning of the book, but it also links with another historical figure. Another 'son of god', in fact. And a coin.

The coin is a denarius. On one side it shows the emperor Domitian. But on the reverse is an image of his son – we don't know his name – who died in infancy. The inscription around him runs: DIVUS CAESAR IMP DOMITIAN IF – 'the divine Caesar, son of the emperor Domitian'. He is naked, and sitting on the globe. His arms are stretched out and between them there are seven stars. This little lad, this 'son of god', is holding the seven stars in his hands.

Domitian and son. The deceased son of the emperor, holding the seven stars in his hand. Used by permission of Classical Numismatic Group. www.cngcoins.com

Nothing gets to the heart of how Revelation works better than this simple image. It is one of the few images in Revelation which is actually explained. John tells us that the seven stars stand for the 'angels of the seven churches' (1.20). So, at the top level, the image is straightforward: Jesus is the one who holds – who commands – the angels, the spirits of these seven churches. (And seven, as we know, means wholeness, completeness. So you could argue that this image shows that Jesus holds *all* the angels of *all* the churches in his hands.)

But why 'stars'? Time to drill down (or up?) to the next level. The seven stars were a shorthand for the whole universe. It probably means, in fact, the seven planets, which the pre-telescope ancient world believed to be the Sun, the Moon, Jupiter, Mercury, Mars, Venus, and Saturn.* So this figure has the universe in his hands.

And then, to give us a whole new angle, there is the coin. Suddenly this is not just an image of Jesus, a statement of his control over his creation at all levels; it's also a subversive sideswipe at the Roman emperors and their claims. The 'divine' Domitian had coins struck showing his dead son as a god, sitting on the earth and holding the seven stars. Now John shows us a Jesus who makes exactly the same claim: the Son of God, holding the stars, thought to be dead, but actually alive and wielding universal power.

*

As we've seen, Domitian was certainly not the first emperor to be deified. But the difference was that most of the emperors (with the odd, insane exception) were only officially deified after their death. Domitian, according to most histories, claimed divinity while he was still alive. The historian Dio Cassius claimed that Domitian 'even insisted upon being regarded as a god and took vast pride in being called "master" and god. These titles were used not merely in speech but also in written documents.'

Now the histories were written by his enemies, and by supporters of the dynasty which succeeded him, so we have to be careful here. Some have challenged the view of Domitian as an out-of-control, delusional tyrant, arguing that the historians who record this all have axes to grind and are over-egging the whole thing. Certainly Domitian does appear rather as a pantomime villain, perpetually plotting against his brothers, pretending to be grief-stricken at the death of his brother, Titus, when he was really rubbing his hands with glee, descending into paranoia and madness, wallowing in blood. Suetonius describes how Domitian's later years saw him become an

---

* These stars were also significant in Mithraism. The seven stars could also refer to Ursa Major (the Plough or Great Bear) or the Pleiades.

'object of terror and hatred to all'. He was accused of cutting off the hands of prisoners, of crucifying a man with whom he had feasted the previous day. He executed his own cousin. He embarked on a massive building campaign which reduced the empire to penury, and confiscated estates to pay for his excesses. There was chaos and disorder on his watch.

Maybe we should take some things with a pinch of salt. But the character assassination is pretty consistent. And Domitian was assassinated, which is not *normally* a sign of popularity. What's more, the audience which was being written to could remember the truth. In Pliny's *Panegyricus*, delivered in AD 100, he describes Domitian's palace, for example, as the 'place where . . . that fearful monster built his defences with untold terrors, where lurking in his den he licked up the blood of his murdered relatives or emerged to plot the massacre and destruction of his most distinguished subjects'. In a letter written around the same time, he says that Domitian displayed 'a tyrant's cruelty and a despot's licence'.

And it is certainly true that Domitian does appear to have been keen on emperor worship. When he ascended to the principate in AD 81, he completed the temple begun for Vespasian in Rome, and dedicated it to the cult of both Vespasian and Titus. He built a Flavian Temple on the site of his birthplace. Statius, the poet, says he has consecrated 'a Flavian heaven'.

When an emperor died, his divinity was usually rubber-stamped by the Roman senate. Now he had done with the inconvenience of being flesh and blood, the dead ruler could truly become a god and take his rightful place in the pantheon. But when Domitian died, the senate, far from ratifying his self-proclaimed deity, issued a decree of *damnatio memoriae*: his memory was to be erased. The images of silver and gold were melted down. The triumphal arches – including one in Ephesus – were torn down or their inscriptions erased. Domitian's name was excised from monuments across the empire. Of course, the senate was not condemning imperial power. Although those in power were glad of a change of emperor, they didn't want an end to the rule of Rome. Nevertheless, all record of Domitian was to be obliterated, so hated was he on his death. In Ephesus the results of this decree are plain to be seen. Many inscriptions have been found which mention the temple dedicated to the *sebastoi*, but in all of them the name Domitian has been chiselled out.

Pliny describes the joy, the bloodlust:

It was our delight to dash those proud faces to the ground, to strike them with the sword and savage them with the axe as if blood and agony could follow every blow. Nobody could refrain from joy, late though our rejoicing was, but everyone sought a form of revenge in seeing those statue bodies torn in pieces, limbs hacked to bits and those dreadful portrait images cast into flames and roasted, so that from such terror and threats, they could be transformed for the use and pleasures of mankind. *

It was like the fall of a modern tyrant – a Ceaușescu or a Saddam Hussein – when the crowds pull their statues down.

This may explain the location where this statue was discovered. It was found hidden away in the basement of the temple. Perhaps, then, this was one of those statues of Domitian which had been subject to destruction. Maybe a howling, riotous mob had toppled the emperor from his pedestal, burnt his wooden body, hacked and crushed his limbs and then rolled the head of their fallen god downstairs to spend the rest of time in dark, shameful obscurity.

*

From the temple of Domitian, I traced the route down Curetes Street, the ancient thoroughfare cutting diagonally through the very heart

---

* Pliny the Younger (AD 61–c. 113), or Gaius Plinius Caecilius Secundus, to give him his full name, was a Roman politician and lawyer. Many of his letters survive, including a famous one asking the emperor Trajan how to deal with Christians. He was a friend of the historian Tacitus, and his staff included Suetonius. The *Panegyricus Traiani* is a speech delivered to the senate in AD 100 and is basically a massive bigging-up of the new emperor Trajan, and an equally massive putting-down of the former emperor Domitian.

of the city. In John's day this was lined with statues and shops, restaurants, elegant houses, public buildings, baths, and even brothels. Past the tomb of Arsinoe IV, murdered in Ephesus in 41 BC by Mark Antony at the bidding of his lover – and Arsinoe's sister – Cleopatra. Another grubby political assassination.

At the bottom, opposite the magnificent second-century library of Celsus, the route goes north to the magnificent theatre where Paul's activities had once caused such a disturbance. Pausing for a moment to climb the seats in the theatre, you can see the harbour quite clearly. It is straight ahead of you, down the Arcadian Way, as it was called in the fifth century AD, or Harbour Street, as it is called today.

If John had been issued with the first-century equivalent of an

The theatre at Ephesus, with Harbour Street leading west. In the distance you can make out the shape of the original harbour.

exclusion order, Ephesus would have been the obvious port of departure. And if that was so, then he would have had to walk down Harbour Street. So I followed him. Sort of. It took a bit of creative footwork, as it were. You're not allowed to walk down from the theatre end: there's a long piece of plastic tape saying 'Do Not Cross'. Obviously, being a good, law-abiding subject of Her Britannic Majesty, I was honour bound to obey such signs. So, I followed a dirt track round, past the ancient Church of St Mary, then cut back through some scrub, and emerged onto Harbour Street just a little way beyond the tape. After all, the sign told me not to *cross* the tape. It never said anything about going round it. No one can accuse me of not respecting the rules.

After a little way, though, the marble street simply peters out, disappearing into the dirt and the dust. You can still trace its course, though. I made my way along what was now a track through the brush. Clambered down and across a wide ditch filled with ancient rubble and pieces of pillars. It's astonishing: in any other country in the world this ditch alone would be enough to stock a museum. Here no one had even bothered to clear up the pillars. They lay there, scattered, as though they had fallen down yesterday. Beyond the ditch you push through some bushes, and duck under the boughs of a low-branched fig tree, the figs fallen and rotting on the ground. Part some more bushes and you come to a chain-link fence. And beyond you is the great harbour of Ephesus.

I climbed a tree to get a better view. Silt was always the enemy, deposited by the River Cayster, clogging the flow in the watery arteries of Ephesus. It was a constant battle. Strabo records that in the second century BC, engineers of Attalus Philadelphus had tried to deepen the entrance, but that only allowed more silt in and made things worse. The outcome was inevitable, and today this once great port

The harbour today. As seen from up a tree.

is miles inland. Despite that, from my perch I could still make out the original shape of the harbour, a shadowy circle, a teardrop stain of darker, deeper green. Still damp and marshy, apparently, fringed with reeds, home now not to ships and sailors but to herons, egrets, waders, and in the air nothing but the frail, plaintive cries of gulls.

Once, it was glorious. Here you could watch the might of Rome in all its commercial strength. Here the ships docked, bringing soldiers and officials, slaves, prisoners, pilgrims and visitors. Through this port passed the goods which made men rich and women beautiful. Ephesus was a city which grew rich through commerce. Strabo said that 'because of its advantageous location . . . [Ephesus] grows daily, and is the largest emporium in Asia this side of the Taurus'.

That word 'emporium' is significant. Ephesus was a wealthy trading city. In a wonderful passage in Revelation 18, John describes the fall of 'Babylon', his shorthand for Rome. The city falls with frightening speed – in just one hour – and its collapse is lamented only by the kings of the earth who lived there in luxury, and the merchants and ship owners who are only sorry because of all the money they are going to lose, 'since no one buys their cargo anymore' (Rev. 18.11). The passage goes on to give a shipping list, a manifest of Roman goods. It's a brilliantly detailed piece of historical and social observation. We start with a long list of big-ticket, luxury goods: 'gold, silver, jewels and pearls, fine linen, purple, silk and scarlet, all kinds of scented wood, all articles of ivory, all articles of costly wood, bronze, iron, and marble, cinnamon, spice, incense, myrrh, frankincense . . .'. But the list also includes everyday things – 'wine, olive oil, choice flour and wheat' – then livestock and military supplies – 'cattle and sheep, horses and chariots'.

Finally, and most damning of all, John sees the merchants weeping because they can no longer trade in 'slaves – and human lives'.

This, in all its rich variety, is exactly the kind of stuff John observed coming and going through the harbour at Ephesus: 'The fruit for which your soul longed has gone from you,' wail the merchants, 'and all your dainties and your splendour are lost to you, never to be found again!' (Rev. 18.11–14). The South African activist and theologian Allan Boesak wrote about Revelation from the perspective of one who had been imprisoned because of his opposition to state ideology.

He wrote that any readers who identify with the lament of the merchants at the loss of trade 'do not know what it is like to stand at the bottom of the list'.

One of John's key messages in the book is that Rome's power was built on the misery of others, and that when the 'souls' of his readers longed for the luxuries of empire, they were colluding with Babylon. Certainly, maritime trade of all sorts was the basis of Roman prosperity. Rome's mastery of the Mediterranean meant prosperity not only for the capital, but also for people in the right positions in the provinces. Our old travelling companion Aelius Aristides described how Rome devoured all the produce of the Mediterranean:

> *Produce is brought from every land and every sea, depending on what the seasons bring forth, and what is produced by all lands, rivers and lakes, besides the arts of Greeks and barbarians. If anyone wants to see it all he must either travel over the whole earth to see it in such a way, or come to this city. For what grows and is produced among individual peoples is necessarily always here, and in abundance.*

Rome was a net importer of goods. It relied on the provinces and its conquered territories to keep it supplied. It has been estimated that to feed the population of Rome with grain alone took 6,000 ships' worth each year. But it was a system built on injustice and fuelled by human misery.

In particular, Rome's economy was founded on slavery.

There were millions of slaves in the empire, and they were seen very much as implied by the order of this list: they were livestock, goods, possessions. When they wore out they could be dumped, like old appliances. To save them the trouble of caring for sick or worn-out slaves, owners would dump them on the island of Aesculapius in the Tiber River in Rome. So many were abandoned there that the emperor Claudius ruled that, if any recovered, they would receive their freedom. But only if they recovered . . .

Christianity, though, gave a voice and status to slaves. Its founder, after all, had died the slave's death and, on the night before that event, had acted in the manner of a slave by washing the feet of his disciples. He had said to them that those who would be 'great among you must be your servant, and whoever wishes to be first among you must be slave of all' (Mark 10.43–44). For the most part, the New Testament writers are quiet on the institution of slavery. They seem to accept it as part of society, and perhaps don't worry about it on the basis that (a) everyone is equal in Christ anyway, (b) we're all supposed to act like slaves and (c) the world is going to end imminently.

Revelation, despite clearly advocating (c), is in fact the most outspoken part of the New Testament on this issue. For John the trade in human souls was part of the great evil of empire. It was so great that he underlines it: 'slaves – and human lives'.

As I hung on to the tree and tried to imagine the harbour in days gone by, my mind drifted back to the duty-free shops in the departure lounge at the airport. There were goods there which screamed luxury, fruits for which our soul is supposed to long: Lacoste, Harrods, Aspinalls, Kurt Geiger, Hugo Boss. The Macallan 1824 Limited Release III whisky was selling at a very reasonable £1,800 a bottle. (As opposed to the Johnny Walker Blue Label Rare Blended Scotch, which was a *tad* pricey at £2,500.)

And I wondered what John would have made of it all, as his Border Agency escort marched him onto the plane for his deportation.

Weep, you duty-free merchants. Weep, you sellers of handbags and designer labels and unfeasibly large bars of Toblerone. Weep and wail, Tag Heuer and Taittinger and Veuve Clicquot. All your dainties and splendours are lost to you, never to be found again.

PATMOS

'The real voyage of discovery consists not of seeking new landscapes, but of having new eyes.'

MARCEL PROUST

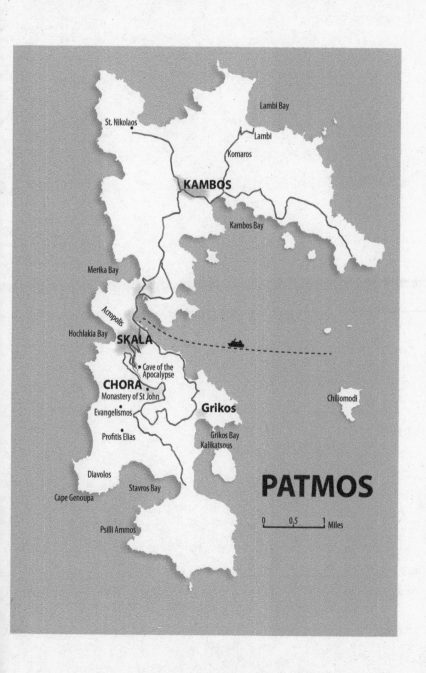

12 The End of the World in Kuşadasi

I set off for Patmos down the same river valley through which the boat from Ephesus would have sailed. The only difference was that where John would have been in a ship, sail flapping, gulls wheeling overhead, I was in a small minibus. Somewhere out in the middle of the shallow valley there is a river of sorts – the road crosses it at the western end, almost where it meets the sea – but travellers today take the road from Selcuk, not the boat.

To my left a heron rose clumsily from the reed beds. We passed apple and peach trees, pomegranate and fig. I tried to imagine the ships coasting along the channel: small, flat-bottomed coasters and full-bellied *corbitae* filled with bales of Lydian wool, or amphorae of wine, fishing boats drying their nets in the sun, military ships – the triremes and quadremes and quinquiremes, oars plashing in the water, the eagle glinting gold.

At the end of the bay we crossed the river, turning south along a coastline full of resorts, many of which looked a little forlorn and end-of-season-ish. Then it was over the crest of a headland, and down into the delights of Kuşadasi.

*

The thing about travelling is that it involves an awful lot of not travelling. There is a lot of just standing around. Sitting in cafés or on park benches, whiling away the time. Or waiting in long queues for people to check, or pretend to check, or hardly bother to check, your identity. You have to go through quite a journey to get to Patmos. Maybe the same was true for John. Certainly no one set sail before consulting the gods. Sacrifices had to be made. The omens – the weather forecast of the gods – had to be interpreted.

After a scary exchange of emails telling me – mistakenly – that my boat was cancelled, I was at the booking desk obsessively early. John may have been reluctant to leave Asia, but I was desperate to head out to sea. The ticket was paid for and the passage booked. And now I had all day in Kuşadasi.

Oops.

Kuşadasi is the modern face of tourist Turkey. Big, brash, filled with not-real Ray-Bans and knock-off Nikes. (Still, it did allow me to indulge my shameful craving for a Big Mac.)

Somewhere under this imitation western resort is the Byzantine town of *Ephesus Neopolis* – Ephesus New Town. It came into prominence as a port when Ephesus finally lost its centuries-old battle against the silt, and the harbour closed forever. Since then, this town has been overrun in turn by Byzantines, Genoese, Venetians, Turks, Crusaders, Italians, Greeks and, finally, Tourists.

But that's history for you. Empires come and go. Cities rise and cities fall. Rivers silt up. Harbours close. Everything comes to an end.

The end. That was the fascination. People were always interested when I told them about my journey, because they wanted to know about *The End*. At least, I *think* they were interested. Although as I recall, their eyes did take on a slightly glazed look. And my increasing resemblance to the Ancient Mariner can't have helped.

On the dolmus to Kuşadasi I met a couple of Australian ladies who were travelling the coast. One was wearing a *Doctor Who* T-shirt.

'Revelation!' she exclaimed. 'I haven't read that for a long time. It's scary, isn't it?'

'Scary?'

'Yes. The end of the world.' She shook her head. 'I'd rather not know.'

'Spoilers,' I said.

I understood her anxiety. Except that, more and more, I was beginning to realise that it was misplaced. It was sitting there in Kuşadasi, on that unintended, in-between day, that I realised that Revelation isn't really about the end of the world at all.

*

A few weeks before arriving in Turkey – and again with time to kill – I had wandered into Tate Britain.

At the end of one of the galleries is an apocalyptic triptych, three enormous, billboard-sized paintings. These are the works of John Martin, one of the most epic of the artists who have taken on the apocalypse.

On the left is *The Plains of Heaven*, all blue and silver and white. On a vivid blue lake golden triremes sail serenely, while a small group of white-clad figures drift, like ghosts, across the canvas, leaving behind them a heavenly contrail. Harps are played. Pines and palm trees wave gently, a far-off waterfall whispers, and the distant mountains dissolve into the silvery-white cloud.

In the middle, *The Last Judgment*: Jesus sits, centre stage, accompanied by twenty-four elders wearing crowns. To his right are the saved, a group of mostly Anglo-Saxon nobility, some in ruffs, most wearing the Bible-black uniform of a Victorian Puritan. To his left are the damned. A sumptuously clad pope claws the ground in terror, a scarlet-robed woman wails in distress. The flashier the clothes, the greater the sinner. Figures already descending into the darkness carry bishop's crooks and wear mitres. Below the pure white majesty of Christ, the sky is the colour of blood and terror. An angel prepares to blow a trumpet. Another stares, wild-eyed, into the abyss, forked lightning in hand.

But it is the painting on the right that always catches the attention. It glows, red hot. Forked lightning zig-zags into the mountains, which are cascading, blasting, shattering, rolling like waves, hurling a huge city (apparently it's Edinburgh) into the fiery furnace. In the sooty, charred gloom at the bottom of the painting, desperate figures huddle together and cling to the rocks. Buxom, Rubenesque ladies tumble to their doom. It is *The Great Day of His Wrath* and it is epically, monumentally terrifying.

I sat there for a long time looking at the paintings. A little boy with his grandparents wandered up. 'Wow. Look at the fire!' he said. A tutor brought a group through and described the picture as a painting of hell. But it isn't. It's the earth. And it's being destroyed.

Martin painted these huge canvases between 1851 and 1853, in what turned out to be the last years of his life. He was a good-natured man 'of lively enthusiastic disposition', but his family history

was troubled. One of his three brothers, William, published philo-
sophical tracts and walked around Newcastle wearing an enormous
home-made medal and a 'helmet of tortoiseshell, mounted and bound
in brass'. Another brother, Jonathan, set fire to York Minster in a
protest against the morality of the clergy. The blaze destroyed most
of the roof and Jonathan was committed to an asylum for the rest
of his life. One visitor went to see him and found him contentedly
drawing a picture of 'a seven-headed bishop rushing into the jaws
of an enormous crocodile'.

Hardly surprising that someone with that kind of background
should be drawn to these kinds of subjects. His paintings are vivid
with all the shades of terror and fear. The critic Ruthven Todd said
of Martin that 'his people perish in the ruins of a world too great
for them to understand, and the vast pointless towers which they
created become tombstones'.

*

The final chapters of Revelation are assumed to depict the 'end
times'. They are, to use the technical term, 'eschatological' – a word
coined by theologians in the seventeenth century, from the Greek
word *eschaton*, meaning 'the end'. Eschatology is the study of the
'last things': the end of an empire, or the end of the world.

In a way, the Romans had an eschatological view of empire: they
thought that the climax of all possible worlds had arrived in the
form of, well, the Roman empire, actually. In Virgil's *Aeneid*, the
god Jupiter ('The Artist Formerly Known as Zeus') concludes: 'For
[the Romans] I set neither bounds nor periods. Dominion without
end I give to them.'

Imperium sine fine. It's an idea which many empires have (rather
rashly, in hindsight) assumed to themselves. The British empire on
which the sun never set, the Nazis' Third (and final) Reich, the
Communist International, declaring the final and irrevocable 'triumph
of socialism'. Even recent historians suggesting the ultimate triumph
of western liberal democracy, brought to you in association with
Coca-Cola.

The Jews saw things rather differently. One of the radical ideas
which they brought to the ancient world, along with monotheism,

the Sabbath and the bagel, was the idea that one day, God would step in and judge. Time would actually end. God would establish his earthly kingdom. When, you ask? Well, there would be signs. There would be terror and suffering. Natural disasters. People running around yelling, 'Woe. Woe.'

No one knew when, exactly. But they were certain that one day, Yahweh, the God of Israel, would instigate a golden age of peace and contentment (with Israel on top, naturally). The idea originated in prophecies from people like Isaiah and Ezekiel, but it was given its fullest, most potent expression in the many apocalypses which were written in the years between the end of the Old Testament and the beginning of the New.

The most influential of these was the book of Daniel. Daniel is, as football commentators put it, a game of two halves. The first half tells uplifting and inspiring tales of Daniel and his compatriots living heroically faithful lives in exile in Babylon. It contains famous stories, like Daniel in the lions' den, the fiery furnace, Belshazzar's feast. Daniel is a kind of prophet, a Joseph-like interpreter of dreams.

The second half is very different. This is a weird, disorientating series of dreamlike visions experienced by Daniel himself. These visions provide Revelation with much of its imagery. For John, Daniel was an image bank on which he drew heavily. In Daniel's visions we see beasts which represent empires, we see a heavenly throne room with a being called the 'Ancient One' with clothing as white as snow and hair like wool, sitting on a throne. (The 'Ancient One' is sitting on a throne. Not his hair. Well, I suppose he might be sitting on his hair. Depends how long it was.) Anyway, this 'Ancient One' judges the beasts and throws them into the fire. We see a 'son of man' – to whom kingship and authority is given. We see angels who guide Daniel and interpret his vision for him. We see heavenly forces at work shaping earthly events.

Above all, we see victory. Daniel is set at a time when Jerusalem has been destroyed, and the people have been taken away into exile. Their nation has been crushed by the Babylonians. Which is the kind of thing to bring tears to your eyes. But Daniel is given a vision of complete victory: the day of the Lord, when the dead will be judged and the wicked punished. This idea nourished and sustained the Jews through the succeeding centuries. Whether ruled by the Ptolemies in Egypt, or the Seleucids in Antioch, or the Romans in . . . er . . . Rome, people took consolation from the thought that this injustice would not last.

Daniel was the most popular expression of this: there are fragments from eight copies of Daniel among the Dead Sea Scrolls, making it the second most popular book after Isaiah. But other writers put the idea into apocalyptic form as well. From the second century BC onwards, apocalypses carried on being produced, each promising a future very different from the present suffering and pointing to a very different reality, of what God was doing 'behind the scenes'.

These works were usually attributed to long-gone Jewish heroes. Like the Book of Enoch, in which Enoch is given a guided tour of heaven by an angel called Uriel ('Fire of God'). The second part of this book represents political and historical figures in the guise of animals. It's known by the Disneyesque name of the Animal Apocalypse – conjuring up images of Mickey Mouse destroying the earth. Another section – the Apocalypse of Weeks – shows that there is a point when the world will be destroyed. Enoch declares that 'the first heaven shall depart and pass away and a new heaven shall appear' (1 Enoch 93.16). Now *that* does sound familiar . . .

The writings known as the Dead Sea Scrolls, which are probably the remains of the library of an apocalyptic Jewish community, contain a number of apocalyptic writings, most notably the War Scroll which predicts, in detail, a war against the Romans. It describes this conflict as a battle between the sons of light and the sons of darkness. It predicts that each side will win three battles over the next forty years and then there will be a final, deciding match, best-out-of-seven, in which the sons of light will triumph. On penalties.

There is a text known as 4 Ezra (written between AD 70 and 100) in which the biblical figure of Ezra sees a series of cosmic visions of judgment on Rome – which the book calls Babylon. (Uriel features again, explaining to Ezra in heaven why God's people are suffering. He is told that the first world is about to pass away and a new one will be brought into existence.) Then you have a work attributed to Jeremiah's secretary, Baruch. Written after the fall of the Temple in AD 70, Baruch is shown that this was not the 'real' Temple: the *real*

Temple is a heavenly building, immune to little inconveniences such as time, entropy and large Roman armies with siege engines. Baruch is guided through his vision by another angel, called Ramiel. (Presumably it was Uriel's day off.)

*

John's Apocalypse, then, was part of an established tradition. The idea of a day of judgment certainly features in Revelation. In chapter 20, 'Death and Hades' give up their dead and all are judged 'according to what they had done'. Then Death and Hades, too, are chucked into the lake of fire, along with anyone whose name is missing from the book of life. After that, 'the first heaven and the first earth' pass away, to be replaced – or upgraded, if you like – with new versions of the same thing. The New Jerusalem descends. Death is no more. Mourning and crying and pain are no more. 'It is done.'

That seems to accord well with the mainstream understanding of the day of the Lord. But then John says something very curious. Because *after* everyone has been judged, *after* the good have been rewarded and the bad thrown into the fire, *after* the arrival of the New Jerusalem, some bad guys appear to be alive, if not well.

Er. What?

The lake of fire should, you'd have thought, be the end of all the evildoers. But two chapters later we find them hanging around outside the New Jerusalem: 'Outside are the dogs and sorcerers and fornicators and murderers and idolaters, and everyone who loves and practices falsehood' (Rev. 22.15). The same thing happens with the kings of the earth. In the climactic battle at Armageddon, the kings of the earth gather to fight alongside the beast and are defeated, becoming food for carrion (Rev. 19.17–21). Yet two chapters later they are invited into the New Jerusalem, which has a tree in it with leaves 'for the healing of the nations' (Rev. 21.24; 22.2).

The implication is that, for John, the end of the world was already happening. Revelation speaks emphatically of the ultimate triumph of God. It speaks of the new creation, of a new heaven and earth, of our bodily resurrection and a time when there will be no more sadness or pain or suffering or death. But the tenses are all over the place. He sees the New Jerusalem descending in the present tense.

This thing is landing *now*. For John, the New Jerusalem is not only a future certainty, it's also a present reality.

At one point, John calls people out of Babylon – by which he means the Roman empire. Practically speaking, how could anyone in John's day leave the Roman empire? They could, I suppose, go beyond the borders, to Parthia, or cross the Danube and join the Goths. Or they could even – though this really would be drastic – go to Hibernia in the north of Britain. But that is not what John is saying. He calls people *out* of Babylon and *in* to the New Jerusalem. It is already there: the doors are already open. In the words of the theologian George Caird, 'in midst of the daily life of Smyrna and Pergamum, Babylon and Jerusalem exist side-by-side. Their citizens rub shoulders in the streets of Sardis and Philadelphia.'

*

The followers of Jesus believed that he was the Messiah, and, though there were different beliefs among Jews about the nature of the Messiah, he was generally agreed to be the figure who would usher in the new age (Luke 3.7–17). For Christians, then, believing in Jesus as the Messiah meant that the new age was here. It had been ushed.

Jesus himself said as much. 'The kingdom of God is not coming with things that can be observed,' he said, 'nor will they say, "Look, here it is!" or "There it is!" For, in fact, the kingdom of God is among you' (Luke 17.20–21). This was a bit confusing to the first followers, because, although they believed in Jesus as the Messiah, there was no apparent sign of the peace and plenty of the messianic kingdom. The Romans were still in charge. There was still poverty and oppression and exploitation. And never mind a time without sickness and death – people were being killed for the faith. How could the new age be said to have begun when so much of the old age was still stubbornly hanging around?

The answer they came up with was that the kingdom of God was both here and still arriving. Its completion lay in the future, but some of the blessings and benefits of that future age could be experienced right now. Thus, the early church lived in a space between the beginning of the end and the consummation of that end. They proclaimed the Lord's death until he comes (1 Cor. 11.26). They believed that they had been forgiven but not yet fully perfected (Phil. 3.7–14). They had been justified, but there was still to be a future judgment (2 Cor. 5.10). They lived in the kingdom now, but they prayed, 'Your kingdom come.'

This duality was something which people at Ephesus already knew about. Paul, writing to the Ephesians some thirty years earlier, says that God has 'raised us up with him and seated us with him in the heavenly places in Christ Jesus' (Eph. 2.6). He's not writing to dead people; he's saying it in the here and now to living, breathing Christians. They are sitting in their house church in Ephesus, and yet somehow they are sitting in heaven as well.

This is the greatest misunderstanding about this book. It is not about the end. Not really. It's about the present. It's about how the streets of London or New York or Kuşadası or Ephesus can be – are, for those who believe – overlaid with the streets of the New Jerusalem. We are not stuck in some cosmic waiting room, waiting for the big day to arrive. The kingdom is here and is continuing to arrive. It is what's known as the iterative present. It has come down, it is always coming down, and one day, it will finally have arrived.

The message of Revelation is that we *can* be in two places at once.

*

It was a long day. A heavy bag, sore feet. Then there was the queue for a boarding pass, a queue for customs, and finally we were off, on a ship called *The Venus*, where I sat on deck and chatted with some tourists who had made a day trip from Samos and were deeply disgruntled at having had to waste time on the obligatory tour of the carpet factory.

An hour and a half later the boat sailed into Samos harbour. After yet more queuing, to get off this time, I trudged up the hill to the guesthouse which was run by a sweet elderly Greek couple who corrected each other incessantly and served me fruit juice and ordered me to sit down. It was like being in a hotel run by your grandparents. I wandered down into town, had a beer at the harbour, and picked up my ticket for the next day's journey. As I walked back up the hill the wind was beginning to rise, and the sea looked angry. That night, the shutters on my window rattled furiously in the gale.

13 Boiled Eggs and Arab Coffee

I spent the night fretting. After so many miles and days of travel I was desperate to get to the island, so it was a big relief when my host knocked on the door the next morning.

'Mr Page, Mr Page,' he said. 'Boat will go. Is no problem. I have called them.'

Distantly in the house, I heard his wife correct him on something. He waved a hand dismissively and trudged off. A minute later his wife knocked on the door.

'Is fine,' she said. 'Don't worry about what he said. The boat will sail.'

I was glad to have that sorted.

Down at the harbour it was still windy, but the sun was out and the rather battered yellow hulk of the *Flying Dolphin* hydrofoil was waiting.

We set off. As far as I know no one made any sacrifices to the gods, although perhaps that was just as well: the gods might have warned them to postpone. Once we were out at sea, the waves started to bounce the hydrofoil up and down like a fairground ride. After a while the waves were so high that the speed was cut. The engines slowed and the hydrofoil stopped hydrofoiling, and we were reduced to trudging through the water like a normal boat. The engines sounded frustrated. Aggrieved.

Looking out through the sea spray, I tried to catch a glimpse of the island. Arriving by boat is the only way to get to Patmos (unless you have your own helicopter). But it is satisfyingly authentic, because boats haven't changed much since John's time, really. What propels them through the water has changed, of course. In John's day it was wind and oar, today it is the diesel engine or the outboard motor. But much of the vocabulary of sailing has stayed the same: hull and keel, rudder and hawser, anchor, mast, sail, rope – all these a sailor from the port of Ephesus would recognise even today. Sea journeys were the fastest means of travel in the ancient world, but also one of the most dangerous. To the Jews the sea was a mysterious force, not to be trusted. In Proverbs, 'the way of a ship on the high seas' is one of the four things the writer does not understand (Prov. 30.18–19).*

In the cosmography of the Hebrew scriptures, water features heavily. Beneath the earth the 'waters of chaos' were lurking, that primeval soup of nothingness home to Leviathan, the sea monster, the embodiment of chaos. 'You shall not make for yourself an idol, whether in the form of anything that is in heaven above, or that is on the earth beneath, or that is in the water under the earth,' says the Old Testament command (Exod. 20.4). Some creatures are better left unimagined. It is no coincidence that the beast of Revelation 13 emerges from the sea. And, at the end of the book, John writes that 'the sea was no more' (Rev. 21.1). For those of us who are rather fond of the sea, frankly it's a bit of a downer. Even on the *Flying Dolphin* that day, as it lurched heavily up and down the waves, I enjoyed myself. But for the writer of Revelation the sea means darkness, chaos, destruction. At the end, says John, there will be nowhere left from where the beasts, the enemies, can emerge.

Sailors from John's time followed the same sea routes as today's. They would keep a lookout for the same capes and promontories, navigate the same channels between the islands, peer through the spray or the sunlight, stay alert for the same rocks. Nowadays we have sonar and radar; they had sailors hanging off the pointy end with long bits of rope. But in the end we follow the same sea lanes and arrive at the same points. The harbour at which we eventually arrived must be the same one at which John disembarked. It is the only ancient deep-water harbour on the island.

We were an hour and a half late. But I had made it. I was finally on Patmos.

*

---

* The other three are 'the way of an eagle in the sky, the way of a snake on a rock' and 'the way of a man with a girl'.

'The idea of holiness clings to islands,' wrote Adam Nicolson in *Sea Room*, his account of the small Scottish islands where he lived. 'Remoteness from the world looks like a closeness to God.' A friend told me about a journey to the Japanese holy island of Miyajima, where the gateway to the island – the Torii Gate – stands in the sea. To go through the gate is to cross the threshold and stand on the sacred.

Patmos is a holy island. It even has the certificate to prove it, having officially been given the title 'Holy Island' in 1981. I couldn't work out who had granted this. The government? The Patriarch of Constantinople? The Greek tourist board? God himself? Anyway, it was about 1,900 years too late – Patmos has been holier for a lot longer than that.

With time on my hands before my room was ready, I dumped my bag in a café and explored Skala, the town by the harbour. The ferry had docked at the eastern end of the port – an ancient wharf which has been used for centuries. This was where John landed in AD 92, where the Byzantines came onshore, where priests and priestesses from Myra and Miletus had set foot on the island. Today, the port has expanded around the bay. On the west, day-tripper boats rub shoulders with the yachts and the super-yachts. Further round, on the north side of the bay, is where the fishing boats dock.

Skala is a beautiful town. From the portside, whitewashed buildings rise up the side of the hills surrounding the bay in a jumble of streets and alleyways. Flowers, yellow and purple and bright, vivid pink, billow over balconies, their names like forgotten Greek gods: oleander, hibiscus, bougainvillea. Cats peek out from every corner. I followed my nose and kept climbing. In Patmos, as I was to discover, it does not take long to reach the limits of any settlement, and five minutes' walking was enough for me to emerge out of the top of Skala, onto steeper, rough terrain, filled with needle-sharp gorse, bronze straw and dark, rough, coffee-coloured boulders. From the top of the hill Patmos lay stretched out before me, the brown hills shimmering, the earth toasted and hot. The sky was a clear, pure blue. Out there over the sea I could see the grey, distant shapes of other islands: Lipsi and Leros, Samos, Ikaria.

They say that on really clear days you can see all the way to the Turkish coast.

Patmos is a curious shape.* It looks like an upside down L. There are really three land masses, linked together by narrow isthmuses. Or isthmusi. Anyway, narrow strips of land. From the top of the hill I could see the point, just north of Skala, where the island narrows to just a few hundred yards wide. For such a small island it seems to have been issued with way too much coastline, which it could only fit in by creating extra coves and bays, promontories and headlands. And while the coastline goes all fractal, the land mass takes every opportunity to head upwards. It's as if there was too much Patmos to fit the space it was allocated.

The two major communities on the island are Skala, down by the harbour, and Chora, the village on top of the hill, where the Monastery of St John is to be found. In the north there is a small town called Kambos; in the south the resort of Grikos. Otherwise there are just small hamlets, tiny settlements, individual hotels and churches. Lots of churches. But in the gaps between these scattered settlements it is the island which really strikes you: brown, burnt, rocky, dry. And with all that coastline, the one thing you notice all the time in Patmos is what surrounds it: the blue, the eternal blue. The sea is a darker, rippled shade, with hints of grey and green and turquoise. But the sky! No words can describe the purity of the Aegean blue sky. There is no other shade of blue to which it can be compared. This is it. This was what God had in mind when he invented blue.

There is blue all around you on Patmos. On a small island you are keenly aware of separation, of detachment. Islands are 'holy' in the truest sense of the word: set apart. On the mainland, life seems unlimited, unconfined. There are borders, of course – customs posts, fences – but nothing like the defined edges of an island. And Patmos is all edge.

Writers like writing on small islands. I think it's because suddenly everything is tight, constrained, concentrated. Life gets narrowed

---

* For the map geeks among us – and we are legion – the best map is the 1:20,000 Patmos Terrain Map produced by Skai Maps Editions, 2009.

down to essentials. It focuses the mind. 'Contained within tight geographical margins, islands are places where memories are intensified and heightened,' writes the academic and critic Jacky Bowring. This is certainly true of Revelation, which is like an intense, heightened act of remembrance. Remember what the Lamb has done; remember who is really in charge. *Focus . . .*

Detachment, of course, comes with the journey. It is not easy to get to an island. This, from early times, has made islands popular with hermits and solitaries. In the sixth century, as the Irish monks

The main port of Skala.

spread around the British Isles, they developed the idea of 'deserts in the ocean'. Islands offered them a destination for what they called *peregrinatio*, where the monk would abandon home, possessions, family and seek isolation. Islands were little lumps of wilderness in the wider wilderness of the sea. Wilderness squared. Our word 'isolation' is rooted in *isola*, the Latin word for 'island'.

Islands are, by their nature, places of separation, of dislocation, even of loss. Perhaps this is why so many death journeys in ancient mythology feature water. In Greek mythology, you had to pay the

ferryman and cross water to get to the underworld. But crossing the rivers of the underworld made you stronger. Invulnerable. One story tells how Achilles' mother held him by the heel and dipped him in the Styx. The rest of his body had 'died', so could not be killed: only his heel, where she held him, remained in the land of the living.

The same is true of the Christian symbolism of baptism. We submerge ourselves in the water. We 'die' – and having done so, we can never really die again.

Most of all, though, islands are liminal places. They are in-between; neither the land nor the sea. They are transit points. Thresholds. Small islands, especially, ask you, 'Where next?' There is always another destination visible, somewhere else to move on to. In Greece, the tourist industry has, for years, been based upon 'island hopping' – moving from island to island, restlessly exploring. Perhaps the first island-hopper of them all is in the Bible; it's just that his next hop took him further than expected.

All this must have had an effect on John. For whatever reason, he was separated from his churches. He had crossed the water, passed into another realm. As he walked the hills of Patmos – and you couldn't be here and not walk the hills of Patmos – he could see the barrier others had placed around him: the great, blue, watery wall between him and his friends and fellow disciples back in Asia. Maybe that was another reason why there would be no more sea in the new creation. The wall will be broken down. No more separation. No more islands.

*

Some 120 years before I landed at Skala, an American called William Geil arrived on the island. Back down in the port, I sat in the café and read his account.

Geil (1865–1925) was a Baptist missionary and traveller. His photograph – he was a proficient photographer – shows a bespectacled man, wavy hair parted in the middle. He looks like a librarian. Or a church organist. Something safe and respectable. But his journeys took him to study the pygmies in central Africa and cannibal tribes in New Guinea as well as exploring the Holy Land. In 1908 he was the first person ever to make the 1,800-mile trip along the length of the Great Wall of China. He travelled everywhere with an aluminium Blickensdorfer portable typewriter and carbon paper – a device which amazed the natives.

At the peak of his fame he was compared to explorers like Stanley and Livingstone. His large mansion in Doylestown, USA, even had its own replica Chinese pagoda. But after he died of influenza in Venice in 1925, his grief-stricken widow sealed off his library, locked away all his possessions, and his name sank into obscurity.

His book on Patmos, *The Isle that is Called Patmos*, was published in 1896 – in Philadelphia, appropriately enough, albeit the US version. He arrived from Izmir on a small Greek steamer, which he described as being in a filthy condition. ('The boiling water and the whites of eyes appeared to me to be the only clean things aboard.') He describes looking out at the island and thinking that the top of the hill was crested with snow. Then he realised that it was actually the white-coloured buildings of Chora. 'Nearly every building on Patmos is pure white,' he wrote. He calls the harbour town 'La Scala', which sounds more like an Italian opera house, and describes it as 'quite a goodly village . . . It is here the twenty Turks reside and most of the business is done.'

Sitting in front of one of the 'three or four coffee shops at the wharf', he 'ordered some boiled eggs and Arab coffee'. In tribute I had a beer and an omelette.

*

A lot of William Geil's information about Patmos came from a previous traveller, Professor Guérin of the Université Française in Athens, who had visited the island some forty years before and documented it in his *Description of the Isle of Patmos and the Isle of Samos*. Guérin found a number of remains on the island, including parts of some white marble columns on Skala quay, and the base of a temple on the ancient acropolis, something I had yet to explore. He is always very precise. The Monastery, he tells us, is at an elevation of 216 metres (700 feet). The height of the grotto of the apocalypse is 4 metres in the outer chapel and 2 metres 30 cm in the inner (roughly 13 feet by 7 feet 6 inches). This man had a tape measure, and he wasn't afraid to use it.

The most notable account prior to the intrepid professor came way back in 1677, from a Greek emigré living in London called Joseph Georgirenes. He was bishop of Samos and Ikaria between 1666 and 1671 and lived on Patmos for two years, having been driven out of Crete as a result of increasing persecution by the Turks. He was described as: 'An indifferent tall man, and slender, with long black hair, having a wart on the left side of his nose just against his eye, a Cut under his eye, and Black Whiskers and very little beard.' His little *Description of the Present State of Samos, Nicaria, Patmos and Mount Athos* includes information about the 'island of Patmos, now called Patino'.

'It is furnished with very commodious havens,' he wrote, 'to which it owes its being inhabited, though not so extensively as in former times, as appears by the many and great ruins in it.' He celebrates John's stay on the island, although like most people he seems slightly baffled by Revelation itself: 'that mysterious and sublime book, which to him indeed was Apocalypse, but to all others Apocrypha; to him a revelation, but to us yet an hidden mystery, like the former prophecies of the Old Testament, that were never rightly understood till actually fulfilled.' He also records the island tradition that John wrote the first draft of his gospel on Patmos.

'The best port of this island,' wrote Georgirenes, 'and of all the *Archipelago*, on the west side toward *Naxos*, is called *Scala*, or the *Wharf*, because of a wharf of stone for the convenient lading and un-lading of ships.' But the village beside the port was now in ruins, an 'entire village called *Phocas*, without an Inhabitant. Here is likewise, among old ruins, a church yet standing which they say was built in St. *John's* days, and they show something like a pulpit where they say St. *John* used to preach.' Other places were also fallen into ruin.

By Georgirenes' time, the former glory of the island had been diminished by what he describes as 'many revolutions': 'Their Ships of Merchandise are all dwindl'd into small Fisher Boats, and the inhabitants are all extremely poor.' The big problem in Georgirenes' day was 'Pirats':

The island is well stored with Vines, Figg-trees, Lemon and Orange Trees, and Corn sufficient for the Inhabitants, if they could keep what they have free from the Robbery of Pirats,

as well Christian as Mohammedan, that often pillage the poor
People who have no other remedy than patience and sometimes
the pleasure of seeing them perish at Sea . . .

In fact, according to Georgirenes, the Patmians complained more of the cruelty of the Christians than of the Turks, so much so that 'the revenues of the monastery are now much diminish'd and the monks become extremely poor'.

And this is the present condition of the Isle of Patmos, once
famous for the residence of that great apostle, St. John, and
for the great and mysterious revelation he had in it; but now
groaning under the yoke of such lords as are common enemies
to the Christian faith, by whom they are both kept in great
awe and slavish obedience, and yet ill-protected against violent
incursion of pirates and robbers, so that poverty is their best
protection against rapine, and patience the only remedy against
the grievous yoke of tyrannical oppression.

The Greeks I met on the island of today made pretty similar complaints. But their 'Pirats' were different: bankers and financiers, Eurozone technocrats.

'It used to be that in the high season the place was fully booked for two months,' the bar owner told me as I sat there drinking my beer. 'This year it was about two weeks.' He waved his hand in the distance where a huge cruise ship was sitting just outside the harbour. 'They have everything on board, all their food and drink. They don't stop in the town to eat. They don't spend money on the island.' Another resident told me about their struggles in the winter to keep warm, how they were reduced to living in two small rooms and taped up all the other doors just to save on energy costs.

*

When Geil came to the island he made his way up to his accommodation mounted on 'a donkey with a merchandise saddle' – which seems to have been three bits of wood used normally for carting masonry.

I rode on a moped, piloted by my landlady's husband. Lean, wiry, grey-bearded, baseball-capped, skin the colour of tobacco. I think he was a fisherman, but no doubt, like many others on the island, he had his fingers in a number of pies. Mopeds are the new donkeys on Patmos. Everywhere you go – from the most off-beaten track to the narrowest of stairways – you find someone coming the other way on a moped. Most often it is a Patmian, cigarette hanging from his lips, one hand on the handlebars, the other working his mobile phone. Sometimes, though, it is a tourist, looking either terrified or unjustifiably confident. On one occasion I was passed by a grey-habited monk, prayer beads flying around him, with a pretty blonde sitting on the pillion, her arms around him. He looked as if he was fleeing his vows in some romantic comedy.

My big black waterproof bag was wedged into the footwell of the bike, while I clung on at the back. There was nowhere to hold on to. (Obviously I couldn't put my arms round my driver. I am English. It would take years of friendship before you could do such a thing.) So I was left relying on my sense of balance as the moped whizzed up through the narrow streets of Skala.

I say 'streets'. Alleys. Corridors. After a couple of minutes' riding we came to an alley which led to a flight of wide, shallow steps. There were about five or six mopeds parked in it: the terminus of the mopeds. We were at the top of the town.

'We walk,' said my driver.

We walked up the steps to a gravel track. A sign said 'Kastelli' – this was the footpath to the old acropolis of Patmos. And there, perched on one of the high points of Skala, was my apartment.

For the rest of the day I got used to my new home. The switch on the kettle had to be stuck down with tape. The bright-green front door was warped and never closed properly. The fridge wheezed and spluttered so noisily I thought it would expire any minute. When the wind blew – which it did quite a lot – the shutters in the little apartment rattled and you felt like you were going to be blown halfway to Samos. Buying groceries – going anywhere, in fact – meant a sweat-soaked, coronary-inducing journey up and down hundreds of steps.

Oh, and it had really good wifi.

In other words, it was perfect.

14 Pottery on the Acropolis

I worked every day at my table by the window, or out on the front terrace. From the apartment I could see down over the port and across the hills to the north of the island. I could see the boats come and go, hear the excited screams of the children swimming in the port, listen to the music drifting across the valley.

Best of all, the track which led up to the house then went onwards up to the Kastelli, the 'Castle', the ancient acropolis of Skala. By sheer chance, I had ended up staying in the nearest possible accommodation to the only buildings on the island which were in existence when John landed here.

On 16 February 1817, a man called Henry Whittington climbed the track past my house to the hill above Skala.*

> We were gratified by finding on the summit very considerable remains of a Greek fortress. The rock is not so lofty as that on which the modern town and monastery are built; but its singular situation, between two ports, renders it even more commanding. The remains are almost exclusively on the northern edge of the hill, and lie between two of those small churches which are so numerous in the island ... There are the remains of a tower thirty feet square near the western extremity, which seems to be unconnected with the outer walls, between which and it there are traces of a few steps hewn in the rock.

* In the book where I found this, his account is listed as merely 'the journals of Mr Whittington'. No first name is given. But an article in an academic journal identifies this man as Henry Whittington. Although I don't know who he is, either.

Not many of today's visitors follow in his footsteps. Although there was a trickle of visitors passing by my front door each day, most travellers opt out of visiting the acropolis. For one thing, in hot weather the climb through the well-paved streets of Skala is hard enough, never mind the further scramble up to the top. Another off-putting factor is the difficulty of finding it. Down in Skala the Patmian authorities have provided helpful signs to the Kastelli. Less helpfully, they disappear the moment you get beyond the houses. The track is easy to follow for a while – up along the edge of the field and then through an old stone gateway – but then you come to a wide expanse of scree and rock, at which point the path seems to run straight into a wall before disappearing entirely. Quite often I would be sitting working and hear people returning not long after they'd gone up, grumbling about not being able to find their way.

But perhaps the main reason why it is not on the main tourist trail is that there isn't much left to see. All that remain are some wall sections, made of large blocks of what Whittington called 'the coarse porphyry of the island', and a short flight of steps which lead nowhere. Geographically, it may be a high point; in tourist terms, not so much.

But for Revelation anoraks it is nirvana, because the acropolis was the centre of ancient Patmos and, in John's day, the only significant settlement on the isle. This, in other words, is the only structure on the island which dates from John's time. Heavens, he might even have stood on those steps.

*

Patmos is only mentioned three times in literature before Revelation. Pliny the Elder tells us it is thirty miles in circumference. Strabo says that it is near Leros. And Thucydides tells us that, during the war against the Persians, some boats from Athens went near it.

And that's it.

The paucity of records, combined with later Christian fantasies about this being a 'prison island', might give the impression that Patmos was uninhabited. But a visit to the acropolis tells a different story.

During the time of the ancient Greeks, Patmos – along with the islands of Leros and Lipsos – was under the control of Miletus, the port-city thirty-seven miles to the north-east. The three islands were known as the 'fortresses' of Miletus, because they formed a kind of barrier to the west, guarding the entrance to the gulf where Miletus was located. From the beginning of the second century BC, these islands were garrisoned by Milesian troops. And those troops would have garrisoned themselves in the acropolis.

It was the perfect viewpoint. Sitting on a saddle of land overlooking the narrowest point of the island, from the walls of the acropolis you can see clearly in every direction. The island stretches out before you, but more importantly, you have a commanding view of the sea lanes and of the distant islands: Lipsos, Leros, Icaria, Samos.

Originally the walls of the acropolis probably ran right down to the port. Geil certainly claimed that some of the houses in Skala were 'partially or altogether constructed of stone brought down from the Acropolis'. At a well just outside Skala he found 'a curiously chiseled stone, which was no doubt at one time a portion of a column – very likely a section of a pillar in an ancient temple, which is thought to have occupied the highest point of the Acropolis'.

But the most striking aspect of the Kastelli is not the walls or the steps, but the rubbish. 'The whole area is thickly strewn with fragments of ancient pottery,' observed Mr Whittington; eighty years later, Mr Geil observed that 'the ground is now covered with underbrush, and much broken pottery can be found'. And today, Mr Page can confirm that nothing has changed. As you walk up the hill, you can't help but kick up the detritus of the community that lived here before. Thousands and thousands of fragments of Byzantine pottery lie scattered everywhere, a carpet of red terracotta, cream-coloured earthenware, shards of white marble, the handles of jugs, lips of bowls. I found a piece with a hole, which may thus have been the top of a simple lamp. To wander on that hilltop is to kick up the dust of history.

And what it shows is that there were plenty of people here, over a long period. The range and diversity of the pottery shards show

Patmos. The ancient acropolis above Skala. Or what's left of it at any rate.

that Patmos was continually inhabited from the middle Bronze Age right up to the time of the Roman empire. Patmos was not a wilderness or a desert isle when John landed down in the bay. People lived here. They ate and drank. They fished the seas and tilled the scanty soil.

There was a vibrant religious and social life. A votive offering slab from the second century BC mentions Hegemandros, seven-times head-man of the gymnasium on Patmos. The inscription also mentions the torch-runners, young men who ran around waving fire at some event held at festivals in honour of fire gods such as Hephaestus. As we've seen, Guérin found the base of a temple at the acropolis, which was probably a temple to Apollo. In fact there were at least three temples on Patmos. There was also a temple to Artemis on the hill where the monastery now stands, and another temple on a strange, misshapen rocky outcrop known as Kallikatsou, on the southern part of the island, near Grikos. These temples had feasts and festivals of their own.

Once again it was brought home to me that Patmos was not an Alcatraz or a Guantanamo. Heaven knows, Patmos has its share of wilderness places — and I would walk many of them, blistered and sun-burnt and wondering what I was doing there — but when John arrived, there were houses and traders and craftsmen and priests and peasants. And these were the people John lived among when he had his vision.

Indeed, the fact that he had his vision on Patmos is surely part of his message. Patmos was a nothing place, hardly mentioned in the histories. But in John's inside-out, upside-down vision of reality, those on the margins are really at the heart of things. The nobodies get to wear the crown. Patmos, then, itself becomes a metaphor: that such a crucial understanding of the cosmos, of the future of the world, could happen in such a 'non-place' is fundamental to John's message.

*

You'd have thought that Revelation would have brought instant fame to Patmos, at least in Christian circles. Yet, even after its name-check in the closing act of the Bible, Patmos seems to have remained relatively anonymous. Despite – or perhaps it's more because of – its association with Revelation, Patmos does not seem to have been venerated like other places were. When Constantine established Christianity as the Official Number One Approved Religion of the Roman empire, big, beautiful churches sprang up in the holy places of Christianity: Jerusalem, Bethlehem, Rome, Antioch.

But not much happened on Patmos.

There was a small fourth-century church, apparently, built high on the hill where a temple to Artemis had previously stood, and, some time in the fifth century, that was replaced by a bigger basilica. But we only know about those because, later, people found their ruins; there are no contemporary accounts of their erection. Their opening ceremonies did not make the news. Once again, you sense a reticence about Revelation, an uncertainty. You get the idea that, because it was mentioned in the Bible, they felt they ought to have a church here, but because it was mentioned in Revelation, they ought not to make much of a fuss about it.

Eventually, the island emptied. The acropolis was deserted, the walls started to crumble. The basilica fell into disrepair and was replaced by a small *exoklissi*, a humble chapel which served mainly as a shelter for visiting shepherds who brought their flocks to graze here from nearby islands. Once a year, perhaps, a priest would arrive by boat to say mass in the chapel and keep it sanctified. And then he'd head back to civilisation and more orthodox pastures.

By the middle ages, the island was deserted. A Byzantine official, Nikolaos Tzazis, the Recorder of the Cyclades, visited the island in 1088: 'Over [Patmos] I walked,' he wrote, 'and found it to be all desolate and laid waste, and darkened with thorns and other litter and untrodden and on account of the absence of water in the place entirely uninhabitable.' At the top of the hill he found only the ruins of the earlier Christian basilica and 'a poor chapel, built in the name of the esteemed Theologian'.

But Tzazis was a man on a mission. Because someone *had* taken notice of Patmos. And that person had applied to the emperor to take over the island. So the emperor had sent Tzazis to make a survey. Tzazis sent his report back to the emperor, who duly signed over the island to the new leaseholder. His name was Christodoulos. He arrived on the island a year later.

He had come to make the island holy again.

*

The Monastery stands high on a hill, at the highest point of the settlement known as Chora. In a small chapel to one side, there is a glass-topped case, a bit like you find in an old museum. It looks as though it should be displaying mounted butterflies, or curious fossils, or geological specimens, but, when I peered into it, I discovered that it actually contains the skull of St Thomas.

Yes, *the* St Thomas. The doubting apostle.

They also have the skull of St Philip. Uh-huh. *That* Philip. The, er . . . non-doubting apostle.

They also have some relics belonging to, as far as I could make out, a monk called Pachomius. Yes, *that* Pachomius – the man who was captured by Tartars and taken to Usaki, near Philadelphia in Asia Minor, where he was enslaved for twenty-seven years before being released and becoming a monk at Mount Athos; then, years later, going back to Usaki–Philadelphia, where he was imprisoned and eventually executed.

No, I'd never heard of him, either.

There were also some chains – the very chains, it is claimed, in which John of Patmos was bound when he came to the island as a prisoner. They looked very strong. And rather recent, if I'm honest.

I don't want to upset anybody, but I'm a little suspicious about the provenance of these relics. But nestled in the case with the skulls and the chains are a pair of sandals. And these, I think, *are* authentic. Because they belonged to the man who is responsible for this building. They are the sandals of Christodoulos – the founder of the monastery. And this is his resting place: the chapel of St Christodoulos.

*

Christodoulos (which means 'servant of Christ') was born, sometime before 1030, in Asia Minor, close to Nicaea. He joined a monastic community at Mount Olympos in Greece, but he yearned 'to travel like a sparrow and live in the desert'. He headed for Rome, but for some reason changed course, ending up in the Holy Land around 1054, where he entered the monastery of San Sabas. It was a time of anarchy and upheaval. Arab tribes were warring among themselves and the Christians – then as now – found themselves caught in the crossfire. So he left and returned to Asia Minor, to join a community in Mount Latros, near the ancient ruins of Miletus. He was a good administrator and he soon rose through the ranks. He became kind of the CEO of the Latros monastery.

But the times were changing. (Maybe it was the end times.) The cataclysmic defeat of the Byzantine imperial forces at Manzikert in 1071 left the monasteries vulnerable to attack by the Turks. Christodoulos moved west with some other monks, first to the port of Skenouros on the west coast of Caria, then even further, out across the sea to Kos.

Kos was too noisy. Nothing changes. But he discovered that the nearby island of Patmos was deserted. So, in 1088, using his not inconsiderable negotiating skills, he persuaded the emperor Alexis I Comnenos to give him the island. Tax free. Alexis sent his surveyor – the aforementioned Nikolaos Tzazis – to see if there was anything worth keeping, and then agreed to sign over the island. Amazingly, the original imperial chrysobull granting the island to Christodoulos is still on display in the monastery museum. It is a six-foot-long piece of parchment. At the top, thin lines of sepia ink weave up and down like a seismograph. At the bottom is the signature of Emperor Alexis, signed in bright-red cinnabar ink. It's a lease on the apocalypse, kept safe by the monastery for over 900 years.

Christodoulos and his brother monks arrived on Patmos and began building in the spring of 1089. He had with him a collection of rare and precious books he had amassed – the beginnings of the famous library. He had also been granted the neighbouring islands of Lipsi and Arkoi, as well as some large estates on the island of Leros. In 1092, however, Turks raided the islands and, with the monastery not completed, Christodoulos and the monks had to flee to mainland Greece. A few months later, exiled from Patmos, Christodoulos was dead. His monks made it back to the island in 1094, taking his body with them. They arrived on 21 October – a day on which Christodoulos is commemorated here annually (as is 16 March, the day he died). So, like John, Christodoulos was only on the island for a little while. And yet these two figures dominate its history.

Skala, with the fortress-like monastery in the distance.

They finished the monastery, a fortress of God on top of the hill. The monastery – and the discovery of the Cave of the Apocalypse – rekindled the fame of the island, and brought wealth and employment for the islanders. In time Patmos became a major centre for ship-owners and ship-building and even a naval base for the Byzantine fleet.

The monastery has continued in use on the island ever since, surviving a siege by Spanish Arabs, an attempt by Normans from Sicily to nick the relics of St Christodoulos, and an attack by an English pirate called Geoffrey. (Abbot Theoktistos mentions one 'Ieffrai' attacking in the 1150s.) Pirate raids were a perennial problem. Some of those pirates were freelancing for bigger powers. One attack in 1258 was attributed to 'the godless Italians', i.e. the Genoese and the Venetians, who outsourced their piracy. After that lot came the

Turks at the beginning of the fourteenth century, and the Crusaders forty years later, when the Knights of St John (appropriately) conquered Rhodes and took *de facto* control of Patmos.

Through all these attacks and changes of ownership, Patmos remained Greek. The monastery lost valuables and men, but never lost its identity. (And it managed to keep hold of most of the relics and the books.) Even when Constantinople fell to the Turks in 1453, Patmos remained a Greek island. It simply surrendered to the Ottomans and carried on. In 1912, the island was occupied by the Italians, who took over all the Dodecanese. In 1943, the Germans arrived.

And through it all, the worship has continued. For a thousand years the monks have rung the bells, burned the incense, chanted the liturgy in the monastery founded by 'Our Father and Founder Hosios Christodoulos'. In one painting in the monastery he is shown standing next to John. He wears a simple brown tunic, his head cowled. In one hand he holds a small church which he is offering to the elder; in the other hand there is an open scroll with a prayer: 'I offer to you, apostle, with all the other monks this church that I have built for you; and you, I beg, do not cease to protect them and act for their benefit.'

15 The Travels of St John

All is silent. Yesterday's incense clings in the air.

There are three monks; two sitting in front of me, one behind. They are grey habited. Brown leather belts. Beads hanging down. Of the two in front, one looks like a history professor: tall, lean, wearing steel-framed glasses. The other is bald, wiry. He could be the killer in a Dan Brown novel. The one behind makes a movement. I realise he is subtly turning off his mobile phone.

To my right a woman is reading a New Testament in Cyrillic. To my left, two women pilgrims sit on the rough granite floor at the side of the cave. Not for them the relative comfort of a chair. They are hardliners.

The cave has a guardian, a verger, a caretaker: a thin, birdlike man, bearded, bald but still valiantly sporting mullet-length black hair at the back. He is dressed in jeans and a black shirt and has a black leather bum bag which holds his cigarettes, his phone and the other tools of his trade. Whatever they are. Unsmiling, busy, quick to scold anyone trying to sneak a photo, he bustles around with broom and with cloth. He speaks no English (I tried) but I have the feeling that even if he could, he wouldn't. On my final visit to the cave I had a nod of welcome from him, but that was as close as our relationship got. I never knew his name, but for some reason I always thought of him as 'Gary'.

Gary had a job to do, and everyone knew it. He was particularly adept at candle recycling. At the back of the cave, pilgrims would light a tallow candle and place it in sand. These candles never got much of a chance to burn. I reckon the average votive candle got ten minutes of burning, max, before Gary whipped it out of the sand and threw it into a bucket. Presumably a tallow-recycling bucket. It seemed a somewhat perfunctory approach to people's heartfelt prayers, but Gary had no time for sentimentality. Being the caretaker of the apocalypse requires discipline.

Every now and then he would pause to answer his phone, retreating to the porch to continue the conversation. I was surprised that he had reception in the cave, but then again, this place has always had a good signal, I suppose.

*

There is no mention of a cave in Revelation, by the way. The only mention of a cave associated with John comes much later, from a fifth- or possibly seventh-century work known as *The Travels of John the Theologian*, or *The Acts of John by Prochorus*.

It purports to be the work of Prochorus, one of the seven deacons mentioned in Acts 6. In the story, this otherwise anonymous figure escapes the New Testament and accompanies John on his travels. Its value as a historical source is minimal, but the legends it contains have made a big impact on the island. Even as late as the seventeenth century, Georgirenes reported: 'The substance of what is related in that Life of St. John that goes by the name *Prochorus* is generally believed in Patmos to this day.'* The work became extremely popular, although it seems ignorant of most of the earlier traditions about John. The book claims that John spent fifteen years on the island of Patmos, then another twenty-six back in Ephesus after his release, finally dying aged over 100. It has been suggested that the author was really an elder from a church in Syria. Certainly he doesn't seem to know much about Patmos, and it is clear he's never been there. He does know some of the names, such as that of Phora, the main harbour and executive centre of the island. But the rest is rubbish. He gives the island a proconsul, something you only got on bigger islands like Cyprus. He describes cities. He says there is a town called Myrinousa, with many temples and statues, and a river running

---

* In Georgirenes' day there was a hermitage near the cave: the hermitage of the Holy Grotto of St John the Divine. According to a local legend, there was a fig tree 'whose figs have naturally the characters of the word *apokalupsis*'. Like a stick of rock with 'Revelation' written right through it.

round it. He seems to think that the island is big enough to accommodate journeys of fifty miles. Admittedly, some of my journeys *felt* that long, but in reality, the only way to travel fifty miles on Patmos is to go back and forth several times.

The Travels sets John's stay in the reign of Trajan (AD 98–117), and it is Trajan who banishes John from Ephesus. However, John reveals that he has always known this punishment was going to happen. He had received a command from Jesus to

> Go into Ephesus, because after three months you will go into exile to an island, which has great need of you; you will be greatly tested, and you will sow many things there.

There then follows a sea journey of a week – slow going for a trip of only fifty miles – during which John's holiness is so apparent that all the guards accompanying him are baptised at the end of the trip. And they are not the only ones: during John's stay on the island he converts two pagan priests, three Jews, over 500 general-purpose pagans, the proconsul Makrinos and the governor Laurentius.

He also has a series of battles with a magician called Kynops, who challenges John to a best-supernatural-power contest. The wizard comes to the harbour and finds John busily baptising. Kynops then demonstrates his power by diving into the bay and emerging with the ghosts of recently drowned Patmians. He then incites the audience to attack John, leaving him for dead.

John, however, is made of tougher stuff, and he survives. The next morning Kynops returns and once again dives into the harbour to show what he can do. But this time, John is ready: he says a prayer and then . . . nothing. Not a ripple. The wizard stays under water. The audience waits for three days – which is overdoing it, frankly – but nothing happens. Kynops has been turned into a rock.

The rock is still there in the harbour at Skala, marked by a warning light. From my house I could watch the local children swim out to it from the tiny beach at the west end of the port. One day I went down there and swam out to it myself. It was not really worth all the doggy-paddling, to be honest.

In a way, what is interesting about the earliest version of *The*

Travels is what is missing: the author makes no mention of John's writing of Revelation, or receiving the vision. The only link between this book and Revelation is the fact that John was on Patmos. In *The Travels*, the text that John receives on Patmos is his gospel. He goes outside the city to a place called *Katastasis* ('Place of Rest'), where he fasts and prays. Then he sends Prochorus back into town to get some stationery supplies (papyrus, ink, etc.), and when the disciple returns he hears thunder and lightning, and John tells him to write down what he dictates. And so he begins: 'In the beginning was the Word . . .' Two days later, and the first edition of John's gospel is ready for press.

It's theological Photoshop. The Apocalypse has been airbrushed out and the far more acceptable gospel inserted in its place. Once again, this reflects an eastern suspicion of the text. Whoever it was who wrote *The Travels of John* was more than happy to link the apostle to Patmos. Just don't mention Revelation.

Only in a later addition to *The Travels* does Revelation get put back in. The manuscript containing this bit dates from the eleventh to thirteenth centuries and it contains the earlier narrative, but adds in a section where John and Prochorus go out of the city to a cave. Prochorus leaves John there for ten days. On the tenth day John hears a voice, commanding him to stay for another ten days, during which he will hear 'many great secrets'. On the twentieth day he receives the Revelation and sends Prochorus for stationery supplies (yes, again). Prochorus then takes down the dictation from John, which, as before, takes two days. They then return to the town and have copies made for distribution, while John reads the original out to the assembled church.

This, then, is the earliest actual mention of the cave. And it coincides with the establishment of the monastery on Patmos in the late eleventh century – exactly the point in time when, surprise, surprise, they found the cave, the *Katastasis*, the very place where John had his vision.

*

Having found the cave, the monks had it gift-wrapped, so that it is now encased in a small church, itself part of a bigger monastic

The Monastery of the Apocalypse. The church containing the cave is in the lower left section of the building.

191

complex – the Monastery of the Apocalypse. This rather higgledy-piggledy building sits on the side of the hill, among the trees, about half a mile below the town of Chora. Entrance to the church is a matter of descending a series of vertiginously winding stairways through the heart of the surrounding monastery, and past the belfry. I descend from terrace to terrace, landing to landing, occasionally catching spectacular views of the sea. Finally, at the bottom, there is a wide, plain entranceway. A church door, in fact, with a white-washed porch. Stooping through the door, you enter the church of St Anne, named after the mother of Christodoulos, founder of the monastery.

It's a tiny chapel. The left-hand wall contains windows through which I can see right down to the harbour.

But to the right the wall is missing. Instead there is a projecting lip of granite, under which I duck. And then, a rock floor, some rows of chairs, many more paintings. This is the cave. This is the *Katastasis*, the 'Rest'.

It is ornately decorated, as is the manner of eastern churches, but not overly so. From the roof of the cave hang seven small lanterns – presumably echoing the seven lampstands in Revelation – and one larger one. All silver, they look like upturned samovars. I have been in Jerusalem where, in some chapels in the Holy Sepulchre, the bling is so intense you feel like you are in an episode of *Pimp My Church*. It's like worshipping in a hip-hop star's bathroom. But here it is more subtle. There is enough to make you realise this is a church, but not so much that you forget it's a cave.

There are icons, of course. A painting of Christodoulos. An icon of the Madonna and Child, and around them the twelve apostles, perched rather precariously on branches. In the big painting in the centre, John's sleep is disturbed by Christ appearing, accompanied by a supporting cast of seven angels. Close inspection reveals them to be the angels of the seven cities, each holding a small church building, like a name tag. The lower-left panel shows a traditional scene: John dictating the vision to Prochorus. The young man wears a red toga. John looks in the other direction: upwards. Towards heaven.

To the right is a small, round opening in the rock, framed in silver. This is, according to tradition, where John rested his head when receiving the vision. It looks a bit like an MRI scanner.

Maybe that's what Revelation is. Spiritual brainwaves. A magnetic map of holy activity. Up and to the right from that niche is another, smaller niche, again chased with silver. This, apparently, was what John used to grip on to when getting up in the morning. An assistive device for the old boy. His Stannah stairlift to heaven. As Geil wrote when he came here a century ago, 'Tradition has striven to make holy each fissure, each ancient water channel, each niche or indentation in the rock, by connecting it with the Gospel of St. John and the Revelation.' So, as well as the hole for his head and the crevice for his handrail, we get the sloping ledge of rock which 'tradition' claims that John – or Prochorus, things get confusing here – used as a writing slope to rest his parchment on. Today a copy of the Apocalypse, bound in crimson velvet, rests there. And above it there is an icon of a man. The body of the icon is almost entirely covered in silver, from which the painted face peeks out, like someone wearing a robo-suit in one of those sci-fi films. This is the man himself. John of Patmos.

He is old, bald, with a curiously bulbous, two-domed head. He looks like the elephant man. Two brains throb inside their casing: something is going on inside that skull, you can tell. A small tuft of hair clings to one of the domes like a palm tree on a desert island.

He sees things, this man. Closeted in his cave, he sees a long, long way.

*

This, then, is where it all happened. Or not. Or maybe it did. Or maybe, you know, it just doesn't matter. You can worship God anywhere, of course. But these places, what the Celtic Christians describe as 'thin' places, do seem to have something about them. Perhaps it is just that we – the pilgrims – bring our expectations, our hopes, our sense of the numinous to the place. Or maybe there really is something there. Perhaps all that worship and prayer has soaked into the rock, laid down a patina of holiness. I don't know.

But I do know that I sat in that room for two hours, and it felt like the blink of an eye.

And on all my subsequent visits it felt the same. There was an air of tranquillity. Of timelessness. 'The nature of time is mysterious,' wrote Peter Ackroyd. 'Sometimes it moves steadily forward, before springing or leaping out. Sometimes it slows down and, on occasions, it drifts and begins to stop altogether.' That's Revelation for you right there. Time goes all over the place.

One day I went, not in the early morning, but at peak time. The cave was plainer. The lamps had been taken down, and Gary was busy cleaning them. A cruise ship had arrived offshore, and the cave was awash with people, wave after wave of tour groups pouring through. Many pass through quickly, but others spend – oh – as much as ten minutes.

Perhaps that's too cynical. Even in a short burst the cave will work its magic on those who will listen. The cave rewards the pilgrim. And pilgrims it gets.

This was a Russian ship, as far as I could tell, and the pilgrims were dressed to the max. Men brandishing their Canon SLRs, irritated that they were not allowed to take photos. Women blinged and bejewelled. An entire family dressed in white – father, mother, five children. It was like a washing powder advert. There was noise and bustle, despite Gary's shushing. Children whispered in that way which they think is a whisper but which is actually still shouting, just at a lower volume.

Great, if perfunctory, reverence is shown. Many kiss the feet of the icons. Others bustle about borrowing pens, writing on slips of paper and placing them in a box. Votives. Prayers. Why do people think that God hears them more in this place? Or that a prayer posted here will be answered when one muttered at sea, or in bed in the bleak darkness of early morning will go unheard?

Whatever their reasoning, they submitted their prayers to Gary, who showed them where they were to be posted. I had no idea what happened to them after that. Perhaps he recycled them, like the candles.

People. So many people. And then, miraculously, the cave emptied. For a brief moment between tour groups, there was silence. I was the only one in the cave. No, not the only one. There was a girl as well. She was tall and slender and her head was covered with a scarf.

Her brown eyes were wide in wonder. She stood at the lip of the cave, trembling slightly. She touched the rock gently, reverentially, fingers lightly brushing the granite. She looked into the cave and her eyes filled with tears.

A moment of grace.

Outside in the porch, Gary's phone went off. The girl looked at me, smiled and then left.

And suddenly, I too was crying, and I had no idea why.

16 The Books in the Library

On 1 June 1795, a Dr John Sibthorpe, Sherardian Professor of Botany at Oxford, came to Patmos, researching his monumental book, *Flora Graeca*. He wrote:

> *Patmos, like most of the Greek islands at this time of year, presented a brown sun-burnt surface, forbidding the botanist to hope for a plentiful harvest. Notwithstanding its arid state I still discovered a few scarce plants.*

Mainly, though, he seems to have spent his time killing things. On his first morning he shot some Greenshank wading birds and 'killed two species of serpent', one of which 'appeared to have all the marks of a species highly venomous . . .'.

The next day he was delayed from leaving Patmos by high storms, so he whiled away the time by going out after dinner and shooting a 'species of Sterna S. Hirundo', i.e. the common tern. He complained that:

> *The island furnishes a very inconsiderable number of land birds; some of the swallow tribe and the wheat-ear were almost the only small birds we saw in the island; the Partridge, the rock Pigeon, the hooded Crow and the little Owl were the only larger land birds.*

If you ask me, all the birds were in hiding. This man was surely the world's most dangerous botanist.

He was still on the island a day later, when he walked to the Monastery of St John to meet with a monk called Gregorio Zeno:

*He understood the ancient Greek and had a large library for
a man in his situation. Among the botanical works he showed
me an old copy of Paul of Aegina and Matthiolus's Commentary
of Dioscorides. He furnished me with the Greek names and
superstitious uses of several of the plants of the island.*

Er . . . probably this was the librarian. Which might explain why
he had so many books. Sadly, for Dr Sibthorpe, the journey to Greece
proved fatal: he developed consumption on the way home, and died
in Bath on 8 February 1796. Rumours that he was pecked to death
in revenge have not been confirmed.*

*

The librarian I met was a studious man, thin, goateed, a twinkle in
his eyes. A Patmian by descent, he was born in exile in Thessalonica,
but returned to the island when he was two. He now guards the
treasures of one of the great libraries of the world.

I had been given his contact details by the Orthodox Information
Centre in the harbour. (I'm not sure if there's an Unorthodox
Information Centre anywhere. Probably a bar, if so.) The kind lady
there provided me with his name, some telephone numbers which
never seemed to get me anywhere, and an email address which later
proved to be wrong. So I went to the monastery itself and asked at
the museum. They told me to ask in the courtyard. In the courtyard
I asked a rather taciturn monk who just said, 'Go to kiosk.'

So I went to the kiosk. There I found that the man who sells the
postcards also runs the telephone exchange for the monastery.
Eventually, after five phone calls, the librarian was located.

'He's coming,' said the kiosk man, with an air of triumph.

From a door on the other side of the courtyard the librarian
appeared. He was charm itself. Of course he could spare the time
to talk. He could do it right away. He led me down some steps, and
punched a code into the electronic lock of a tiny door. We entered

---

* *Flora Graeca* – 'Greek Flora' – was eventually published in ten volumes
between 1806 and 1840. The first edition ran to a mere thirty copies, probably because it contained 966 colour plates.

into a cool stone hallway, then through another door, and there we were: in the library of the Monastery of St John.

*

I am used to old libraries. Much of my time is spent in the Bodleian in Oxford, which dates back to the late fifteenth century. The library of the Monastery of St John, though, is 500 years older.

The books arrived with Christodoulos, who had started acquiring them while running the monastery at Latros. Through all the attacks by 'Pirats' and sundry other vicissitudes of history, the library survived and even flourished, to become one of the foremost libraries in the Byzantine world. For some 900 years this library has continued on Patmos without interruption. Visitors have come to see the monastery and its famous library. Some of them, mind you, have not left empty-handed: in the British Library is a copy of the works of Plato known as *Codex Clarkianus*, which was taken from the library by one Daniel Clarke in 1801. 'It is enough to say,' he wrote, 'that I rescued from the rats and the worms in the library of the convent, many valuable works.' Hmm. One man's rescue is another man's theft.

Nowadays the security is better. Indeed, the library looks more like the underground lair of a Bond villain. You descend through a grey granite doorway to a room with plush red carpet, long tables. I half expected the bookshelves to slide aside and reveal the map of the secret laser weapons.

An inventory from AD 1200 lists over 300 manuscripts. Today the library contains nearly 1,000 manuscripts, about 50 of them illustrated. Many of these are theological works: lectionaries, commentaries, copies of biblical books. There is also a remarkable archive of official documents, including over 125 Byzantine imperial documents from the eleventh century onwards, and thousands of documents covering the four centuries (the sixteenth to the nineteenth) of Ottoman rule. It's like a 900-year-old filing cabinet. Here are letters from Byzantine emperors, official documents from Mehmed II The Conqueror, a letter from the Tsar, a document signed by the Doge of Venice.

Some of the finest and most ancient texts are on display in the museum. There are some pages from *Codex Petropolitanus*

Purpureus – a sixth-century Greek New Testament written in silver on purple-stained vellum. This fabulously expensive document was originally created by imperial scribes in the scriptorium in Constantinople, where it remained for six centuries until it was broken up – probably by Crusaders – with half of it remaining in the east and the other fragments disappearing into the west. The Patmos fragments were discovered in the library in 1864. (Good thing no one knew about them earlier, otherwise Daniel Clarke would have had them.) There is a copy of the *Homilies of Gregory of Nazianzus*, its golden pages rippled with age, decorated with blue and red flowers, peacocks and what seems to be a dog with a blue beard; and a twelfth-century copy of the gospels where Mark sits writing his wonderful words, bearded, blue-cloaked against a background of melted gold.

Downstairs in the secret book lair, we sat in the anteroom and talked, in suitably hushed voices, of John, his links with Patmos, and of the building of the monastery.

'Christodoulos was only two years here. Then he went away, and he died there. Then the monks who were with him bring his body back to Patmos. So . . .' The librarian carefully selected his words. 'We know that in two years he made the Katholikon. But we know nothing about the walls outside. We don't have this information about the monastery.'

'How do the islanders feel? Are they proud of the connection with John?'

'Yes they are.' He paused. 'But it's not the same feeling like twenty years ago. Many things have changed the people. The tourists – year by year there are more and more. So . . . Twenty years ago all the people go to church every Sunday. Not all of them, but many of them. Now, it's almost nobody. But this is not just a problem in Patmos, but everywhere in Europe. Still, all of Patmians can tell you something about the history of St John and the story of Kynops the magician.'

We talked briefly on why I was writing the book, of people's nervousness about Revelation.

'Most people are afraid,' he agreed. 'They know about the book. But they are scared. Confused. It's not . . .'

He shrugged. His hands waved uncertainly in the air. The words would not come.

I knew just how he felt.

*

The monastery has had a long association with scholarship and learning. Because the Turks never settled on the island, it always remained Greek and even flourished under the *Pax Ottomanica* of the sixteenth century. And the survival of the library meant that it became a home for scholars and researchers. After 1713 a school was established in the monastery, based around the well-stocked library. It became one of the centres of Orthodox learning. The fifty-one students studied theology as well as 'physics' and Aristotle. The Patmian school fell into disrepair in the later Victorian period, and in 1907 financial problems forced it to re-locate to Samos, but forty years later, after the liberation of the island from the Italians, the school was re-established in new buildings just above the monastery. Today it even has its own Facebook page. The skull of the school's founder, Makarios Kalogeras, is, apparently, kept in an engraved silver shrine in the Chapel of St Anne. Gives a whole new meaning to the title 'the Head of the school'.

Some of the manuscripts contain entertaining warnings and marginal notes. On one manuscript, written in 1180:

> *I, Neilos, great sinner and unlettered peasant, do the little book, penned by me, dedicate to the greatly venerated and holy convent of Patmos, that the saint might be mindful of me . . . Whosoever would deprive this Holy Monastery of this, Neilos' gift, on any pretext, be it just or no, let him be accursed and damned. So be it! Amen!*

Another manuscript from 1494 warns:

> *if anyone giveth this book to the pupils while at lessons, thus causing its destruction, may the curses of the 300 saintly and godly fathers at the Synod of Nicaea and the leprosy of Gehazi*

fall upon him and may he have the great St John and the Blessed Father Christodoulos as his accusers on the Day of Judgment.

A curse to warm the hearts of school and college librarians everywhere.

John, of course, added his own imprecatory warnings to the end of his vision. If anyone adds to the words of the book, John warns, 'God will add to that person the plagues described in this book; if anyone takes away from the words of the book of this prophecy, God will take away that person's share in the tree of life and in the holy city.'

Keep out. No trespassing. You can look, but don't touch.

John never said anything against writing books *about* Revelation, though. And it is a scholar-monk, far away from the Patmos school, who is responsible for one of the most influential books on Revelation.

*

Joachim of Fiore was born in Calabria, Italy. He became a monk, then an abbot, before founding a new monastery in Fiore. And it was there that he began to study Revelation and think about the shape of history.

It didn't go that well to begin with. He'd only got ten verses into Revelation when the obscurity and mystery 'stopped him like a stone'. It took a year of prayer before he had an epiphany. On Easter morning 1184, the book snapped into focus and suddenly Joachim Knew What It Was All About. 'I suddenly perceived in my mind's eye something of the fullness of this book,' he wrote, 'and of the entire harmony of the Old and New Testaments.'

Revelation, he now understood, described specific historical events. Joachim divided history into three ages, each of which corresponded to one of the persons of the Trinity. The first age spanned history from creation to the crucifixion; the second age was still in progress and would end with the advent of the antichrist. Then would come a battle between God and Satan, as described in Revelation 12, and after that would dawn a third age, an age of peace and perfection.

Leaving aside the details, the key thing is that Joachim treated the book of Revelation as history: history that had happened and was in the past, and a history which was to come. He believed that hidden amongst its symbols and imagery were real, datable historic events. Scouring its details, he found not only the obvious ones, such as the persecution of Christians by Rome, but also the heretics of the middle ages and the conflicts with the Arabs and the Turks of his own day. Joachim lifted the bonnet of Revelation and identified all the moving parts. The heads of the beasts, for example, were all those who had persecuted the church, including Herod, Nero, Henry IV (who at the time was engaged in a massive row with the Pope over who had the right to appoint senior clergy) and Saladin, who had recaptured Jerusalem. The seventh head was the antichrist, who had not yet been identified.

The antichrist is a figure that pops up a lot in apocalyptic studies, but John, in fact, never mentions him – he seems entirely unaware of the character. For all his appearances in the sermons and writings of fundamentalist Christianity, not to mention a number of appearances in films, the word is only used in the letters of John (not, as we have seen, the same John who wrote Revelation), and there he is not a person, but many different people: 'Many deceivers have gone out into the world, those who do not confess that Jesus Christ has come in the flesh; any such person is the deceiver and the antichrist!' (2 John 7). John's antichrist is anyone who rejects Jesus. The antichrist is already living in the world.

Over the ensuing centuries, there have been many individual candidates for the antichrist. But, biblically speaking, the antichrist is not a person: it's a state of being. Augustine stated this clearly: 'whatsoever is contrary to the word of God, is antichrist.'

What was actually significant about Joachim was that he set a precedent for seeing detailed analogies between the events of Revelation and political events in the world around him. Perhaps rather dangerously from the point of view of his career prospects in the Catholic church, Joachim believed the antichrist, the seventh head of the beast, would be an evil Pope who would exercise power over all the earth. On the flipside, the angel from the sun who features in Revelation 10 was going to be a virtuous, angelic Pope. It was good Pope, bad Pope. The only tricky issue was identifying which was which.

Joachim of Fiore became a well-known and respected figure. King

Richard I went to meet him on his way to the Third Crusade, and the first question he asked was when the antichrist would be born. After his death, the poet Dante pictured Joachim in paradise. The man was a prophet, after all.

What was different about Joachim was that he saw the Apocalypse as a roadmap of history: the events in the book were not just metaphors, they were coded versions of the future. This approach, which became known as futurism, launched the idea of Revelation as a code to be cracked by those with specialist insight.

One of Joachim's big ideas was that the 'two witnesses' in Revelation 11 were two monastic orders, orders which were still to appear. And then, guess what, two monastic orders did appear: the Dominicans and the Franciscans. And the Franciscans took Joachim to their hearts, particularly a group of Franciscans known as the Spirituals. The Spirituals were hardline Franciscans who believed that the church had lost its way. One of them, Peter Olivi, wrote a hugely influential book which argued that the church was so depraved and corrupted that it had 'turned, as it were, into a new Babylon'. His writings were condemned and burnt, and the authorities clamped down hard. But they couldn't stop others taking up the cause. Olivi's disciple, Ubertino da Casale, wrote a tract which confirmed a definitive ID of the two beasts of the Apocalypse: they were Pope Boniface VIII, and Benedict XI, both of whom, it so happened, actively persecuted the Spirituals. So it was the Spirituals – Catholic monks, let's remember – who were the first mainstream group to identify the church with the malignant forces in Revelation.

In some cases they preached – and organised – revolution. The Joachimite Fra Dolcino of Novara advocated the abolition of all property, and of marriage, and established a peasant commune in Piedmont. He was captured by the authorities and, under torture, proclaimed that the antichrist would arrive in three and a half years. He was burned at the stake in 1307. A monument to his memory was erected to commemorate the sixth hundredth anniversary of his death in 1907, but was later gunned down by Fascists.

The response of the church to this excess of prophetic interpretation was to argue that of course Revelation prophesied certain events, but all those events had already happened. The Jesuit Catholic scholar

Luis de Alcazar argued that Revelation chapters 4 to 11 described Jewish persecution of early Christians and the downfall of Jerusalem, while chapters 12 to 19 described the foundation of the church, the fall of pagan Rome and Constantine's conversion of the empire to Christianity. The millennium was an undefined period following Constantine's reign, which would lead to the return of Christ. And the New Jerusalem was already here in the form of the Catholic Church. Known as preterism, this approach saw Revelation as a largely (past) historical document – and had the added bonus of ruling out any possibility of identifying the beast with current or future Popes.

These two strands have largely dominated the interpretation of Revelation ever since. Futurism blossomed into all the strange varieties of millenarianism. Preterism has turned into historical criticism that sees everything in Revelation as explicable in terms of historical equivalences. What they have in common is that both are attempts to 'break the code', as it were. They're not so far removed from each other – and generally speaking, once any theological group gained power, they moved from futurism to preterism. After all, once you've got power, the last thing you want is Jesus walking in and taking over. The effect is that futurism rarely stays mainstream: it keeps moving outwards to the fringes.

And out there on the fringes, in the early nineteenth century, was a man called John Nelson Darby.* Darby was an heir to Joachim. A Church of Ireland clergyman, he left the church in 1830 and became part of a dissident group known as the Plymouth Brethren. Darby came up with two of the most enduring ideas about the end times.

The first was a development of Joachim's ideas of ages. Darby believed that God had arranged history in a series of epochs, which he called dispensations, each of which corresponded to one of the seven letters to the churches.† He believed that we were in the sixth dispensation.

---

* His middle name comes from the fact that his uncle fought with Horatio Nelson at the Battle of the Nile in 1798.

† Since Darby's pioneering work, others have identified different dispensations. Some theologians believe there are nine. Some have gone as far as thirty-seven.

But when would the seventh and final dispensation begin? Well, that's where Darby's second big idea came in. He said it would begin with an event called 'the rapture'. The rapture, like the antichrist, is a word which doesn't appear in Revelation. It's based on passages in Matthew 24, and Paul's first letter to the Thessalonians. In Matthew 24, Jesus describes his return. The Son of Man, says Jesus, will come 'on the clouds of heaven'. Of two men working in the field, 'one will be taken and one will be left'. Meanwhile, in 1 Thessalonians 4:17, Paul talks of how the dead will rise first, and then 'we who are alive, who are left, will be caught up in the clouds together with them to meet the Lord in the air; and so we will be with the Lord forever'.

Darby was a literalist. If Christ said he was coming on the clouds, that's how he was arriving. If Paul said we would be whisked up into the air, that was what was going to happen. Darby took these references and formed them into the idea of the rapture, where Christ would return and the believers would be lifted up to meet him. Darby argued that this would happen, not at the last judgment, but before a seven-year period of tribulation, which would then be followed by the thousand-year reign of Christ on earth.

And so, he was able to confidently set out an agenda for the end of days: the rapture, the arrival of antichrist, seven years of tribulation, Armageddon, the millennium, the return of Satan, the defeat of Satan, the resurrection, the last judgment, any other business, date of next meeting, etc.

(Darby himself made a very specific prediction. He believed the rapture would happen in 1882. Oops.)

Darby's ideas inspired thousands of followers, who attempted to put finer detail on his outline. One of them was C. I. Scofield, a veteran of the American Civil War who had a religious conversion in 1879 and subsequently began to study the Bible. He developed the Scofield Reference Bible which, with its copious notes and cross-references, became, literally, *the* Bible of the dispensationalists. By the 1990s it had sold 10 million copies. As the Scofield Bible put it, 'we have before us the millennium'.

Ah yes, the millennium.

*

In Revelation chapter 20, an angel descends from heaven, binds Satan and throws him into the abyss for a thousand years. During this thousand years – the millennium, as it is known – the souls of all those who 'had not worshipped the beast or its image' come to life and reign with Christ. Belief in a literal, thousand-year reign of Christ is known as millennialism – or chiliasm, from the Greek word for 1,000.

This short passage in Revelation is one of those tiny bits of Bible text which have had a disproportionate impact. The question is simple: is it literally true?

The notion of a blessed time preceding the last judgment is found elsewhere in Jewish writings of the New Testament period. The Apocalypse of Ezra prophesied a messianic kingdom of 400 years. The Ethiopic Enoch argued it would be for three weeks. Bit of a difference of opinion there, but the principle was the same.

There are hints of something like it in Paul's writings, too. In 1 Corinthians he seems to suggest that Christ's reign would begin with the resurrection of the dead (1 Cor. 15.23–25).

But the *millennium* – a thousand years – was something which came in with Revelation. The earliest writers on the book – people like Papias, the Montanists and Victorinus – believed there would be such a reign, although they had different ideas about how the thing would actually work. Some believed that the redeemed would live for a thousand years with Christ, after which there would be a last judgment and the New Jerusalem would descend from heaven. Others thought it would happen the other way around – the New Jerusalem would descend, and *then* the millennium would begin.

Gradually, other voices began to come to the fore, though. Tychonius, one of the first to write a commentary on Revelation, believed that the millennium was simply a way of describing the time between the first and second comings of Christ. In fact he believed in a pretty quick millennium, since he interpreted the three and a half weeks in Revelation 11 as being 350 years. So he probably believed that Christ would return around AD 380. But he rejected a literal reading of Revelation which saw a resurrection of the faithful at the start of the millennium and then another for the rest at the end.

Essentially, though, as the church became more established, millennialism fell out of favour. The historian Eusebius had started out as a chiliast, but when Constantine adopted Christianity and started an ambitious building programme of churches and began transforming Constantinople into the greatest Christian city on earth, he came to believe that the New Jerusalem had arrived. Christianity didn't have to believe in a golden rule in the future, because it had access to quite a bit of gold, and rule, in the here and now.

In the west, Augustine of Hippo developed what became the official line. Revelation was a sort of allegory of the Christian life. If you turned to God, then Satan was bound. The City of God, the New Jerusalem, had already descended in the form of the grace of God, and persisted in the form of the church. He was not opposed to the idea of a literal thousand years; he just thought it meant the period between the first and second comings of Christ. Hence the second coming would pitch up in around the year 1000. His opinion was echoed by the Council of Ephesus in 431, which decided that the millennium had already begun with the birth of the church. It was all symbolic, and that was OK.

Thereafter, official church teaching gently began to edit out any mention of the millennial reign of Christ. Literally, in some cases: Irenaeus of Lyons was keen on the idea of the second coming, but over the years, as his works were copied and translated, his comments on the subject were quietly omitted. Lost in translation, you might say. When, in the sixteenth century, an early copy of his works emerged, complete with his original comments about the second coming, everyone was rather embarrassed to find that one of the founding fathers of the western church was saying exactly the same sort of thing as some of those mad, heretical, radical Protestants who seemed to be springing up everywhere recently.

Not that all Protestants were eagerly awaiting a new millennium. Luther believed it had already run its course, from the time the Apocalypse was written, to the rise of the Turks. John Foxe, whose book celebrating the deaths of Christian martyrs was the big publishing hit of the seventeenth century, believed it ran from the time of Constantine to about 1300.

Dispensationalism, the millennium, the rapture – these are ideas which appeal to outsiders. They are the ultimate cosmic 'told you so'. The powerful and apparently pious will be left behind; the overlooked, the dispossessed, the marginalised gain the kingdom. Darby rejected the established church and, indeed, wrote: 'I believe the notion of a Clergyman to be the sin against the Holy Ghost in this dispensation.' And since his time an emphasis on this kind of millennial eschatology has been a hallmark of radical Protestant groups.

Nowadays, those who advocate a literal millennium break into two camps. The premillennialists believe Christ will one day return and set up his thousand-year rule. The postmillennialists believe that Christ will return *after* the millennium. There will be a golden age for the church, and the resurrection referred to will be a supernatural, spiritual event, not a physical happening. And then Christ will return.

To put it far too simplistically, premillennialists believe that the world is getting worse, but eventually Christ will arrive to sort things out. Postmillennialists believe that the world will get better, and then Christ will return as a culmination. Premillennialists expect violent, abrupt change. Postmillennialists expect to see gradual human progress towards a messianic kingdom.

The final brand of millennialism that we need to touch on is amillennialism, which is the belief that Revelation's account of the thousand-year reign of Christ is purely symbolic. It is a kind of allegory, or picture, of the spiritual perfection of the human soul.

Certainly there is no reason to think that we are heading for – or currently in – a literal thousand-year rule. Numbers in Revelation simply don't work that way. The number of 144,000 for the tribes of Israel isn't literal. The recurrent uses of the number seven aren't literal. How can I say this clearly enough? NONE OF THE NUMBERS ARE LITERAL. When it says a thousand years, what it means is 'a flipping long time'.

But why am I bothering? Big, shouty, uppercase text won't make any difference. Those who believe they have cracked the codes will remain convinced. The millennium, the antichrist and the so-called rapture are very minor parts of scripture. Each of them is only mentioned once. (Come to think of it, the whole idea of 'being born again' only features in one verse in the Bible as well.) And yet the lack of detail seems only to feed the fires of debate: these issues have become huge battlegrounds in Christian theology, tests of who is in and who is out, while issues that are mentioned hundreds of times (money, for example) seem to pass us by.

Personally, I think that we should always bear in mind that Revelation is a two-track vision: stuff happens in heaven; stuff happens on earth. Which means the millennial rule may well be in full swing, but not where we can see it.

The early Christians definitely took for granted that Christ was already reigning in heaven. What they prayed was that his kingdom should come in the same way on earth. And scripture implies that the binding of the Satan has already happened. In Matthew 12.29, Jesus says, 'But if it is by the Spirit of God that I cast out demons, then the kingdom of God has come to you. Or how can one enter a strong man's house and plunder his property, without first tying up the strong man? Then indeed the house can be plundered' (Matt. 12.25–29).

So we know – or should do – that whether we take these passages literally or not, whether our views are post-, pre- or a-millennial, Jesus is already reigning. The strong man has been bound.

17 The Angry Monk

The road up to Chora coils like a garden hose. The buses and coaches toil and grumble up through the trees to the car park by the cave, then on to the little plaza below the town.

Mainly, though, I walked, descending from my apartment into the backstreets of Skala, then up along the cobbled track towards the woods. Though obviously renovated quite recently, this route probably follows that of the simple donkey track built in 1818 through the generosity of a man called Nectarios. It rises steady and straight until you reach the shade of the woods, with their pine and eucalyptus, at which point the cobbles disappear and the track becomes more dirt than anything else. By the time I reached the woods, I was always grateful for the shade, although its benefits were rather negated by the final section of the climb, which meant ascending the steep steps by the Greek School, and then yet more climbing through the alleys to the centre of Chora.

Chora, the small town which surrounds the monastery, is a rabbit-warren of alleys and tiny streets, a maze of white walls with blue shutters, where each turn takes you to a new junction or reveals a stunning vista. It is one of the most remarkable places in the world. What it must be like living there I can't imagine. You'd think it would drive you mad, but everyone I encountered said 'Kali spera' quite cheerfully.

The town grew out of simple necessity. The monastery was the most fortified place on the island, and the biggest building. According to Georgirenes:

> the inhabitants that lay scatter'd in the Isle desired leave to build Huts near the Monastry, for their better Shelter and defence in case of any sudden Attaque by Pirats. In process

of time these Huts were chang'd into fair Houses, and by Trade and Commerce became a great Town, to the number of 800 Houses, and there Inhabited by rich Merchants, that traded into all parts.

However, Georgirenes goes on to admit that by the time he was writing, 'Attaque by Pirats' had become so frequent that Chora had fallen into disrepair and poverty. Today it looks like the rich Merchants are back, and the quietly elegant, beautiful old houses sell for millions of euros.

As Christodoulos could have told you, it's all about location.

*

At the high point of Chora stands the Monastery of St John. From a distance, it looks more fortress than monastery, its dark-brown stone in sharp contrast to the white houses of Chora beneath it. Crenellated battlements line its walls, and at its peak the five-belled belfry looks like a bombed-out ruin.

Below the gate souvenir stands are opening for business, hanging out their beads and their replica icons. Some of them are lighting incense, the religious equivalent of frying onions at a burger van. It gets your holiness salivating. I mount the steps to the huge, castle-like gates through clouds of incense. Disinfected. Please shower before entering the pool.

Inside, the climb continues, through a narrow tunnel, which opens out into a small central courtyard paved with pebbles and flat stones. All around are the buildings of the monastery, stairways and passages and balconies, shuttered windows and mysterious doors. Monks come and go across the courtyard, hats like chimney pots, black capes flapping like the wings of crows. In the middle of the square is a huge storage cistern, which once held wine, but, in a reversal of the wedding at Cana, now holds holy water. And on every level there are smaller chapels, some of them freestanding, like little huts. Monasteries in the Orthodox world are full of tiny chapels, because the Orthodox Church only allows one ceremony per altar per day: hence the more chapels you have, the more daily services you can hold. I don't know how often they are used now, mind you: I rarely saw any of these smaller chapels open.*

When Geil came here, he 'learned that there are forty monks and sixty cats in the monastery'. I should say that the number of monks has gone down, but the number of cats has gone up. There were a lot of them about. On one side of the courtyard is the entrance to the main chapel – the *Katholikon*, as the main church of an Orthodox monastery is known. The porch – the outer narthex, to give it its proper name – is decorated with wall paintings showing scenes from *The Travels of St John*. Over the main entrance he is shown raising a young man from the dead in Ephesus. To the right, he rescues a young man who has fallen overboard from their ship. Further along still we see him drowning the sorcerer Kynops. Worn away in places, fading to white at waist height, the porch is nevertheless a riot of colour. The white floor is inset with patterned marble tiles the colour of ox-blood and amber.

The entranceway uses materials from the older basilica of St John which originally stood on this spot. The balustrade and the pillars are certainly a riot of styles. There are plain and patterned marble pillars, and one with a kind of spiralling corkscrew pattern carved into it. There are Doric and Ionic capitals. Some of the pillars may come from the even earlier temple of Artemis which occupied the site. It's a tribute to the art of ecclesiastical architectural salvage.

Beyond the outer narthex, three doors give access to the unimaginatively named inner narthex. This dates from the twelfth century and, again, is smothered with wall paintings and icons. To the left Mary holds Jesus – who, as so often, appears as a tiny little old bloke, rather than a baby. On the central pillar is an icon of St John, bearing the legend '*o theologos* – 'the theologian'. This is the *proskynesis*: the most venerated icon of the monastery. It is first mentioned in a twelfth-century inventory of the icons of the monastery, and out of the eighteen icons in that list it is the only one to survive to this day. Tradition (again) has it that it was a gift from the emperor.

* The monastery has ten chapels in all, three of which are actually outside the walls in Chora.

The Monastery of St John. The paintings on the outer narthex show scenes from the 'life' of St John.

To the right is a particularly striking portrait: *Agios Sisoes*. This is Sisoes the Great, a fifth-century Egyptian hermit. On his deathbed, he was heard murmuring, arguing. When the monks in attendance asked him what he was saying, he told them that the angels had come for his soul, but that he was trying to persuade them to give him a bit more time to repent.

'You have no need for repentance, Father,' said one of the monks, to which Sisoes (who had spent sixty years as a desert father) replied, 'I do not think that I have even begun to repent.'

I stood for a while looking at his remarkable portrait. His monk's cowl is of the deepest blue, the blue of the Aegean where it meets the shadows of the rocks. Austere, he stares out with concern at a world which has certainly not even begun to repent.

To the right of Sisoes is a door which leads to the chapel of Christodoulos. Above this a mural of the last judgment features a terrifying two-headed demonic sea beast, painted against a vermillion sea. Just as terrifying is the picture on the other side, which shows a naked hermit, supermodel-thin, his modesty protected by a long and strategically placed beard.

This is St Onoufrios – a man of whom there are several representations in the monastery. The name, apparently, is a variation of the rather unpronounceable Egyptian name Wnn-nfr, meaning 'he-who-is-continuingly-good'. The story goes that a man called Paphnutius went into the desert on a kind of monastic 'taster' session, to see if it suited him. After wandering in the desert for sixteen days, he came upon a wild figure covered in hair, wearing nothing but a loincloth of leaves. Understandably, Paphnutius was so scared he ran away, but the figure called him back: 'Come down to me, man of God, for I am a man also, dwelling in the desert for the love of God.'

The figure introduced himself as Onoufrios, formerly a monk but for seventy years a wandering hermit. He invited Paphnutius back to his cell for some bread and water, which appeared miraculously. But the next morning, Onoufrios died. The ground was too hard for Paphnutius to dig a grave, so he covered the body with a cloth and walked away. As he walked off, behind him the hermit's cell crumbled to the ground.

Onoufrios subsequently became an immensely popular figure in art, as well as a venerated saint. He is always depicted as a wild man, naked, wearing underpants made out of leaves. His skill at weaving these made him the patron saint of weavers, although as a naked leaf-wearing wild man, he wasn't what you'd call a big supporter of the textile industry. I had seen a monastery dedicated to him once before without realising it; it's in the valley of Hinnom outside Jerusalem. It marks the traditional site of Akeldama, the place where Judas Iscariot is supposed to have hung himself.

Beyond the narthex, I dive into a dark, mysterious world. The *Katholikon* glitters softly with gold and silver. Everywhere there are icons and carvings, wall paintings in scarlet and blue and emerald green. In 1150, Athanasios of Antioch described this building as 'a church of astonishing beauty, here ablaze with the brilliance of its marbles, there lit up with golden flashing of its holy icons'. It hasn't changed much.

Inside the church, the world outside seems far off, remote. This is a church which still reflects the glory of the Byzantine empire, even though that came to a final end in 1453. The abbot's chair is topped with the two-headed eagle of Byzantium – an image later co-opted by the Holy Roman Empire and the Habsburgs. The seats on which the monks sit during the services are elaborately carved, with the heads of animals on the tops. I think they are lions and eagles, although, to be honest, the eagles look a bit like ducks. Or possibly dodos.

To the right of the *Katholikon*, a small door leads into the Chapel of the Virgin. The walls are lined with dark-brown wooden seats for the monks. But above and around are marvellous frescos which were painted in the late twelfth century. Right above me, Mary holds Christ on her knees. Saints and angels swoop along the archways and the architraves. There are intricate patterns painted in crimson and deep blue, almost like Celtic knotwork. At the east end of the room is an ornately carved iconostasis, all gold and purple. The shallow step beneath it is marble. The stone apparently bears Greek inscriptions and may have come from the ancient temple which once stood on this site. Couldn't see it myself.

*

On my third visit to the monastery, the monk shouted at me.

I had seen him before, striding around the courtyard. He was a big man, with a forbidding air to him. Grey hair tied in a bunch at the back, grey beard flowing free. His black shirt was buttoned up at the top three buttons, with the rest left loose to allow his stomach room to breathe. Periodically he would come out and berate the noisy tourists in the courtyard.

I had gone into the church and sat down, as I had before, in one of the side seats. Notebook in hand, I was gazing up at the ceiling painting of Christ Pantocrator, Christ the judge, when all at once I received a judgment of my own.

'You can't sit there. No sitting!'

I looked round. There he was, rather angry.

'No sitting. And you show no respect. You cross your legs.'

My legs weren't crossed, but even if they had been I wondered how this would have been disrespectful, God having both (a) given me two legs and (b) arranged things so that I could cross them.

'You always lie to me!' he continued. 'You take photos.'

'Excuse me?'

'You lie to me! You take photos. No photos.'

This was too much. 'I am not taking photos,' I replied. 'I am taking notes. I have sat here before like other people. And I don't like being called a liar. I am not taking photos.'

I stood up. He stormed out.

I was shaken. It's quite frightening being shouted at by an Orthodox monk. I think it's the costume: all that black.

I tried to carry on looking, but really I was thinking about slipping out through the other door. Soon, though, my fright turned to anger. How dare he accuse me – a citizen of Her Majesty the Queen – of lying. And, more to the point, of Disobeying A Sign. No, I was not going to slink out and avoid a scene. I was English, damn it. I was going to walk out right past him.

So I did. I went out to the porch, and there he was. Now for it.

'I am sorry,' he said, holding out a hand. 'I shouldn't have said that.'

Well, *that* was a surprise.

Turned out he'd had a trying morning. A few minutes before I arrived he had found a tourist sitting in the seats taking surreptitious photos. 'People lie,' he said. 'They sit and pretend to pray and take photos. That is not a good man. Don't pretend to pray. So I no longer allow people to sit down.'

'I'm sorry,' I said. 'But I was just taking notes.' I told him I was writing a book about Revelation and Patmos.

'A book about the apostle!' Suddenly he was all enthusiasm. 'Ah,' he said, 'sit down, sit down.' He patted the seat next to him. I decided not to cross my legs, just to be on the safe side. 'I will tell you about the apostle.' And, after a short break to tell off another tourist, he did just that. 'Look,' he said, pointing up at the frescos that lined the porch. 'There is life of the apostle.'

He took me through the frescos, all of which showed events from the apocryphal life of John. 'There he is in Ephesus,' he said. 'He worked in the baths. A Roman came and his son had died. He prayed to Artemis – no good. But the apostle prayed and the son came to life.'

'Wasn't there a temple to Artemis here?'

He nodded. 'Before Hosios Christodoulos. Some parts of the church are built out of that temple.' He carried on, running me through the story. John and Prochorus being sent in chains to Patmos. Being shipwrecked. His battles against the magician Kynops – 'His name means "dog face",' he said – and the stone in the bay. As he pointed to each painting, the tales bubbled out of him.

We told – together – the apocryphal story of John in old age in Ephesus. The Christians had gathered to hear the words of the apostle. He was carried in on a stretcher, and he just said to them, 'My children, love one another. If you do that, it will be enough.' And that was it.

'I found that story in London,' the monk said. 'I found a very old New Testament and that story was written in the back.'

I asked what he was doing in London. 'Oh,' he said. 'I have been to these places.'

Legends grew around John. But they also grew around

Christodoulos, the founder of the monastery. The monk told me that Christodoulos had once turned a pirate ship (or three pirate ships, he wasn't terribly clear) into rocks, which can still be seen outside Skala bay.

'Just goes to show,' I said. 'Never attack a monastery.'

'Yes! I turn you into a rock. Or salt!' That seemed to remind him of something. 'And I will tell you an amazing thing,' he said. 'The cross, you know the cross? Where did the wood come from to build the cross?'

'From the crossbeams the Romans had in stock,' was on the tip of my tongue, but I sensed it was not the answer he wanted. And I was right.

'I tell you. This is important story. You write it in your book.' And he started in on a long, fascinating tale. How the wood for the cross was given by the angels to Abraham, to use for the pyre on which he was going to sacrifice Isaac; how Abraham's nephew Lot planted it in the ground and watered it for forty years to find a sign that God had forgiven him; how Solomon had some of the wood from the tree cut down to use in the Temple, but it wouldn't fit. 'The builder would measure it perfectly, but when he came to put it over the door – no! – it would never fit. So they knew it was cursed. And then, finally, the wood from this tree was used to create the cross on which Jesus was crucified.'

He told me that he had learned this story in Israel, in the Monastery of the Holy Cross in Jerusalem. 'Used to be big monastery,' he said. 'Now only one monk there.

'But I believe this story. I have been to these places.'

*

Jewish stories and images ripple through Revelation like a seam of gold running through a rock. When Jesus appears in heaven, he appears as a slain Passover lamb. When John wants to describe the full number of the servants of God, he does so by using the imagery of the twelve tribes of Israel. At one point he brings both of these images together with the Lamb and the 144,000 standing together on Mount Zion. When the seventh trumpet is blown, John sees an ecstatic celebration in heaven, at the end of which 'God's temple in heaven was opened, and the ark of his covenant was seen within his temple'.

The heavenly version of Jerusalem mirrors its earthly counterpart – no, more than mirrors – because the heavenly version contains lost items: along with Mount Zion, the heavenly Jerusalem has God's Temple and even the Ark of the Covenant. The Temple was destroyed in AD 70, the Ark of the Covenant lost many centuries before that. But there they are, alive and well in heaven. Not just a mirror, more like the perfect backup.

And those who played a part in the destruction will face punishment. 'The nations raged,' sing the twenty-four elders in heaven, 'but your wrath has come, and the time for judging the dead, for rewarding your servants, the prophets and saints and all who fear your name, both small and great, and for destroying those who destroy the earth.' The destroyers destroyed. It's payback time.

And before this song is sung, Revelation shows us the destruction the elders are singing about. It is a story full of Jewish imagery, a story straight out of the lives and words of the prophets: the story of the two witnesses.

*

This is one of the strangest passages in this strange book, but it helps to understand that it is stuffed full of references to the Jewish prophets. John starts by eating a scroll – just like Ezekiel.* He is given a measuring rod to measure the Temple – just like Ezekiel. And he sees two witnesses, described as olive trees and lampstands – just like . . . no, not Ezekiel, actually; this one's from Zechariah.† Put all that together and you get a strong sense that what we are witnessing here is the climax of Old Testament prophecy.

John is told to measure the Temple of God, the altar 'and those who worship there'. A measuring rod is a biblical symbol for judgment. He is literally checking to see whether the place measures up. But he omits the courtyard, because that has been given over to the

---

* Ezekiel 2.8–3.3. Ezekiel's scroll tastes sweet, unlike John's, which gives him an upset stomach.
† Zechariah chapter 4, in case you're interested.

nations to trample it for forty-two months. During this time, authority has been given to two witnesses to prophesy. At first they seem powerful – they can stop rainfall (like Elijah) and turn waters into blood (like Moses). They can ward off fiery attacks. But then they are killed by the beast from the bottomless pit, and their bodies lie in the street for three and a half days (there we go again) while the people gloat and celebrate and 'exchange presents'. Happy holidays, everyone.

Then, just when all the presents have been unwrapped, or taken back and exchanged, the witnesses return to life. They go up to heaven in a cloud while the people watch. Then there is an earthquake, a tenth of the city is destroyed, 7,000 people are killed. And there we have it. Clear as crystal, right?

Perhaps not. But let's have a go at clarifying things.

What does all this mean? First, it's about Jerusalem. John describes the city as one which is 'prophetically called Sodom and Egypt, where also their Lord was crucified'. The last phrase is the giveaway. Why Sodom and Egypt too? Perhaps because, in the Old Testament, they were places of depravity and slavery, both of which were punished by God. Second, it's to do with the Temple, because that's what John is tasked to measure with his rod. Third, there is the amount of time: forty-two months. This number comes from another Jewish prophet, Daniel, where the fourth kingdom – a kingdom utterly opposed to God and his holy ones – is allowed to rule for 'a time, two times and half a time' (Dan. 7.25). Three and a half 'times' in all, therefore – three and a half years, or forty-two months, or 1,260 days. These numbers crop up throughout this section and, indeed, throughout Revelation. They are apocalyptic shorthand for 'temporarily'.

But the beast is involved in this story, too, making its first appearance (somewhat prematurely, since it hasn't been called out of the sea yet). And in Revelation the beast is *always* Rome. Tellingly, forty-two months is also roughly the time the Romans took to crush the Jewish revolt: from spring of AD 67 to late summer of AD 70. At that time the rest of Jerusalem – all of the city outside the Temple – was profaned. But the Temple survived until it was finally burnt down. Why doesn't John measure the Temple, then? Well, maybe because he sees the Temple itself as having a heavenly counterpart. The physical building might have been destroyed, but the heavenly version still existed.

So what about the witnesses? Who are they? In Zechariah the olive trees and lampstands are linked to Zerubbabel the king and Joshua the high priest. Kings and priests. Christians, in the updated context of these times. Certainly the reference to 'their Lord' being crucified identifies them as disciples.

So this appears to be another version of the siege of Jerusalem. Certainly the picture of corpses left to rot on the streets fits in with reports of the siege of Jerusalem as depicted in Josephus, who describes piles of dead bodies. The witnesses are the faithful Christians in the city who perform miracles and are protected from harm – right up until the beast arrives. Then they are apparently crushed, destroyed, killed, much to the delight of people who hated them. But they cannot be killed, in fact: they rise like their Lord, and go to heaven while the city itself is, literally (in the original Roman sense), decimated.

The witnesses may have been real people. We know that James, the brother of Jesus and leader of the Jerusalem church, was martyred in the city around AD 63, in the tense years before the civil war. More likely is that John is painting a picture of the church in Jerusalem, the mother church of the faith. In the run-up to the war it came through unscathed, on the whole, but during the siege it was caught in the crossfire. And yet, and yet, John says, the enemies who thought it dead have severely underestimated it. It will rise again. It will always rise again.

*

Across history, Revelation-watchers have been keen to identify the two witnesses in their own time.* Perhaps the most radical – and tragic – identification occurred in the early sixteenth century. This too ended with bodies on the streets, a terrible siege and a city given over to depravity.

---

* Blake thought they were Wesley and Whitefield, the founders of Methodism.

Melchior Hoffman was an itinerant preacher from Strasbourg. After studying Revelation he came to believe that he was one of the two witnesses of Revelation chapter 11. Strasbourg, he believed, would be the New Jerusalem, and from this shining city he would send out an army of evangelists (144,000 of them, naturally) to share the good news. All this would be achieved before 1533, because that was when (1,500 years after the death of Christ) the millennium would begin. Sadly, the authorities in Strasbourg disagreed with his thinking. Hoffman was arrested and locked in a cage, where he spent the rest of his life.

Hoffman's ideas could not be locked up so easily. A Dutch baker, Jan Matthys, had been inspired by Hoffman, and he acquired followers of his own. He sent two of them to the city of Münster where they were greeted as – yes, you've guessed it – the two witnesses. Their teaching fell on fertile ground. The area already had its share of apocalyptic troubles: it had been devastated by bubonic plague and the region was ruled by a Prince-Bishop who imposed heavy taxes on the citizens in order to pay for a war against the Turks. Soon, one of Matthys's messengers, Jan Bockelson (aka John of Leyden), gained control of the city council at the head of a group of apocalyptic revolutionaries.

Thrilled by this confirmation of his prophetic powers, Matthys arrived from Holland to oversee the establishment of the New Jerusalem. Catholics were exiled from the city, as were any Protestants who disagreed with the new leaders. There was complete social equality, all goods were held in common, and the city declared itself no longer bound to any earthly ruler or authority. Suddenly, the city became famous, and from all parts of Europe revolutionaries began to arrive – radical reformers, apocalyptic Anabaptists, disaffected Lutherans, anyone and everyone who had been hanging around waiting for the end times to pitch up.

Naturally, the authorities were monitoring the situation. Uniquely, the opposing forces were an alliance of Catholics (who obviously didn't like being kicked out) and Protestants (who didn't like the idea of being tarnished by association with what these radical loonies stood for). Their combined army gathered outside the city and put it to siege.

By now, Matthys had completely identified the situation with that of Revelation. He believed that this was the great battle, as foretold in chapter 19. The evil alliance mustered outside Münster were the forces of the beast and the kings of the earth. And he, he was the white rider. He would go out to conquer them. He rode out alone, confident that the prophecy would be fulfilled. Unfortunately, he was cut to pieces before the horrified eyes of the Münsterites.

After that the city spiralled into a kind of collective cabin fever. Jan Bockelson assumed complete control and imposed strict austerity on the city. Then he switched around completely. He took fifteen wives for himself, arguing that he was following scriptural precedent. Any woman who was reluctant to join him in this (many-sided) union, he threatened with death. Enemies within were summarily beheaded in the town square. While Bockelson, the self-styled king of the New Jerusalem, dined in splendour, there was starvation on the streets. It was a reign of terror, pure and simple, and it could only have one outcome. The city was captured, and the leaders were executed and hung in cages from the tower of the city church. The strange, rectangular, crate-like cages still hang there today, dangling from the central windows of the tower like wind chimes.

18 Vera and the Squirming Goats

The icon of John in the monastery museum is Cretan, from 1500. His eyes look old, weary. He holds a copy of the Apocalypse. Actually, he is not so much 'holding' it as clinging on to it for all he's worth.

The museum in the Monastery of St John, reached by way of some more winding staircases, describes itself as the finest museum in the Aegean. It might have a point. The treasures to be found here are remarkable. There is the imperial chrysobull signing the island over to Christodoulos, and granting some very lucrative tax incentives along with it. There is a lantern reputedly given to the monastery by Mehmet, the conqueror of Constantinople, when emissaries from Patmos went to meet him in Adrianople in 1454 – a year after the fall of the great city. And so many beautiful pictures: a tiny, delicate mosaic of St Nicholas from the eleventh century, its detail intricately worked out in gold; more pictures of John, either solo, or dictating to Prochorus. There are even a couple more pictures of Onoufrios and his foliage-based underwear.

But I was headed upstairs, where you can find the very few remains of Roman Patmos. There is not much. We are not talking, say, Ephesus. More like Philadelphia territory. There are some inscriptions from the fifth century BC. Some pediments and capitals from long-lost columns. The votive offering slab from the second century that talks about Hegemandros. The heads of statues, worn and battered, but still showing the small holes where their metal wreaths were fixed. A fine head from a statue of Dionysius. Some funerary inscriptions, several of which mention Artemis.

And then there is a particularly long inscription:

With good fortune.

[Artemis] herself, virgin huntress, chose as her hydrophorus [i.e. priestess] Vera of Patmos, the noble daughter of Glaukios, to offer sacrifices of squirming new-born goats under favourable auspices. Vera was raised as a young girl in glorious Argos, but she was born and nourished on Patmos, the very venerable island of Letos's daughter [Artemis], which emerged from the depths of the sea to become her throne, who the war-faring Orestes snatched from Scythis, and installed there [in Patmos] and afterwards she calmed his terrible madness, caused by the murder of his mother. Now she the tenth [priestess of Artemis] Vera, the daughter of the wise physician Glaukios, by the will of Scythian Artemis, has crossed the perilous Aegean Sea in order to celebrate gloriously the feast and sacred meal as the divine law prescribed.

Good luck!

It's a fascinating inscription, and not just because of the squirming new-born goats.

Let's start with the Greek myth bits. First, there is the story of Orestes, who murdered his mother Clytemnestra because *she* had murdered his father Agamemnon, because *he* had sacrificed (i.e. murdered, with a side order of religious weirdness) their daughter Iphigenia. (And then gone to the Trojan war. And come back with a new woman. No wonder Clytemnestra was a bit tetchy.) Anyway, according to some versions of the myth, after killing his mother Orestes went insane. He then stole or borrowed or otherwise obtained a 'statue' of Artemis from Scythia and took it to Athens, where it was honoured and named 'Scythian Artemis'. In gratitude for this, Artemis cured Orestes, at which point he stopped hearing the voices, butchering people, etc.

The interesting thing is that the slab I was looking at now claimed that Orestes placed it on Patmos, not in Athens. This means that there must have been a cult statue of Artemis in a temple on Patmos. And not just for a short time, but well established. Although the inscription comes from the second or third century AD, if Vera the squirming goat killer was the tenth priestess, the temple must have been there way back when John arrived in AD 95. In fact, the shrine seems to have gained wider fame: an inscription found at Leros mentions Artemis Patmia, and a second-century AD papyrus fragment from Egypt lists famous shrines and includes 'Artemis at Pathmos [sic]'. Patmos had a reputation in this area.

Now, all this is Quite Interesting. What makes it more important for Revelation is that the existence of this temple, and the claim on the inscription that Patmos 'emerged from the depths of the sea to become Artemis' throne', takes us straight to the heart of one of the most baffling sections of Revelation: the story of the woman and the dragon.

Chapter 12, located at the very centre of Revelation, tells a weird story of a woman 'clothed with the sun, with the moon under her feet, and on her head a crown of twelve stars', who is attacked by a giant red dragon. The woman is in labour and about to give birth, and the dragon is waiting to devour her child. However, her son ('who is to rule all the nations with a rod of iron') is snatched away by God. The woman flees into the wilderness, and a war breaks out in heaven. Michael and his angels defeat the dragon and his angels, and the dragon is cast down. It is revealed that the 'great dragon' is 'that ancient serpent, who is called the Devil and Satan, the deceiver of the whole world' and 'the accuser of our comrades'.

Down on earth the dragon pursues the woman. From his mouth gushes water, but it is swallowed up by the earth. Furious, the dragon goes off to make war on the rest of the woman's children – defined as 'those who keep the commandments of God and hold the testimony of Jesus'. And his first act of war is to stand on a seashore and summon a beast from the sea . . .

This story has fed into many bits of Christian doctrine, not least the fall of Satan, and the idea of Mary as the queen of heaven. But actually, what it is is a history lesson, using Hebrew imagery, and parodying Greek myth. This is John's version of 'Previously . . .'.

The woman waiting to give birth is often identified as Mary – mainly because the son she gives birth to is so obviously Jesus. But the human Mary, while respected, was not venerated in the earliest decades of the church. And if she is Mary, then why is she attacked afterwards? And how come *all* the followers of Jesus are also her children?

Israel, on the other hand, was often portrayed as a woman in Old Testament imagery. In many places she is depicted as being in labour: 'For I heard a cry as of a woman in labour, anguish as of one bringing forth her first child, the cry of daughter Zion gasping for breath,' writes Jeremiah (Jer. 4.31). The imagery of birth-pangs was commonly used to describe the advent of the Messiah. Isaiah describes the distressed, anxious, suffering Israel as being 'like a woman with child, who writhes and cries out in her pangs when she is near her time'. The same passage in Isaiah then goes on to describe how 'On that day the Lord with his cruel and great and strong sword will punish Leviathan the fleeing serpent, Leviathan the twisting serpent, and he will kill the dragon that is in the sea' (Isa. 26.17–27.1).

Biblically, then, it looks like this woman is Israel (the twelve stars on her crown being a reference to the twelve tribes – as when Joseph dreamt of the sun, moon and eleven stars bowing down to him), pictured in the years of suffering and oppression, waiting to give birth to the Messiah.

The dragon wants to devour the child, but, in the space of a sentence, the child is whisked away to heaven.

(Blink and you'll miss it – that was Jesus whooshing past.)

Then, or perhaps at the same time, there is a cosmic war in heaven, in which Satan is defeated and thrown down to earth. 'I watched Satan fall from heaven like a flash of lightning,' says Jesus when his disciples return from their mission proclaiming the arrival of the kingdom of God (Luke 10.17–18). Back in Revelation, the heavenly choir sum all this up, singing, 'Now have come the salvation and the power and the kingdom of our God and the authority of his Messiah, for the accuser of our comrades has been thrown down.'

OK, on to phase two. The woman has fled into the wilderness. Here we have to understand how John sees the 'new Israel' as describing the followers of Jesus. In Revelation he uses common metaphors for Israel, such as the bride and the twelve tribes, to describe Christians.

In this he is following other early church writers: in John's gospel, Jesus refers to his followers as God's vineyard (John 15:1–11); Paul claims 'God's temple' as a metaphor for the Christian community (1 Cor. 3:16–17; 2 Cor. 6:16); Peter says that Christians are 'a chosen race, a royal priesthood, a holy nation, God's own people' (1 Pet. 2:9–10). Now, then, the woman is not the old but the new, true Israel: the church. More specifically, Jewish Christians in the Jerusalem church. And her flight into the wilderness – aided by eagle's wings – is probably a reference to the flight of the Jewish Christians in Jerusalem during the first Jewish revolt. According to Eusebius, during the Jewish uprising in AD 66 the Christians left Jerusalem before the siege, 'because of an oracle given by a revelation', and settled in a town called Pella.* Situated in the foothills of the Transjordanian Mountains, Pella certainly counts as being in the wilderness.

This, then, is John's vision-version of the birth of Jesus, his ascension to heaven, and the escape of the Christians from Jerusalem. Israel brings forth the Messiah, Satan attacks and loses his place in heaven, but then attacks the Jewish Christians in Zealot-controlled Jerusalem, who escape to the wilderness. The woman–church is described as being there for 1,260 days. There's that number again.

*

So far, then, the story seems to relate pretty well to some actual historical facts. But then the dragon attacks the woman in the wilderness – using the rather un-dragonly method of opening his mouth and breathing water. Not your *fire*-breathing dragon, then.

At this point we need to move away from the world of biblical imagery and return to Patmos, to the temple and Vera and the myth of Artemis. The myth has a lot of variants, but it goes something like this:

Python was a huge dragon, who lived on Mount Parnassus. It

---

* They weren't the only ones who tried to detach themselves from the situation. During the siege of Jerusalem by the Romans certain rabbis left and set up home in Jamnia – on land which, according to Josephus, was donated by the Romans. Followers of other brands of Judaism also left. The Qumran community (who may have been Essenes) went to live by the Dead Sea.

was prophesied that he would be killed by the offspring of a woman called Leto. Zeus, head of the gods and well-known serial adulterer, slept with Leto, who (of course) fell pregnant. When Python found out that she was pregnant, he decided to kill her. That wasn't Leto's only problem, though. Hera, Zeus's wife and well-known serial aggrieved spouse, had found out about her husband's shenanigans and decreed that Leto would never be allowed to give birth on land.

Ever resourceful, Zeus ordered a wind to carry Leto away and put her in the safe keeping of Poseidon, god of the sea. Appropriately enough for a sea god, he tried to steer a middle course, and keep both Zeus and Hera happy. He hid Leto from Python and raised up a floating island for her to give birth on – so it was not technically land.* Python came looking but could not find her, and returned to Parnassus. Leto duly gave birth to twins, Apollo and Artemis, to whom the god Hephaestus gave arrows. A mere four days after his birth, Apollo went to Parnassus and, using the arrows, slew the dragon. Not bad for a babe in arms.

The island on which Leto gave birth to Artemis was generally agreed to be Delos. In the inscription I read in the museum, two lines talk about how Patmos 'emerged from the depths of the sea to become Artemis' throne, and she became its guardian'. Clearly the Patmians believed that their island had risen from the sea, like Delos, only this time to make room for the statue of Artemis which Orestes had stolen/borrowed/otherwise obtained from Scythia. This was not a unique claim, by the way: at least a dozen other islands made similar claims for their statues.

Which brings us back to Vera.

Vera is described as a *hydrophoros* of Artemis Patmia. The *hydrophoroi* were the priestesses of Artemis. Vera is not the only such woman associated with Patmos; in Miletus, a third-century AD marble tablet mentions Aurelia Dionysiodora Matrona, naming her too as a *hydrophoros* of Artemis Patmia. The *hydrophoroi* were elected annually in their cities, although the post often passed from mother

---

* In one version, though, just to be sure, the island remains covered with waves and Leto gives birth underwater. How she survived is not made clear. I guess she was probably on gas and air.

to daughter. They were clearly posh girls, because almost all the inscriptions mention the wealth, status and achievements of their fathers and grandfathers. If you were elected *hydrophorus*, Daddy would have had to stump up.

Although the precise nature of their role is unclear, it certainly involved distributing meat from the sacrificed animals, and hosting a feast for citizens and dancers. As a priestess, she also performed various rites and mysteries, and as the name implies, these were somehow concerned with watery things. We do find some details in an inscription about a *hydrophoros* called Theogenis from the shrine of Artemis at Didyma. Her tasks included paying for 'the underground canals, cisterns and reservoirs' in the grove, and 'she hallowed the water of the spring before the temple at her own expense to the gods of the sanctuary'. Theogenis's role, it seems, was to take water from the sacred spring to the altar of Artemis, where it was incorporated into some sort of offering. This is where we might find a link into Revelation and that water-breathing dragon. If it was common for the *hydrophoroi* to pour water out in some kind of ritual, that might start to explain the bit about the water gushing from the dragon's mouth and disappearing into the earth.

We don't know how much water was poured out, or onto what. But, on Patmos, it must have been sea-water. And with a bit of casting around we do find that in the temple of Hierapolis in Syria there was a similar ritual (albeit a long way away, and involving a different goddess) where the writer Lucian describes how 'twice a year sea-water is carried to the temple and not only the priests, but whoever comes from the whole of Syria, Arabia and even from the other side of the Euphrates, descends to the sea and brings the water. They pour it at first in the temple, and then it flows down to the cleft. However narrow the breach is it is capable of swallowing great quantities of water.'

*

So what do we make of all this? Well, simply that Patmos at the time John came to the island had a strong pagan religious tradition of its own. It had its own temples and its own myths. In one of these temples was a famous statue of the goddess; a statue which, local legend had it, was the *raison d'être* of the island – the island had risen up out of the sea only in order to house it. And in Revelation, this local myth mixes with biblical images and actual events to provide a rich, powerful re-imagining of the history of the church.

Myth feeds poetry and history and prophecy and revelation. The stories are far from identical, of course; but there is enough overlap to show that Revelation creatively uses local myth to retell the history of the early church and the story of how the serpent tried to kill the one who was to defeat him.

The museum in the monastery was the right place to think about such things, because that was, in fact, where the statue of Artemis stood. When he came here in 1088, Christodoulos chose the hill of Chora for the site of his monastery. It was high up and easily defended. But more importantly, there was already a religious building in place, a little chapel, built in the ruins of an earlier Byzantine basilica.

The story of Christodoulos also says that another kind of religious object was found on the site: a white marble statue of Artemis, which he destroyed. If so, then it seems likely that this was where the temple of Artemis stood, this was where the statue which Orestes had brought to the island was placed, this was where Vera came to worship with the other *hydrophoroi*, to pour out the water and sacrifice the unfortunate goats.

In the story in Revelation, the dragon is thwarted in his plan to kill the Messiah. And he is thwarted in his plan to water-cannon the church to death.

So he switches to plan B.

He goes to the beach, and summons a beast from the sea.

19 The Mountain and the Monsters

I visited Patmos's highest peak the stupid way: I walked.

I hadn't intended to do so, but the early morning bus to Chora either wasn't running or had been and come and gone. The morning was clear and bright, the sky a cheerful, optimistic blue. Time for a nice morning walk. How hard could it be?

Quite hard, as it turned out. Patmos sometimes seems to defy the laws of physics, geography, thermodynamics and common sense. I swear there are more ups than downs. It's a landscape out of an Escher drawing.

That walk took me two hours. I climbed up through Chora, over the top and down the other side, skirting the huge medieval walls of the monastery through a maze of trench-like streets. This early in the day no one was awake in Chora and nothing was moving, not even the cats. Perhaps the Pirats had returned and everyone was

The view from Profitis Elias, looking east. Kallikatsous rock can just be seen, jutting out into the bay.

hiding. The silence increased the eerie sense that at any moment I could stumble upon another world. Everywhere in that mysterious town were strange little gates, small secret doors, suddenly revealed stairways, low archways through which I had to stoop. It was like a kind of urban potholing. You become like water, letting gravity set your direction, searching for the route downwards. And, indeed, at certain points I did find myself following a stream through the streets, where a resident had been cleaning their steps and the water from the hose ran off down the hill, revealing the shortest route out.

I was carrying some maps, but they were of limited use in such disorientating terrain. Herr Dieter Graf, author of *Walking the Greek Islands: Samos, Patmos and Northern Dodecanese*, assured me that somewhere to my right there was an ancient nunnery – Aghia ton Agion ('Holy of Holies') – built in 1279. I would have explored, but I was no longer sure which direction *was* my right.

Eventually the walls lowered, the houses thinned out and I emerged onto the south side of Chora. And there, ahead of me, was my destination: the mountain of Profitis Elias and, on the summit, the small white cube that marked its church.

I crossed a road, climbed some white-painted steps, and followed an old goat track past two small churches (both shut). The track was more like a riverbed. Once again I was walking in a water

channel, this one made by the winter rains as they ran down the slope.

To my right and far below, the landscape fell away to the cliffs at Kambi. Down there I could see the grey, square buildings of the Evangelismos nunnery. A modern building with medieval styling, it looks like the architect had been overdosing on *Minecraft*.

South of Chora the landscape is harsh. Unyielding. This is a landscape of heat and solitude. Hermit territory.

*

The earliest hermitage on the island was at the Kallikatsous rock, a solid lump of strangeness, 30 feet high and 250 feet round, which sticks out into the bay at Grikos. Its other name is simply Petra – that is to say, 'Rock'. A work associated with Christodoulos mentions the Hermitage of Petras, and you can still trace where these early hermits carved steps into the rock, made openings for ovens and water storage, and hammered out post holes for the beams which would have supported primitive hermitages.

Not far from Evangelismos, meanwhile, is the Kathisma, a group of cells founded 900 years ago by a monk called Savas, a contemporary of Christodoulos. The will he left behind – written sometime between 1119 and 1127 – describes how much he spent building the church and the cells, cultivating the gardens and looking after guests who came to stay. His will appointed someone called Theoktistos 'to serve as monk and to chant', and 'Monk Loukas, to care for the gardens'.

Eight centuries later another Theoktistos came to the same area. Of all the hermits I have read about who lived on Patmos, he is one of my favourites. There's an air of mystery about this Theoktistos. His biography, contained in a charming book about the hermits of the island, simply says, 'He never mentioned anything about his personal life before he came to Patmos.' Some said he was a bishop, but he kept his past life a secret. He was a huge man and immensely strong – capable of moving boulders single-handed. Dark eyed, olive-skinned, with a beard down to his knees, which he plaited and threw over his shoulders when he worked. He was usually barefoot, although he did wear socks when he went to the monastery. For forty years or so, he lived as a hermit on Patmos and its surrounding small islands, always preferring the harshest of places. His pattern was always the same: he would move to a place, build a hermitage from whatever he could find, raise a garden and grow crops. Then he would move on and start all over again.

Geil met him when he was living, for a short time, in a hermitage in the ruins of the old Patmian school near the Cave of the Apocalypse.

'I met an 80 year old man who was modest, sweet, kind and holy,' Geil wrote. 'He offered us lunch under a tree . . . He was dressed in an attire that resembled a fireman's uniform. It was black from the shoulders down to the ankles and he wore a belt . . . He invited us into his small home. It was a small room built in a corner of the ruins.' Geil describes how his bed was the floor, while 'an old rug and box covered with cloth were his pillows . . . He offered me the only chair and the others sat on boxes . . . A strong fishy smell revealed that he had an octopus nailed to a stick near the ceiling.'

Even today you often see octopuses hung out to dry in Greece, draped over string like shirts hanging on a line. On a foray to a beach near Kallikatsous, I met a man there with his daughter. He went out swimming at one point and returned, triumphant, having caught an octopus. Cheerfully he showed me the correct way to kill it. Delicacy prohibits me from describing the operation in detail, but it involved a surprising amount of hitting the octopus against a rock. At one point, I'm pretty sure he turned it inside out and removed the ink sac as well.

A few years after that meeting with Geil, Theoktistos moved to the area south-west of Profitis Elias, the promontory of Genoupa. This was devil territory. On my map the promontory is marked as Diabolos – 'Devil' – while the south-west corner is called Cape Genoupa – a word derived from the name of Kynops, the magician who challenged John when he arrived on Patmos. According to *The Travels*, Kynops lived in this area. Like John, he is associated with a cave, this one smelling of brimstone and sulphur. When Geil came here he was told stories of a cave full of demons on the cape. Once, they said, a man was lowered down on a rope to have a look and when they pulled him up he was dead. People died or went blind simply walking by. Sounds like the Plutonium all over again. A local superstition had it that when the sun set you should close all the windows facing Genoupa.

None of that impressed Theoktistos. 'I will go and beat him in his cave,' he roared. And he did, setting up home in another cave on the mountain. Theoktistos makes a satisfyingly Elijah-like figure. Wild, big-bearded. When a young man visiting him saw a snake and went to kill it, the monk stopped him: 'He is one of my friends. Every night a dozen of them come to sleep with me in the cave.'

He was still living in Genoupa in 1908. But eventually, with his eyesight failing and his once upright frame stooped and bent, he moved into the monastery, and ended his days there. Towards the end he lost his sight completely, but he was still able to see things that others couldn't. A few days before his death he said that he had seen a vision: 'My angel told me to be ready. On a certain day we will leave together.' When the head of the monastery asked what he had seen, Theoktistos replied, 'Don't ask too much.'

'When he died,' said his biographer, 'they found nothing in his cell, not even a second cape in which to bury him.'

*

I could see why people had felt this part of the island was dangerous. The landscape is unearthly. Alien. It has not changed much since Guérin described it: 'One walks with difficulty among the huge rocks, which appear in all shapes within a magnificent disorder. One could say they accumulated there, thrown by giant hands.' An enormous bee bumped around, black and orange, its body seemingly too heavy for its wings. A matt-black beetle droned past like a tiny spy plane. Small, grey-blue birds, twitching nervously on the boulders; a whinchat perched on a fence. There were not even any crows up here: they all stayed down in the valley. Everything looked slightly dusty. Even the birds.

It was the vegetation that really unnerved me, though. It was all the wrong shade: either burnt, tobacco brown or a sickly, pale green. There were large plants with pale blue-green leaves which felt like velour, like some bad 1970s furnishing fabric. There were dandelion-like flowers, only massive and with fearsome, spiny heads. There were thorn bushes with needle-sharp thorns in geodesic patterns; half-hidden tubers from which strange, grey, spindly stems rose to end in white, conical clusters. It was like the Chelsea Flower Show re-imagined by a diseased mind.

In Chora and Skala you saw flowers, bright colours, pinks and scarlets and yellows. Here it was drab. Dusty. Monstrous. You can see why the beasts would feel at home on Patmos.

*

Eventually I reached the goal of my journey: the peak of Profitis Elias. Many Greek islands have a 'Profitis Elias', usually their highest peak and usually with a church or chapel on the top. Patmos is no exception; it too has a church, and a hermitage to boot. Built in 1746, the church is a stuccoed white boxlike building which sits on a great brown outcrop of rock at the summit. From the rooftop a modern antenna points upwards to heaven.

The church was closed, of course. Its small, chocolate-coloured door was firmly locked and there was no sign of life. For a moment I toyed with the idea of climbing onto the roof of the building, but in the end discretion – and the fact that I had walked for two hours at this point – got the better of me. Instead, I walked right around the church, map in hand, identifying the landmarks.

The view was magnificent. To the north in the distance were the hills of Samos, to the east Arki, Lipsi and Leros. I could see almost the whole of the island – where it curved round to the Cape of Geranos in the north-east and then south where the island narrows to a tiny strip near the village of Stavros, before broadening out again onto another promontory. Somewhere along the north-west coast of that promontory is the island's only truly sandy beach. It is called, imaginatively, Psilli Ammos – Greek for 'fine sand'.

John sees so much of his vision from high places. 'Come up here,' says the angel, 'and I will show you what must take place after this.' At the end of the book he is taken away to a high mountain. Perhaps John did literally go up, to the high point of the island. If he did he would have seen across to other islands, maybe on a clear day to the mainland from which he was exiled. He would have seen wilderness and rock and desolation. Most of all he saw the whole of time and history and the complete cosmic plan laid out. In this monstrous landscape, he saw the beast.

I saw it too.

It rises out of the sea in the distance, just south of Stavros Bay. A single, vertical cone of rock, slightly curved, pale in colour. It looks like a tusk. Or a horn. Or, perhaps, the long neck of a monster coming out of the sea. It stands just off a small, gravelly beach. Later I found out that the locals call it *Stavrou*.

There are other rocks as well, hump-like, breaking through the surface, and I had the strangest feeling that this was where John had stood and that was what he had seen, and through his 3D 'kingdom of heaven' spectacles everything got changed and twisted and warped, and suddenly a rock becomes a vision of the beast.

The Beast. Or maybe just a rock.

Probably I was a bit light-headed after all that clambering.

From Profitis Elias, I tried to find my way down to get a closer look at this strange, misshapen rock. The journey took me onto the ominously named Diavolos headland. But I couldn't get any nearer. It's a mining area now, fenced off, and the road I was walking along came to an end at a locked gate. Below was some kind of church and what looked like a large and very exclusive luxury house. If Kynops was at home, he was not welcoming visitors.

And anyway, by that time I had calmed down. I'm not sure this rock would even have been there in John's day. Two thousand years is a long time in the life of a coastline. Maybe it was this rock, maybe it was something else, maybe he was thinking of something else entirely.

What we do know is that he saw something beastly. Two beasts, in fact. One from the sea, and one from the land.

*

The strangest chapters in Revelation – chapters 10 to 14 – are the burning, wild heart of this book. The opening chapters call the seven churches to authentic witness, whatever the cost; the opening of the scroll reveals the heavenly truth that the Lamb is in charge of history and that judgment will come. But in chapters 10 to 14, the community of Christians confronts the beast.

It starts with John seeing the dragon standing on a beach – *ammon*, literally 'the sand' – of the sea. Some have speculated that the beach in question was Psilli Ammos, as most of the other beaches are stony. He could certainly have seen it from the vantage point on the top of Profitis Elias. Whatever the location, though, what matters is that out of the sea there emerges a beast.

There are two beasts in Revelation, although only one is called a 'beast' with any frequency. That is the first beast: the beast from the sea. He dominates chapter 13, where he is mentioned fifteen times, and reappears in chapter 17, where he gets nine mentions. He is specifically tagged in the book thirty-six times overall. But the second beast – the beast from the land – is only called a beast once, in chapter 13. Everywhere else that second beast is called the 'false prophet'.

The Greek word for 'beast' here is *therion*: it means, simply, 'wild animal'. It's used to describe the animals in the wilderness in Mark 1.13 and even the snake which bites Paul on Malta in Acts 28.4–5. But people could be beasts as well: Paul describes Cretans as 'beasts' in Titus 1.12; Apollonius of Tyana called Nero a *therion*; while the Sibylline Oracles call him *ther magus*, a 'great beast'. But John's beast here deserves a special category: it comes from an unnatural world. It has ten horns and seven heads, 'and on its horns were ten diadems and on its heads were blasphemous names'. The whole earth follows the beast and stands in awe of its power: 'Who is like the beast, and who can fight against it?'

Well, I think we can all see where we're going with this one. John means only one thing when he starts talking about blasphemous names: the emperors and their cult. We can take our pick of the many, many epithets which would have been blasphemous to John: coins marked with the name of the divine Julius or Augustus or Domitian, titles claimed by the emperor such as saviour, lord, god. The heads are emperors. The beast is the Roman empire.

From the time of Daniel, the idea of the beast was the standard apocalyptic symbol for the wicked ruling empire. For John, of course, it is the Romans. And the whole world knew that you could not fight against Rome. It was too powerful. But John sees where the beast's power comes from: it comes from the dragon, Satan (Rev. 13.2–4). He calls this beast out of the sea – the sea being the archetypal place of chaos and darkness. (John may also have a poetic image in mind: every year a new Roman proconsul or governor would arrive at Ephesus, sailing in a galleon up the Cayster River, into the harbour.)

The message is pretty clear: the Roman empire is fundamentally evil. Far from being an empire of law and order, as it would claim for itself, it is a creature full of chaos and disorder, and it holds power only because it is backed by Satan.

But there is a curiosity about this beast: one of its heads has received what should have been a mortal wound, but it has somehow recovered. What is that about?

Well, the general consensus is that it refers to a legend. A legend about an emperor called Nero.

*

On 9 June AD 68 whatever then passed for the *Rome Tonight* evening news started to receive reports that Nero had committed suicide at the villa of his freedman and confidant, Phaon. Abandoned by his palace guard, and with Galba's army marching on Rome, Nero had fled in disguise. As the sound of horses approached the villa, he cut his own throat. When the soldiers arrived, they tried to revive him, with no success. Nero was dead.

Or *was* he? Because, despite whatever *Rome Tonight* might have said, the Roman equivalent of Twitter had other ideas. Rumours spread: Nero hadn't died. It was all a set-up. Fuelled by the fact that hardly any witnesses saw either his corpse or his burial, rumours began to circulate that he had fled east, across the border to Parthia. Fictitious edicts were posted in Rome under his name, threatening vengeance on his enemies. The idea grew that Nero would return; that, like Elvis, he was alive and well and working in a burger bar in Persia, biding his time for the big comeback tour.

This belief took two forms. Some believed in *Nero Redux* – i.e. that he hadn't actually died and he would return. Others, though, believed that he had died, but would come back to life. This theory is known as *Nero Revividus*, Nero revived. (Sounds like a great Roman pub name: 'Fancy a quick pint down the Nero Revived?')

And then, in AD 69, just a year after his 'suicide', the stories came true. Nero – or someone who claimed to be him – popped up in Asia. This new Nero – Nero 2.0 – looked like the old emperor, *and* he could sing and play the lyre as well. 'About this time Achaia and Asia Minor were terrified by a false report that Nero was at hand,' wrote Tacitus. 'Various rumours were current about his death; and so there were many who pretended and believed that he was still alive.' He gathered an army of deserters and set sail from Greece, but a storm forced him to go in the opposite direction, and he wound up on the island of Delos in the Cyclades, where his ship was taken and he was killed.

This first attempted comeback tour was followed, eleven years later, by another, headed up by a Nero lookalike called Terentius Maximus (that's Big Terry in English). He too passed the singing and playing and looking-a-bit-like-Nero-in-a-certain-light test, and gathered a number of followers whom he led to the banks of the Euphrates. In the end he seems to have been given hospitality by the Parthian leader Artabanus, and nothing is known of what became of him.

Finally, in AD 88, a third pretender appeared, 'a person of obscure origin', according to Suetonius, 'who gave out that he was Nero, and the name was still in such favour with the Parthians that they supported him vigorously'. In the end he was handed over to Rome, however.

Behind the stories of these many and varied pretenders lies the same basic myth: that Nero would return at the head of a Parthian army, that he would cross the Euphrates, march on Rome and retake the throne. Now, what makes this interesting is that while Rome may not have been keen on the idea of the second coming of Nero, in the east he was surprisingly popular. Especially during the reign of Domitian. Writing at that time, the historian Dio Chrysostom said that 'even now everybody wishes [Nero] were still alive. And the great majority do believe that he is.'*

Even as late as the fourth century, Augustine of Hippo wrote that:

> some suppose that [Nero] shall rise again and be Antichrist. Others, again, suppose that he is not even dead, but that he was concealed that he might be supposed to have been killed, and that he now lives in concealment in the vigour of that same age which he had reached when he was believed to have perished, and will live until he is revealed in his own time and restored to his kingdom. But I wonder that men can be so audacious in their conjectures.

This legend began to appear in Christian works, too. For Christians, unsurprisingly, the returning Nero is a bogeyman, a monster, the incarnation of evil. This was a man who had launched a savage attack on Rome's Christian community – an attack from which it took fifty years to recover. In the Christian parts of the Sibylline Oracles Nero is clearly plotting a return:

* Dio Chrysostom (c. AD 40–c. 115) was a writer, orator and historian. Chrysostom means 'golden mouth', which refers to his oratorical skills, not his dentistry.

One who has fifty as an initial will be commander,
A terrible snake, breathing out grievous war,
who one day will lay hands on his own family and slay them,
and throw everything into confusion,
athlete, charioteer, murderer, one who dares ten thousand things.
He will also cut the mountain between two seas and defile it with
gore.
But even when he disappears he will be destructive.
Then he will return declaring himself equal to God.
But he will prove that he is not.

And that's just Thursday.

There are clear references to the Nero myth in Revelation. In chapter 17, John talks of seven kings, and then mentions the eighth king who is at the same time one of the seven:

they are seven kings, of whom five have fallen, one is living,
and the other has not yet come; and when he comes, he must
remain only a little while. As for the beast that was and is
not, it is an eighth but it belongs to the seven, and it goes to
destruction.

John doesn't really make clear what he thinks of this myth. Does he actually believe Nero will return? I don't think so. I think, once again, he is creatively using the stories of the world around him to make statements about the empire itself, and to contrast it with the reign of Christ. He is reworking the ideas, the illusions, the memes of the late first-century world to make his point hit home.

First, there is the very obvious contrast with another wounded king. The idea of Nero – fatally wounded, healed but only back in any kind of way for a short space of time – is a kind of perversion of John's image of Jesus, the slain Lamb, who still stands and will live and rule forever. Christians, after all, had their own *revividus* story. Any alternative version, no matter which part of the empire it came from, even (especially) Rome itself, could only be a dim, reflected perversion of the truth.

But perhaps the reference to this story reinforces another of John's key messages. The beast from the sea (that is, the empire) has seven heads (that is, emperors), one of which 'seemed to have received a death blow, but its mortal wound had been healed' (Rev. 13.3). Why such a serious wound? Nero's suicide didn't wound the empire in any real way – far from it. It was actually the powers that be in the empire who wanted him out and engineered his defeat. The empire in John's day was as strong as ever.

Perhaps, though, the importance of this wound should be interpreted in a more subtle way. Don't forget, for John the chief evils of the empire were idolatry and exploitation. So to have your 'god' commit suicide brings what, in PR terms, is known as 'reputational damage'. What has been wounded the most is Rome's claim that the emperors are gods. Nero's attempted suicide showed the true weakness of imperial megalomania. The failure of Nero laid bare the faultline running through the cult of emperor worship. Betrayed by the senate – ostensibly so keen to perpetuate the idea of the divinity of the emperor – their so-called god died alone, afraid, and in disgrace.

*

Let's just nip back to the Sibylline Oracles for a moment. One of the clues that text gives about the identity of the man it is talking about is that he 'has fifty as an initial'. In Greek numerals, the letter N stood for 50. That leads us on to one of the most hotly debated passages in the whole of Revelation: the number of the beast.

The image is actually found in a passage describing a second beast. This one comes from the land, and has a clearly defined role: 'It exercises all the authority of the first beast on its behalf, and it makes the earth and its inhabitants worship the first beast, whose mortal wound had been healed' (Rev. 13:12). So the purpose of the second beast is to get people to bow down to the first. To do this, it deceives people into worshipping an image of the first beast. And, in a telling phrase, 'it was allowed to give breath to the image of the beast so that the image of the beast could even speak and cause those who would not worship the image of the beast to be killed' (Rev. 13:15).

That's straightforward enough. This is our old friend the imperial cult – the whole religious system which built up around worship of the emperor. And that is why, for the rest of the book, John describes it not as a beast, but as a false prophet. The beast from the land exercises the authority of the first beast and insists that the first beast should be worshipped. And woe betide those who resist.

In order to implement this directive, the second beast has a fool-proof system:

> [The Beast] causes all, both small and great, both rich and poor, both free and slave, to be marked on the right hand or the forehead, so that no one can buy or sell who does not have the mark, that is, the name of the beast or the number of its name. This calls for wisdom: let anyone with understanding calculate the number of the beast, for it is the number of a person. Its number is six hundred sixty-six. (Rev. 13.17–18)

Over the years, people have been obsessed by these two ideas: the mark and the number. Barcodes. That was a big one a few years ago: apparently, every bar code in the world had the number 666 encoded. Then there was the one about Intel computer chips. Somehow, the number was being put into every computer sold around the world.

Take a deep breath. Remember, everyone: *It's not literal*. Actually, John's Old Testament word-bank helps solves this. Deuteronomy 6.4–9 is what is known in Judaism as the *Shema*. It's a proclamation of the two greatest commandments: 'The Lord is our God, the Lord alone', and 'You shall love the Lord your God with all your heart, and with all your soul, and with all your might'. The text commands obedient Jews to remember the commands, 'to bind them as a sign on your hand, fix them as an emblem on your forehead, and write them on the doorposts of your house and on your gates' (Deut. 6.4–9).*

---

* In a fine example of missing out on the whole 'it's not literal' thing, ultra-orthodox Jews actually do put the text of these commands in small boxes and bind them to their wrists and their foreheads. These boxes are known as phylacteries.

In other words, what the second beast does here is replace the *shema* with his own form of worship. This is not about being labelled with some kind of high-tech barcode; it's a symbolic way of asking, 'Whose commands are you listening to about who and how to worship? Who is your God? Is it Rome, or the Lord?'

The mark has one very specific attribute associated with it: no one without the mark can buy or sell anything. Yes. We're talking about money. Moolah. *Cash*. In John's world, the single biggest purveyor of the myth of emperor worship was money. For a Jewish Christian like John, every coin in the empire had an idolatrous image on it: that of the emperor-whom-you-must-worship. This placed those who did not want to engage in idolatry in an impossible position, because no one could buy or sell without entering into some form of compact with the beast.

OK – so what about the number? For once, John appears to give us a definite clue: anyone with understanding can 'calculate the number of the beast, for it is the number of a person. Its number is six hundred sixty-six.'

Greeks, Romans and Jews did not have separate symbols for numbers like we do. Our system of numerals (1 to 10) comes from the Arab world, and was adopted in the west in the thirteenth century. Before that everyone used letters of the alphabet to double for numbers. In Greek and Hebrew, every letter had a numeric value. The first ten letters of the alphabet were 1 to 10; then the next lot were multiples – 20, 30, up to 100; and the remaining letters were 200, 300 and so on. So any word could also be a number, because every letter stood for a numeric value. The Romans had a simpler system, using only seven letters – I, V, X, L, C, D and M – to represent 1, 5, 10, 50, 100, 500 and 1,000 respectively. Most people today still recognise this system because it is used – for reasons I don't really understand – on the copyright screens of films and television programmes.

It means that words could also, always, be numbers. This system is called *gematria*. Sometimes it was used for simple coded messages. A piece of graffiti in Pompeii says, 'I love her whose number is 545.' The Christian Sibylline Oracles say the Messiah's name will add up to 888. And wouldn't you know it, 'Jesus' in Greek adds up to – kerching! – 888. Sometimes there were deeper, political meanings.

A famous one was a political statement about Nero which pointed out that the name Nero and the phrase 'he killed his mother' both add up to 1,005. You do the maths.

The problem is that if all you have is the number, such codes are almost impossible to crack. Despite John's confident assertion, a great many 'men of understanding' have had a go at cracking the code and none of them have come up with a definitive answer. And there's another problem. Because the number of the beast may not be 666 at all. Some other manuscripts of Revelation have '665'. And a fragment of papyrus which is the earliest actual manuscript of that part of Revelation says '616'.*

Writing in AD 180, Irenaeus makes the earliest known attempt to solve the riddle. He knew about the 616 variant, but decided that 666 is the official version. He theorised that the answer must be a Greek word, since John was writing in Greek. He suggested *Lateinos*, which could mean any Latin ruler. But he preferred the idea that it stood for *Teitan* – which implied a more general tyrant or ruler. But in the end even he wasn't sure. No one could accuse Irenaeus of not being someone 'with understanding', but in the end he admits defeat.

Nowadays, however, the most popular solution is that 666 is the Greek phrase 'Nero Caesar', transliterated into Hebrew and then added up.† That seems nice and neat, but first, it relies on a rather unusual way of transliterating the words; and second, John is writing to a Greek-speaking audience, and this solution only works in Hebrew. So in order for this to work, when John writes, 'Let anyone with understanding', he really means, 'Let anyone with a working knowledge of Hebrew who is prepared to transliterate the title of one of the emperors in a very specific way . . .' One might argue that would require not so much understanding as psychic powers. Third, this is the *whole* beast we're talking about. The beast is not Nero; he is just one of its seven heads.

---

* P.Oxy. LVI 4499, in case you're interested. Having said that, this fragment of papyrus is not that early – it dates from the late third or early fourth century (i.e. AD 275–325).

† Nero Caesar in Hebrew is *qsr nrwn* – Neron Caesar. Add that up and you get 666 (qsr=360 + nrwn=306).

In the end, we just don't know.

Which, of course, hasn't stopped people trying to work it out.

*

'Pin the number on the beast' has always been one of the most popular Revelation games. And attempts to crack this code – and the other apocalyptic numbers in Revelation – have had some surprising side-effects.

Michael Stifel was a former Augustinian monk and an early fan of Luther. In 1532 he published *Ein Rechen Büchlin vom End Christ. Apocalypsis in apocalypsim* ('A Book of Arithmetic about the Antichrist. A Revelation in the Revelation') in which he calculated that the day of judgment was near and, via some rather obscure numerology, that Pope Leo X was 666 – the beast. Later calculations led him to believe that the day of judgment would arrive at 8 a.m. on 18 October 1533. When the day came, the local peasantry put down their tools and went, *en masse*, to the village of Lochau, where Stifel was pastor.

Nothing happened.

Stifel was sacked. However, his experiments with Revelation had inspired in Stifel a love of mathematics and eventually he became so good that he was appointed Professor of Mathematics at Jena University, where he invented exponents. (Whatever they are.)

Maths and Revelation seem to fit together like hand in glove. A contemporary of Stifel, John Napier, eighth Laird of Merchistoun, was also fascinated by Revelation. In *A Plaine Discovery of the Whole Revelation of St. John* (1593), he calculated that the seventh trumpet would be blown sometime in 1541, and the end of the world would occur in either 1688 or 1700. In order to help him with his calculations, he invented logarithms.* (Whatever they are.)

Perhaps the most famous of all Revelation-obsessed scientists was Isaac Newton, discoverer of gravity. (Whatever that is.) Throughout his life, he wrote millions of words on the end times and devoted thousands of hours to trying to work out the approximate time of the second coming. Newton believed that the world would end in 2060,

---

* He also invented the slide rule.

at which date Christ would return to establish his worldwide thousand-year reign. When Newton entered Cambridge in 1660 it was because he 'wished to test judicial astrology' – in other words, he wanted to find out whether predicting things by the stars actually worked. A few years after that a comet lit up the sky; the year after that a great fire swept through London, and no one was terribly surprised.

It was, after all, the year 1666.

Even without cracking the 'Gematria Code', many, many people and organisations have been suggested as the beast. But, to paraphrase Nietzsche, he who identifies someone as the beast should look to it that he does not get identified as the beast himself. For example, Frederick II, the Holy Roman Emperor, declared that Pope Gregory IX was the beast from the sea. For good measure he added that the Pope was also the red horse, the dragon, *and* the angel from the abyss. In return, Pope Gregory IX denounced the emperor in a letter entitled *Ascendit di mari bestia* – 'the beast risen from the sea'. Right back at you. Two hundred years later, Luther aimed much higher and went for the organisations that lay behind both of these chaps: the papacy was the beast from the land, the Holy Roman Empire the beast from the sea. In return, the Catholic cardinal Robert Bellarmine identified Luther as the antichrist and said that his name could add up to 666.

One thing we do know. All identifications have been wrong. And, in fact, all such attempts are futile. Both beasts have names, but they are not the personal names of emperors or kings, popes or pastors or politicians. Those people are just how the real, threatening power is manifested from one moment to the next. To waste our time matching individuals up with these mythical beasts is, to use Leonardo Boff's powerful phrase, to be those who 'can count every hair in the beast's coat, but never look it in the face'.

The fact is, we *know* the identities of the beasts.

The first beast is empire itself, with its military might, the brutal power of the legions, the steamrollering, stormtrooping, shock-and-awe power of Rome. The second beast is the spin, the PR machine which makes gods of mere men, which painted the emperors as benign deities bringing peace to the world. In one beast you have Satanic power, in the second beast you have those who tell us that such power is good, even godly.

If we want to identify the beasts in the here and now, we have to ask what idolatrous, uncaring power it is that presently dominates our lives. And what secondary power there is that seeks to persuade us that this domination is the divine order. Ask an African, or a poor South American, to interpret this passage, and in their minds the first beast is those powers, those impersonal multinational corporations which stripmine their land, raze their forests, ransack their country for minerals and metals and people. The second beast is the long chain of petty dictators, cruel tyrants and tinpot generals who have made this the only way for such countries to be, who have queued up to borrow western cash only to spend it on arms at the trade fairs. When a group of South Americans were asked to give names to the seven heads of the beast, they chose things like 'multinationals', 'foreign debt', and 'the law of National Security'.

In a slum in Brazil, meanwhile, women were asked to name the 'images' of the beast in their world: they chose pans to symbolise the arduous cooking in smoke-filled unsanitary conditions; alcohol because so many of their men drank to excess every night; and the central committee of the camp which told them what they could and couldn't do, and which was composed entirely of males. These were the things which made their life beastly, the things that they were always told could never be changed.

The first beast tyrannises; the second beast lies. It is propaganda and state-controlled media and censored news; but it is also gossip columns, and Photoshopped models and advertising agencies and PR. Anything which seeks to persuade us that the false gods deserve our worship. And those who question are demonised, labelled as the bogeyman: counter-revolutionaries, fascists, anarchists, capitalists, commie pinkos, liberals, feminists, killjoys . . .

Make the beast look good, and make its opponents look stupid or evil.

There were many people who benefited from the rule of the Roman empire in the first century. But they were blind to the idolatry that lay behind it. John sees things more clearly. He sees the empire for what it is: a ravening beast, supported by a load of toadying, smooth-talking con-men. And he preaches revolution.

What John has given us through these images is a book which

inspires us to fight, not against some petty ruler, or a long-lost pontiff, but against all the monsters of history. Throughout history, bestial regimes have risen to power, and then used lies to portray themselves in the best possible light. And the biggest lie of all, the one that really crushes the spirit and the soul, is that uttered by the beast's worshippers throughout the earth: 'Who is like the beast and who can fight against it?' The idea that there is no alternative is power's greatest weapon. The inevitable triumph of communism. The market is always right. Economic growth is all that matters. *Imperium sine fine.*

That's just the way life is.

If you'd said that to John, he'd have thrown you out of his cave. Because the message of Christianity – real Christianity, the wild faith which has always thrived at the margins – is that you *can* change things. The way life is now is not the way it has to be. Revelation calls us to buck the system, rock the boat, upset the apple-cart. It calls us to identify the beastly powers, to witness against them, to refuse to bow down to them and, most of all, to believe that things can change.

And those other numbers – 42 months; 1,260 days; three and half years; a time, times and half a time. We know what they mean as well. They mean that the beast's power is limited. They mean the clock is ticking. They are apocalyptic shorthand for 'temporarily'. They mean that the beast does not win in the end.

*

Footsore, parched and dusty, I reached Chora again in the late afternoon. I sat in a café perched on the edge of the village and looked down towards the harbour in the far distance, drinking a chilled Mythos beer and eating an enormous tomato stuffed with rice. I deserved a treat after all that walking.

The café owner chatted to me about his life. A Greek who'd returned from America, he regaled me with stories of his previous restaurants, of people who had cheated him and others who had stood by him. I sat and let the waves of anecdotes wash over me. The conversation ranged from illegal betting on boxing matches to the best way to stuff a tomato. Business was slow. This man had time to talk.

'Ah, what can I say, times are hard,' he said. 'No one has it easy, eh?' He shrugged.

I thought about this a lot on the island. Greece, after all, is definitely in a position to understand how the beast works these days. The high priests of the market – the bankers and the politicians and the media moguls – have spoken: there is no other way. No one can stand against the beast. Sacrifices must be made. Jobs. Families. Homes.

As I made my way home at the end of that day, after my long, arduous trip, I passed a derelict building on the outskirts of Skala, in the shadow of the monastery. The windows were smashed, the metal already rusting. And on the walls someone had graffitied the word 'Change'.

20 Four Horsemen, Five Battles, No Contest

The lady who lived across the track from my apartment was called Shakira. She was elegant, grey-haired, beautiful and she really liked grapes. Every morning when I went out she would make her way up the field, snorting in anticipation, and I would feed her some grapes. She was my very own horse of the Apocalypse. Her field, though nice and roomy, was steeply terraced. Not much room to run around in. But then that's true of the whole island. It's not exactly horse country.

The lovely Shakira. My favourite horse of the apocalypse.

Horses in the ancient world were closely associated with the military. Many people had donkeys or asses to carry goods around, but horses were more expensive. High maintenance. In Revelation horses only appear when bad things are happening.

The four horsemen of the Apocalypse from Revelation 6 are one of the most enduring images of the book. They have popped up in many books and films, inspiring art as diverse as Clint Eastwood's *Pale Rider* and Terry Pratchett's Discworld books, whose scythe-carrying figure of Death rides a horse called Binky.

Perhaps the most famous image of this cosmic cavalry charge comes from a remarkable set of drawings by Albrecht Dürer. In 1497–8, Dürer published a set of fifteen woodcuts based on the Apocalypse. Self-published, in fact. Like Luther, whom he admired, Dürer really understood the emerging technology of print. He made his prints affordable and widely available. He invested in his own printing press, had his own shop, and franchised agents in major cities. Sometimes he gave away advance copies of prints to stimulate demand. He even created his own logo. As an artist and as an entrepreneur, he was a genius.

He was also a deeply religious man with a strong personal faith, and his visionary, other-worldly, even grotesque interpretations brought John's work to life as never before. They burned their way into the cultural consciousness of western Europe.

Dürer's drawings capture perfectly the otherness of the book, and particularly the sense of a group of people who absolutely do not know what's going on. The opening print of the series shows the war in heaven. Michael skewers a dragon with a spear, while his comrades fire arrows and wield swords against the demons, but below on earth all is serene: an ordinary landscape, houses and churches, ships on a calm sea. No one down below seems to realise what's happening. As the Whore of Babylon parades around, she is admired by well-dressed members of the elite, hands on hips, hats at jaunty, relaxed angles. They don't seem at all put off by the grotesque seven-headed beast she is riding, nor by the goblet of blood (which resembles a sundae dish), nor even by the fact that, in the distance, the city is being completely consumed by fire.

Yet for all his genius, even Dürer struggles at times. In perhaps the strangest of the prints, John is seen attempting to eat a book which has been handed to him by an angel who appears to have two legs made out of pillars. Frankly, John looks like he's swallowing a pillow.

Dürer certainly made his interpretation of events highly political and highly contemporary. Those worshipping the beast wear crowns and coronets; the rulers of the world fleeing from judgment wear bishop's mitres and monk's tonsures.*

And in his famous print of the four horsemen of the Apocalypse, royalty and clergy join ordinary peasants in being trampled underfoot. One of the most influential aspects of this was that it showed the horsemen as a quartet. This was not how previous generations had read the text. Earlier interpreters – dating right back to the first known commentary on the text – identified the first horseman as Christ, with the power of the gospel spreading through the world. Then the subsequent three riders were the wars, famines and pestilences announced in Matthew 24.14.

Dürer is probably on the money here. Just because Christ appears as a horse-riding warrior later on in the book doesn't mean it is him here. In fact, the first horseman would have been readily identifiable to John's listeners, and not as anything to do with Christ. Dressed in white, carrying a bow, this is a Persian cavalryman, the feared invader from the east, bringing war and conquest. The bow was not a Roman weapon; it was used much more commonly in the Near East, especially in Parthia.

The *Pax Romana* brought peace and stability to the empire. But there was still trouble around the edges. At the eastern frontier the Roman army often repelled incursions from the Parthians, or from nomadic raiding tribes such as the rather mundanely named Alans. In Revelation one of the main threats to empire comes from the east: when the sixth bowl is poured out, it dries up 'the great river Euphrates . . . in order to prepare the way for the kings from the east' (Rev. 16.12).

So, that's the first rider: military invasion. The second rider also

---

* Having said that, they don't go as far as the engravings of Dürer's contemporary, Lucas Cranach, which included recognisable portraits among the worshippers of Babylon, including Ferdinand I, George of Saxony, and Emperor Charles V.

brings death, but of a non-militaristic kind. He is mounted on a red horse, the colour of blood. He carries a 'great sword', but the Greek word used here is not the short and relatively light sword carried by legionaries, but the large sword of the executioner. The right of the sword, or *jus gladii*, was the higher Roman magistrates' authority to condemn wrongdoers to death. So this horsemen represents not more warfare, but killing of a different kind. This is a magistrate on a mount: this is judicial murder.

John says that 'this rider takes peace from the earth' – a swipe at the *Pax Romana*. Rome claimed that Augustus 'brought war to an end and has ordained peace for the world'. But the supposed beneficiaries of Rome's peace knew otherwise. 'To plunder, butcher, steel, these things they misnamed Empire: they make a desolation and they call it peace,' said Calgacus, a tribal leader in northern Britain.

It is fundamental to the myth of empire that imperial violence is always an act of justice and peace, the act of a father who occasionally has to take a disciplinarian approach. Whether the *jus gladii* or lethal injection or the 'surgical strike', acts of violence can always be rebranded as prevention, justice, peace-keeping. John is having none of this. He knows that Rome murders its opponents. Revelation is full of references to Rome as murderer or executioner.* 'In you was found the blood of prophets and saints,' cries the angel when Babylon is destroyed, 'and of all who have been slaughtered on the earth.'

The third rider is mounted on a black horse and carries a set of scales. Traditionally this rider is thought to represent famine. When John sees him, he hears a voice: 'A quart of wheat for a day's pay, and three quarts of barley for a day's pay.' Dürer, provocatively, dresses this rider in luxury and opulence, a rich merchant dressed in his finery. This is not nature's famine, this is exploitation. This rider is getting rich on scarcity. Again, I think Dürer has picked up on one of the main critiques of the empire: it exploits the world for its own gain. Supply and demand, my friend; survival of the fittest.

Finally, we have the fourth horse. John tells us the name of the jockey: 'Its rider's name was Death.' In Dürer's wonderful engraving, the horse's ribs are showing through a painfully thin body. Its rider

* E.g. Revelation 6:9; 13:15; 16:6; 17:6; 18:24.

is a wizened old man, eyes sunk back in his skull-like head, legs more like those of a bird than a man. The fourth horse is described as 'green'. The Greek word is *chloros*. The colour of vegetation, or maybe mildew. Mould. Green as in sickness. Bilious. We're talking about plague. In a world without modern medicine, without penicillin and antibiotics and even basic hygiene, the threat of plague was viewed with terror. Mysterious, random, invisible, plague was an act of God – what else *could* it be?

And, of course, Revelation says all of this is an act of God.

The four horsemen are 'given authority over a fourth of the earth, to kill with sword, famine, and pestilence, and by the wild animals of the earth' (Rev. 6.7). Clearly the reference to 'wild animals' doesn't correlate with the horsemen – rather, what John seems to have in mind is a verse from Ezekiel where God talks about 'my four deadly acts of judgment, sword, famine, wild animals, and pestilence' (Ezek. 14.21).

And this is how horses generally appear in Revelation. They are warhorses, yes, but the wars are pictures of judgment. There are three episodes in Revelation where a run of seven judgments is released, revealed or generally let loose: the seven seals, the seven trumpets and the seven dwarfs. Sorry, bowls.

In the opening of the seven seals, the first four seals release the four horsemen in turn. The fifth seal reveals the martyrs appealing to the Lord to 'judge and avenge' the blood of those who have been slaughtered for their testimony. They are told to rest a while, but John shows that their prayers will be answered. That leads to the opening of the sixth seal, after which the sky turns black, the moon turns to blood, stars fall to earth, the sky rolls up like a scroll, mountains and islands 'are removed' and everyone tries to hide.

After this there is an interlude where John sees four angels holding back the four winds, delaying the final act until the servants of the Lord – the 144,000 – are sealed. And then when the seventh seal is opened there is a silence in heaven, a silence which may well make the loudest noise in the whole of this noisy book.

This episode is followed by the blowing of seven trumpets. We are not talking about a brass band here: trumpets were instruments which signalled announcements or arrivals. Think fanfares. Think police sirens, even. The trumpets are blown in response to the prayers of the saints. Broadly speaking, the first four trumpets release disasters onto the earth, with each of which a third of the earth is destroyed. Trumpet one releases hail – fire mixed with blood – which burns a third of the trees and green grass; trumpet two casts a mountain into the sea, destroying a third of the fish and a third of the ships; with trumpet three a star falls from heaven and a third of all rivers and springs are poisoned; with trumpet four the sun, moon and stars are struck and a third of each is darkened, although how you darken a third of the sun I don't quite know. Maybe some kind of enormous cosmic dimmer switch.

After that, the emphasis changes. Trumpet five sends a star to earth: the angel of the abyss, whom we met way back in Hierapolis. He releases a load of locusts – like horses equipped for battle. Locusts with faces. Locusts with women's hair. The sixth trumpet releases what are recognisably more traditional cavalrymen from across the Euphrates, 200 million strong. Well, I *say* more traditional. These riders wear breastplates 'the colour of fire and of sapphire and of sulphur' while their horses' heads are like 'lions' heads, and fire and smoke and sulphur came out of their mouths'. A third of humankind is killed.

After the sixth trumpet, there is another interlude, where John has a mysterious vision of seven thunders (which he never describes). He is then handed a tiny scroll and told to eat it, and doing that reveals the episode of the two witnesses. Only after that is the seventh trumpet blown. This time the work is completed: 'The kingdom of the world has become the kingdom of our Lord, and of his Messiah, and he will reign forever and ever' (Rev. 11.15).

Finally we have the seven bowls full of plagues, poured out like offerings from a *phiale* offering bowl, only this time the altar is the earth and, specifically, the kingdoms of the beast and the dragon. The plagues carry echoes of those inflicted on Egypt before the exodus: sores afflict those who bear the mark of the beast; river, spring and sea turn as red as blood; the sun first burns everyone and then is extinguished, plunging the kingdom of the beast into darkness. Bowl six dries up the Euphrates and allows the 'kings of the east to cross' (and it's a big welcome back to our old friends, the Persians!). The emphasis is clearly on the Roman empire facing its enemies – facing its nemesis. But here it gets weirder, because John sees three spirits coming from the mouths of the dragon, the beast and the false prophets, calling on the kings of the world to assemble for battle, for the great day of God the Almighty. (We don't see their battle, though; nor do we know the outcome of their battle until later.)

The seventh bowl brings finality. A great voice comes from the throne in heaven, saying, 'It is done!' The great city splits into three. Cue lightning, thunder, earthquake. Babylon is destroyed. The islands sink; mountains fall; huge hailstones descend. 'And every island fled away.'

Much has been written about these three series of seven, especially with regard to whether they show three completely different sets of seven, or whether they reflect three different perspectives on the same seven events. This latter approach is known as the recapitulation theory, and it first appears in the earliest extant commentary on Revelation, written by Victorinus of Pettau, a martyr who was killed sometime around AD 304, during the persecution under Diocletian. Victorinus rejected the idea that Revelation was a linear narrative: he saw it as a cycle of visions, chronological up to the end of the sixth seal, but then repeated. It's not possible to give a definitive answer on this, but Victorinus's view is widely accepted today. Certainly events and images from Revelation reappear in different forms through the book. And there are strong similarities between the series – like the pause or interlude between the sixth and seventh events in each case. Between the sixth and seventh seals we see the sealing of the 144,000; between the sixth and seventh trumpets there is the episode of the two witnesses; and between the sixth and seventh bowls, although it's not placed there in the text, there is one of the most famous, or infamous, images in Revelation: Armageddon.

This image of a final climactic battle has had a huge influence in our culture. 'Armageddon' has become a shorthand for any massive, world-changing conflict. It features in film titles and newspaper head-lines. The Clash sang about 'Armagideon Time'.* Hal Lindsey thought

---

* The Clash song is actually a cover version. The original was written and recorded by reggae artist Willi Williams. Revelation has a long association

it referred to World War III. Many people believe that there will be a final battle, whatever form it may take.

But the strange thing about Revelation's battle of Armageddon is that it never actually happens. In fact, none of the battles in Revelation are actually played out. There are at least five occasions when armies prepare for battle in this book – Armageddon being only one of them – but we never see anyone actually fight.

*

In the text, the sixth and seventh trumpets follow each other immediately. This leaves us in a state of suspense: we see the armies called to battle by the frog-spirits (now *there's* a phrase I never thought I'd type), but the action isn't taken up again until three chapters later.

And when we do come back to it, everything starts with another horseman. 'Then I saw heaven opened,' says John, 'and there was a white horse!' Few images reinforce the futility of a literal reading of Revelation more than this figure. He is a royal figure, wearing many diadems on his head, but you have to say it's a confusing, not to say incoherent, image. John says the rider is called 'Faithful and True'; he then says that 'he has a name inscribed' – presumably on the diadems he is wearing – 'that no one knows but himself'. A verse later, though, we are told that 'his name is called The Word of God', and, finally, 'On his robe and on his thigh he has a name inscribed, "King of kings and Lord of lords."'

---

with Rastafarianism and reggae. When Emperor Haile Selassie I was crowned in Addis Ababa on 2 November 1930, among the many titles he was given was 'Conquering Lion of the Tribe of Judah'. Many miles away in Jamaica, those who had been reading their Bible remembered their Revelation: 'See, the Lion of the tribe of Judah, the Root of David, has conquered.' Street preachers like Leonard Howell started to preach that Haile Selassie was the Messiah. Howell later wrote a tract called *The Promise Key*, which described Haile Selassie and his wife as King Alpha and Queen Omega, and referred to 'the poison 666'. Revelation still influences the culture, religion and music of Rastafarianism. Babylon is a common metaphor, symbolising the white political power system that has held the black race down for centuries. Even the use of cannabis has been called 'the healing of the nation', a phrase based on Revelation 22.2.

So let me get this straight. Nobody knows his name, despite the fact that it appears to be written all over his clothing, engraved on his headgear and, apparently, tattooed on his thigh. And it is not one name, but four. Or possibly five. Or six. What's more, this rider is leading out the armies of heaven to battle. They are dressed in pure white, but he is wearing a robe dipped in blood, which is rather odd considering the battle hasn't started. And, of course, he has a great big sword sticking out of his mouth.

This is Jesus, clearly. But it's a Jesus constructed out of all the many images which have been used of Christ throughout the book. He rules nations with a rod of iron, as previously featured in chapter 12. He has a sword coming out of his mouth, as seen in chapter 1. The eyes like flames of fire come from chapter 2. The blood comes not from his enemies, but from himself: he is the Lamb who was slain, as related in chapter 5. The name 'Faithful and True' comes from chapter 3. And so on, and so on . . .

Nor is it just this figure; this whole section is full of episodes which are sort of different, but which may well be the same. Although it is punctuated with the repeated phrase 'Then I saw . . .' it's never clear if what is being described are different, consecutive events, or if John sees the same things over and over again, through different lenses and from different perspectives.

After the white horseman, the next scene sees an angel call all the carrion that fly in 'mid-heaven' (which I like to imagine is the bit above Middle Earth) to feast on the bodies of the kings, captains, horses, riders, free and slave, small and great. But although the beast and the kings of the earth have gathered to wage war against the white rider and his angelic army, we don't actually hear about the battle – we never see any battle in Revelation. All we see is the outcome: the first and second beast are captured and thrown into the lake of fire; the rest are killed – and we have to be precise here – 'by the sword of the rider of the horse, the sword that came from his mouth'.

A little later the same thing happens again. After being imprisoned for a thousand years, the Satan is released. He goes out to deceive the nations, gathers Gog and Magog from the four corners of the earth and surrounds the camp of the saints. Then there is a big battle . . . oh, no, sorry – there isn't. Fire comes down and consumes the enemies. And the devil is thrown into the lake of fire and sulphur, where the two beasts are.

In Revelation 16, as we've seen, there is a similar elision. The sides gather at Armageddon. And they all fight a big battle . . . oh, hold on. No, no they don't. The seventh angel pours out his bowl and a loud voice says, 'It is done!'

In Revelation, then, Armageddon is a complete non-event. There is no armageddon at Armageddon. No actual final battle. Why? Because it's not about a literal battle. It's about the defeat of evil by the power of God. None of this is in fact the remit of humans. The followers of the Lamb never do take up arms; their only weapon is the testimony of Jesus. And this is the truth we see reflected in that confusing figure – a figure which, I might add, John sees in heaven – the warrior with the sword in his mouth, the man whose words alone can cut evil down to size.

In the world John lived in, victory was achieved through violence. Armies lay slaughtered on the field, gladiators lay writhing in the sand of the arena. The whole point of Roman coins was to show the empire victorious over its subject peoples. John steals this imagery, but that's all it is: imagery. Just as we use the word 'fight' metaphorically to describe a dispute or an argument or a struggle. Used symbolically, it doesn't always imply that physical violence was involved.

We use language in exactly this way every day. A rugby player comes off the pitch. 'That was a brutal battle,' he says. A trader comes off the floor of the stock exchange after a bad day. 'It was a bloodbath out there.' A contestant in reality TV says she wants to crush her opponents. None of that is literal. (All right, the rugby one might be. I've seen a few matches which would count.) We 'cross swords' with opponents. We are 'shellshocked' by events. John's method is no different. He is describing the defeat of the forces of evil, using the strongest images he can find, which, in the first-century world, meant using the language of warfare.

But the amazing thing about Revelation is that victory comes through apparent defeat. The Lamb in Revelation conquers, not through killing others but through being killed: he achieves victory through being made the victim. Revelation urges its listeners to stand strong, in the knowledge that it may cost them their lives. Shockingly, perversely almost, for Revelation that is victory: non-violent, intentional resistance; standing up in personal witness against the beast. That is the only battle which matters. And through that, God grants the victory.

*

Among those who believed in the literal arrival of Armageddon was, alarmingly, a man who later had access to the nuclear button. In 1971, Ronald Reagan offered up his belief that 'the day of Armageddon isn't far off . . . Everything's falling into place. It can't be long now.' And when Reagan assumed the role of President, one of his staff said, 'I have read the Book of Revelation, and yes, I believe the world is going to end – by an act of God, I hope – but every day I think that time is running out.' Worryingly, that staff member was the Defense Secretary, Caspar Weinberger.*

America has always had a complicated relationship with Revelation. One of its chief patriotic songs – the Battle Hymn of the Republic – has lyrics straight out of the Revelation Songbook:

Mine eyes have seen the glory of the coming of the Lord
He is trampling out the vintage where the grapes of wrath are
stored
He hath loosed the fateful lightning of His terrible swift sword.
His truth goes marching on.
Chorus
Always look on the bright side of life . . . etc.

In fact, the very foundations of the USA are bound up with the Apocalypse. Christopher Columbus had some very strong – and quite strange – apocalyptic beliefs. He thought, for example, that the Spanish king and queen would reconquer Jerusalem and that would herald the end of the world. Columbus reckoned that the end

---

* Even more worryingly, Reagan's full name was Ronald Wilson Reagan – three names, each six letters long. You don't think . . .

of the world was 'about 155 years away' but that, before the end could come, 'the good news of the kingdom will be proclaimed throughout the world, as a testimony to all the nations; and then the end will come' (Matt. 24:14). Later, he saw his discovery of America as part of an apocalyptic plan. 'God made me the messenger of the new heaven and a new earth of which he spoke in the Apocalypse of St John,' he wrote. 'And he showed me the spot where to find it.'

Those who followed him across the Atlantic were likewise influenced by Revelation. Roger Williams, for example, was an English minister who travelled to America in 1631 and, in 1636, began the colony of Providence Plantation, which provided a refuge for religious minorities. Williams advocated fair dealings with Native Americans and organised the first attempt to prohibit slavery in any of the original thirteen colonies. His radical views saw him attacked by other Puritan leaders in America, and actually expelled from the colony of Massachusetts. But he saw Revelation as a proclamation of religious liberty and his struggle against the forces of officialdom in the colonies as an apocalyptic battle. John of Patmos, after all, was encouraging Christians to stand strong in the face of state-enforced religion. 'Forced worship stinks in the nostrils of God,' Williams said. He argued that any nation which claimed 'the title of Christ's land or Christian land' was, in fact, one of the kingdoms of the beast, and he identified Charles I as one of the beastly kings. In his own writings Williams quotes more from Revelation than any other biblical book.

Williams is just one of many, many dissenters who saw in America a new set of possibilities. Here was a place where groups could realise their dream of a New Jerusalem; here was an ark where refugees from godless Europe could hunker down and wait for the second coming. So it is perhaps not surprising that America has seen more millennial and apocalyptic groups than any other country. Sometimes with terrible consequences.

One of the most well known of these groups – albeit more for their beautiful furniture than any knowledge of what else they stood for – are the so-called Shakers. They originated in Lancashire, England, where they called themselves the United Society of Believers in Christ's Second Appearing. In the face of persecution, their leader, a blacksmith's daughter called Ann Lee, led them across the sea to America, where they established communities entirely shaped by the idea of the imminence of the second coming. They were celibate communities (after all, if the new creation was coming soon, they would not need to think about future generations; no need for procreation if you've got the new creation). They held their goods in common. Like the long-lost Montanists, they experienced ecstasies and visions during which they would shake and shudder (hence the derogatory nickname given to them by opponents). 'Do all your work as though you had a thousand years to live,' said Mother Ann, as she was known, 'and as you would if you knew you must die tomorrow.'

In 1805, meanwhile, a spiritual leader called Johann Georg Rapp was expelled from the German Duchy of Württemberg. He and 800 followers went to America – or as Rapp called it, the 'land of Israel' – where they attempted to build the New Jerusalem. They established three communities, named Harmony, New Harmony and Economy, so were known as the Harmonites (better than being known as the Economists, I suppose). Rapp believed that Napoleon was the antichrist and that Jesus Christ would return on 15 September 1829. When he failed to materialise a third of their members left.

The Harmonites and the Shakers quietly dwindled away, but not all the apocalyptic movements in America died down so quietly. Some of them *burned*.

*

In 1836, William Miller, a salesman from Vermont, USA, published a book called *Evidence from Scripture and history of the second coming* which claimed that the second coming would happen on 22 October 1843. When it didn't turn up, either Miller, or a follower called Samuel Snow, gave a revised ETA of 20 October 1844. Thousands of people prepared themselves. Many of them abandoned their homes; farmers stopped tending their crops and their livestock. As the date neared, some gave away all their money. One storekeeper shut up shop and put a sign up, saying, 'This shop is closed in honour of the King of kings who will appear about 20 October.'

He didn't. Appear, that is. And the event, or non-event, became known, rather understatedly, as 'The Great Disappointment'.

But while Miller returned to Vermont to buy a new slide rule, some of his followers circled the wagons and joined together in the movement known as the Adventists – people who were waiting eagerly for the advent of Christ. They began to celebrate the Sabbath on a Saturday, as the Jews did, and from 1861 became known as the Seventh-Day Adventists. Among their number was a visionary teenage prophetess called Ellen G. Harmon, whose zeal for the second coming was matched only by her enthusiasm for the nutritional value of vegetables and roughage. Inspired by her teachings, a wealthy Adventist established a health sanatorium and created a range of healthy fibre-rich foods. His name was W. K. Kellogg. And so it was that Revelation was responsible for giving the world cornflakes.

Over the years, the Adventists were fragmented by one theological dispute after another (it is a common feature among these Revelation-inspired groups that they are endlessly dividing, like cells). In the 1870s Charles Taylor Russell, a Pennsylvania draper and member of the Seventh Day Adventists, announced that the second coming was going to happen in 1874. Four years after that, according to his inter-pretation, the bodies of the true believers would transform from flesh to spirit and then, in 1914, the kingdom of God would materialise on earth after the battle of Armageddon. In the meantime they were to shun all earthly religions and nation states, immerse themselves in the Bible, and warn as many people as they could about the impending end. He called the movement The Watchtower. Later they became the Watchtower Bible and Tract Society. Still later, in 1931, they became Jehovah's Witnesses. Astute readers will have spotted that, by then, the first deadlines had passed. When the kingdom of God failed to show up in 1914, it was postponed to 1918; then to 1925 by Russell's successor, 'Judge' Joseph Franklin Rutherford, who was certain that 'our generation will see the great battle of Armageddon' and that 'millions now living will never die'. The latest update given by the Jehovah's Witnesses was 1974. Since then they have given up predicting the date. Or at least, they've stopped publicising it.

Rutherford was a zealous separatist. In 1929 he declared the secular state of America to be demonic and ordered the Witnesses not to salute the national flag, nor to stand up for the national anthem; Christmas and birthday parties were pagan rituals and Mother's Day was a feminist plot. We can see how all this is rooted in an extreme reading of Revelation, where John does, indeed, call on the witnesses – the martyrs – to separate from the state.

But there's separation, and then there's downright antagonism.

Vernon Howell was a member of the Adventists who was utterly convinced that the millennium would arrive any moment. He joined a splinter group from the Adventists known as the Branch Davidians. (In fact, in 1959 the Branch Davidians had split off from the Davidian Seventh Day Adventists, who themselves had left the Seventh Day Adventists in the 1920s. A splinter group of a splinter group.) Obsessed with Revelation, Howell changed his name to David Koresh and identified himself as the Lamb of the seven seals: only he was equipped to explain the meaning of the book.

He took his followers to the Mount Carmel compound, and began to amass a huge store of provisions and weaponry to help them survive the disasters following the opening of the sixth seal – which would happen sometime not long after March 1993. The presence of all this weaponry alarmed the United States Bureau of Alcohol, Tobacco, and Firearms and, on 28 February 1993 their officials attempted to search Mount Carmel. There was a gunfight during which four agents and six members of the cult were shot and killed. Immediately the FBI were called in and laid siege to the compound. Well, they *said* they were the FBI, but Koresh knew who they really were. They were the beast. Koresh and his followers prepared for the end. It came fifty-one days later when the FBI launched a final assault. A fire broke out in the compound. Seventy-six people died in the conflagration.

Today this kind of apocalypticism remains a highly visible part of American life. America is the natural home of survivalists – preppers, as they are sometimes known – people who are determined to be fully prepared for the big meltdown. It's never quite clear what this meltdown will be – some say natural disaster, others say nuclear war, others say climate change. It doesn't matter. Whatever the cause, they are making their stand in a long line of American apocalyptic groups who have all been waiting for the end of the world. When it comes, they will be prepared.

21 A Jewel of a Place

The bus driver was playing New Order. Then it was The Smiths. It was the bus the eighties forgot.

I was heading north on the island, to see the two oldest churches on Patmos. Or the locations of the earliest churches, at any rate. From what I could see, the buildings themselves weren't so ancient.

There were clouds in the sky, but the heat was intense. Perhaps those were not clouds up there, but roiling steam. Perhaps the earth was boiling. The bus was filled with walkers, their faces Andy Warhol-white with sun-block. After a brief delay caused by slow-moving goats on the road, we drove on through a sandy, beige landscape, accompanied by the strains of Duran Duran.

At Kambos beach, we emerged blinking into the harsh light. The beach is fringed with tamarisk trees, their wispy grey-green foliage and thin trunks twisted and wrenched into strange shapes. The beach itself is not covered in sand – more of a fine gravel. At this end of the season, it was more or less empty and had that forlorn air of all beaches when the sunbathers have left. There were no heavenly parties going on in the Patmos Paradise hotel at the southern end of the beach, and all the cafés were deserted.

From Kambos I followed the instructions in Herr Graf's book and walked due north along the road, through a valley between rocky hills. Eventually I descended into Lambi, a small, practically deserted beach. Here there were more tamarisks, the bases of their trunks painted with whitewash, for some reason. I sat under their shade and drank iced tea, and looked at the stones getting wet in the turquoise sea. Lambi's beach is nothing special, save for one thing. Its otherwise unremarkable pebbles are transformed in the water. They become deep red, marbled with veins of white and yellow. Some take on an almost translucent quality. They become like gems.

Gems, of course, are a feature of the Apocalypse, notably in its descriptions of heaven. I'm not sure if the Patmos Paradise hotel has floors made of gemstone, but the real Paradise is full of the stuff. John routinely describes what he is seeing in geological language.

The jewel which appears the most in Revelation is jasper. The glory of God looks like jasper, which also makes up the wall of the New Jerusalem. Jasper can be found in many colours: red, green, brown, blue, yellow or white. In a jeweller's shop on Chora I met a lovely lady who specialised in making jewellery out of the twelve gemstones of Revelation. We had a nice chat. When she heard that I was writing a book on the subject she solemnly took my name and wrote it in her visitors' book in case she had any questions for me at a later date. Interestingly, she had substituted diamond for jasper. John certainly talks of crystal-clear jasper, which is confusing, since jasper – *iaspis* – generally referred to an opaque precious stone. It is possible that he meant diamond. But then again, he also talks of streets of crystal-clear gold, so I think he was just being poetic.

And what poetic names they are: jasper and agate, sapphire, emerald and onyx, carnelian and chrysolite, topaz and chrysoprase, jacinth and amethyst.

And beryl.

Can't win them all, I suppose.

What all this adds up to is the idea that the heavenly city is created out of the finest possible materials. Even the foundations of its walls are precious stones. But John is also, as ever, referencing some Old Testament passages: first Exodus 28.16–20, where detailed DIY instructions are given for the design and manufacture of the breast-plate of the high priest. It was to be adorned with twelve jewels, on each one of which was engraved the name of one of the tribes of Israel. Ten of these jewels feature in Revelation's list.* More significantly, perhaps, John is thinking of Isaiah 54, a jewel of a passage where God promises that Israel, disgraced, destroyed, exiled though she is now, will be greater than ever before. No longer will his people fear oppression or terror or fear. 'O afflicted one,' he

---

* The two differences are that Exodus has turquoise and moonstone, whereas Revelation has chrysoprase and topaz.

says, 'storm-tossed, and not comforted, I am about to set your stones in antimony, and lay your foundations with sapphires. I will make your pinnacles of rubies, your gates of jewels, and all your walls of precious stones' (Isa. 54.11–12).

At the beginning of this section of Isaiah, Israel is likened to a woman, widowed, desolate and barren. But then God says this: 'For your Maker is your husband, the Lord of hosts is his name.' God's people – Israel – are getting dressed up for a wedding.

*

The day before, as I sat nursing a small glass of something chilled and trying to write, my attention was caught by the sound of car horn. Loads of car horns. A convention of car-horn-pushers. It was a wedding procession, of course, down in the port. A long line of cars, horns blaring and hooting, wound through Skala and then out, up into the hills from where their horns continued to bleat, like the sounds of distant animals. I don't know how far they went through the island, but they returned later, horns still blasting, and that evening my work was accompanied by the sound of very bad disco music drifting up from below. I gave up trying to write, and raised a yet larger glass of something chilled to toast the bride and groom.

The image of Jerusalem as the bride is one of the most compelling images in Revelation. It's drawn from both Christian and Jewish tradition. Isaiah 61 proclaims the year of the Lord's favour and promises a home for returning exiles. The Lord, Isaiah says, 'has clothed me with the garments of salvation, he has covered me with the robe of righteousness, as a bridegroom decks himself with a garland, and as a bride adorns herself with her jewels' (Isa. 61.10). Perhaps this is reflected in later rabbinic writings, which claimed: 'In the future the suburbs of Jerusalem will be filled with precious stones and jewels and all of Israel will come and take them.' In 2 Corinthians, Paul says to the church at Corinth, 'I feel a divine jealousy for you, for I promised you in marriage to one husband, to present you as a chaste virgin to Christ' (2 Cor. 11.2). It is clear that the idea of the church as the bride of Christ already had some currency.

In John's brain, soaked as it was with Isaiah's messianic visions, this picture of the bride becomes the climactic vision of the book.

In chapter 19, he hears voices from heaven celebrating: 'for the marriage of the Lamb has come and his bride has made herself ready'. Up next is the defeat of the beasts, the casting of the Satan into the abyss, the millennium rule of the saints and the judgment of the dead – so it is what you might call a long engagement. After all that, John sees 'the holy city, the new Jerusalem, coming down out of heaven from God, prepared as a bride adorned for her husband' (Rev. 21.2). An angel shows him around the 'bride, the wife of the Lamb', and that's where we get all the jewels described. The gems are not just foundation stones, but bridal jewellery. This is a wedding, and judging from the amount of bling, it's a royal one at that.

The New Jerusalem is more than a place, then: it's a relationship. It's bridegroom and bride, a relationship made architectural; love and security and perfect peace expressed through urban planning. The image might strike us as odd, but it was not unusual in the ancient world for a city to be depicted as a woman. And a little earlier in this book another woman-shaped city appears – but she is hardly a blushing bride. No, her blushes are purely cosmetic.

*

In a house in Ephesus archaeologists discovered some graffiti: 'Rome, queen over all, your power will never end.' Picturing Rome as a woman was commonplace in the empire. The city and its rule were embodied, immortalised in a goddess: Roma. Smyrna, Pergamum and Ephesus all had temples dedicated to Roma, and her figure appears on many Roman coins. The most common representation of her is as a noble, female warrior, reclining serenely with sword in hand on the seven hills where Rome was built.

John doesn't exactly follow this picture – he makes it his own, shall we say. He portrays her as a drunken whore, dressed up to the nines, 'all fur coat and no knickers', as the saying goes. And instead of the seven hills of Rome we see the seven heads of the monster on which she rides. She has mislaid her sword, and instead is swigging from a cup filled with offal and sewage and filth. So a *slightly* different take on the official line, then. She is clothed in 'purple and scarlet, and adorned with gold and jewels and pearls'. In Rome, only those of a high social class were permitted to wear purple and gold, so this is not some commoner. This is a high-class courtesan. One with a double-barrelled name. One with connections. But appearances should not deceive us. She may look posh, but she is a blood-thirsty harlot, whose name is written for all to see: '"Babylon the great, mother of whores and of earth's abominations." And I saw that the woman was drunk with the blood of the saints and the blood of the witnesses to Jesus' (Rev. 17.4–6).

This is one of those few occasions in Revelation where John is specific about the interpretation. The seven heads of the beast represent seven mountains. 'The woman that you saw,' the angel explains later, 'is the great city that rules over the kings of the earth.'

That'd be Rome, then. The city built, famously, on seven hills. The city where, in AD 64, hundreds of Christians were brutally executed by Nero in reprisals for the great fire. The city where Peter and Paul were executed. This lady has blood on her hands.

And John foresees judgment. Rome says, 'I rule as a queen; I am no widow, and I will never see grief,' but she is wrong and by the end of the section, the city – no longer a woman – is ruined and desolate. No trade takes place, nobody bakes any bread, no lamps are lit. No car horns blare out in celebration, no more disco music is played: 'the voice of bridegroom and bride will be heard in you no more' (Rev. 18.21–24).

Two cities, then. Two women. And clearly we are meant to note the contrasts between them. John gives both sections virtually identical introductions:

> Then one of the seven angels who had the seven bowls came and said to me, 'Come, I will show you the judgment of the great whore who is seated on many waters . . .' So he carried me away in the spirit into a wilderness, and I saw a woman sitting on a scarlet beast that was full of blasphemous names, and it had seven heads and ten horns. (Rev. 17.1, 3)

And:

> Then one of the seven angels who had the seven bowls full of the seven last plagues came and said to me, 'Come, I will show

you the bride, the wife of the Lamb.' And in the spirit he
carried me away to a great, high mountain and showed me
the holy city Jerusalem coming down out of heaven from God.
(Rev. 21.9–10)

There are plenty more comparisons to be had, too: Babylon/Rome is dressed in purple, New Jerusalem in white linen; Babylon/Rome is a whore, New Jerusalem is a bride; Babylon/Rome has a cup overflowing with blood, the New Jerusalem overflows with the water of life; Babylon/Rome is brought to darkness and ruin, in New Jerusalem there is no night; Babylon/Rome is the dwelling place of demons, the New Jerusalem is the dwelling place of God; in Babylon/Rome there is weeping and wailing and mourning, but in Jerusalem these things will be no more.

*

Even after they'd lost it, Jews never gave up the idea that God would restore their city – and greater than before. The language of Isaiah 65 – echoed in Revelation 21 – is a poignant, emotional plea for security and hope, for a place where 'no more shall the sound of weeping be heard in it, or the cry of distress' (Isa. 65.19). The New Jerusalem is a place of perfect safety: 'the gates are never shut and there is no night there', writes John. Today our cities are so huge and sprawling, we forget that once all cities had walls and gates, which were shut at night. Jews already theorised that God's revived Jerusalem would be spectacularly large. In the Talmud, rabbinical writings claimed that the 'Holy One' would make the city so big that if a horse ran away its owner would be able to recover it within the city's limits. One rabbi claimed: 'In the future all the nations and kingdoms will be gathered unto Jerusalem.'

All this is reflected in Revelation. And magnified. Never mind 'as far as a horse can run'; John's city is 12,000 *stadia* – some 1,500 miles – on each side. This city is bigger than the entire empire.

And that's not all. It's 1,500 miles up as well. It's a cube. There is only one other building in the Bible that is a cube. I say 'building'; it's a room: the Holy of Holies in the Temple. This was the most sacred place in the Temple, in the world, according to Jews. Only the high priest was allowed in the Holy of Holies, and then only on one day a year. So the implication is that in this New Jerusalem, the people of God will be living within the Holy of Holies itself, a Holy of Holies the size of the Roman empire.

*

From Lambi I struck out west, across the headland to Panaglia, up past Aghios Georghios, and out along a road north-east of Kaliva. The rock in the north is lighter in colour, more like caramel, rather than the dark brown of the Kastelli. And it is noticeably volcanic, more sponge-like, a bit like tufa. I trudged west, through a landscape dotted with small chapels and hermitages, bright white. In the distance, goats were being herded along a ridge. Near me, on the fence, a small brown bird whirred to a stop, eyes ringed bright red. A Sardinian warbler. The terrain reminded me of an English moor. Exmoor in the Aegean – but without the bogs. Everything was bone dry.

As I neared the goats, the goatherd appeared. He was a big man, dressed in a Gothic-black T-shirt and jeans. Satisfied that all the goats were in place, he shut the gate and returned to the road where he had left his moped. We exchanged greetings and mimed at each other about the heat. Clearly he thought I was mad to be walking anywhere on the island in such heat, let alone in this remote spot.

The landscape in the north of the island. On reflection, walking was not a great move.

He intimated that he was going home to sleep and puttered off on his moped. I envied him his cool house and restful bed. I walked on for fifteen minutes, then turned down a track towards what Herr Graf assured me was the oldest church on the island. My feet were blistered with the heat of the roads, my head aching. Outside the small church of Aghios Nikolaos, I sat beneath a tree and dozed for a while.

Once the temperature of my feet had moved from 'volcanic' to merely 'boiling', I went to explore the church. For once, the door was open. Reputedly, this church was built a year before the monastery. It's hard to see any evidence of that. The outside looks like a traditional Greek chapel. The inside, however, looks like a Greek transport café. There was the familiar smell of incense, but the inside had been 'remodelled' at some point and everything was painted white and glossy brown. It was only missing the Formica and a mug of tea. The walls were hung with some not very well-painted icons, and, most curiously, in the narthex of the church there was a mattress, still wrapped in its plastic.

There are so many of these little chapels or hermitages on the island. Many of them are surrounded by their own little gardens, like a homestead. But I never saw any signs of life within. I imagine they must be used on certain feast days, or occupied by monks

during times of hermitage. This one had quite a large compound and a little way away there was a garden full of prickly pear. Many hermitages on the island have a garden attached, growing tomatoes, cucumber, melon, perhaps. A fig tree, the shade of a vine.

When Guérin visited in 1850 he found a hermit with the wonderful name of Apollo at a place called Thermia. This is out to the east of Kambos, along towards Geranos. He had lived on his own in a remote part of the island for thirty-five years. By the time M. le Professeur found him, Apollo was quite infirm and only left his cell to go to the chapel or to work a little in his garden:

> He had planted all the trees that were about his chapel, and he used the two springs, which were near at hand, one of them being warm and the other cold, to water his vegetable garden. A vine which he planted when he arrived on Patmos had become very large, and in his old age, in the summer time, he would sit in its shade and meditate.

Apollo was named after an Egyptian hermit from the fourth century, although his nickname was 'the Peloponnesian', since he hailed originally from Mount Athos. He arrived in Patmos in 1816, moved to Thermia in 1818 and lived there for the next forty years. Guérin described his unvarying daily routine:

During the day he goes to his little church twice to pray. At night, he repeats the same prayers with the three monks who live under his supervision.

Guérin stayed with Apollo, and that night at midnight heard the monk get up and go with three other brothers to the little church he had built. Guérin wrote:

I could not help but be moved, when in the stillness of the night, at the foot of a deserted mountain, a few steps from the sea, I suddenly heard those four voices. Their chanting and prayers mingled with the hollow moaning of the sea with its eternal cry and this gave life to the desert.

Guérin recorded their words:

. . . in your courtyard, I praise You, Saviour of the world and, kneeling, I worship Your unbeatable power.

Apollo lived to a ripe old age. As Guérin wrote:

Freed from the worldly cares which others have, he peacefully awaits his death which seems to avoid him, respecting his bald head and long white beard.

Eventually I returned over the hill to Kambos, past a deserted windmill. Back in the town I sat at a café and drank iced tea and ate olives. In Kambos there is a triple church – a church with three naves, the central one of which dates from the twelfth century. I thought of going to have a look.

But I was outvoted by my feet. So I sat there, waiting for the bus to take me back home.

THE CAVE

'And it is utterly true that he who cannot find wonder, mystery, awe, the sense of a new world and an undiscovered realm in the places by the Gray's Inn Road will never find those secrets elsewhere, not in the heart of Africa, not in the fabled cities of Tibet. "The matter of our work is everywhere present", wrote the old alchemists, and that is the truth. All the wonders lie within a stone's throw of King's Cross Station.'

ARTHUR MACHEN

22 The Mystery

My final visit to the cave was on the Saturday morning, for the service.

I was late and the walk up the hill had left me, as usual, dripping in sweat. My only hope was that the darkness of the cave would hide my state, and the incense would mask any other effects.

The cave was crowded and the service already in full swing. In the gloom, I eased my way through the throng and positioned myself next to a pillar. If I'd hoped to arrive unnoticed, it didn't work. The lady at the jewellery shop had told me that the priest leading the service had a beautiful voice, and as I stood there I felt a hand on my shoulder and her face appeared next to me: 'You see?' she asked. 'Wasn't I right? Beautiful.'

She was right. Although it was hard to put your finger on what the nature of the beauty was. This was no classical singer. There was that reedy, almost nasal quality that seems to be an essential part of sung Greek liturgy. But in the cave the notes swooped around like birds. I let the sound of Byzantine Greek wash over me. The sounds, the smells, the *mysterium*. The priest kept appearing and disappearing behind the iconostasis: making the journey between heaven and earth, piercing the veil. In the dark sanctuary, lights flickered, figures moved about, shadows on the wall. I felt that disconnected feeling, as if my ears were blocked. Was it the pressure? Some kind of spiritual altitude sickness? Some words surfaced from the sea of Greek: *Kyrie eleison* – 'Lord have mercy'. *Hagia ton theon*. Names of saints and apostles. *Ioannes. Apocalupsos*.

The congregation were entertainingly Greek. People stood and sat, came and went. When they surged forward to kiss the icons, there was no sense of order, just enthusiasm. Nobody queued, and if there was a system I never fathomed it. When the priest brought out the wine he was surrounded by people as if they were clamouring for an autograph. Which in a way they were. When, at the end, he brought out the basket of bread for the faithful, there were no mealy-mouthed morsels or wafers which stuck to the roof of your mouth. It was a party.

And then it was over. The window shades were opened and suddenly the cave was filled with sunlight. Gary started to sweep up. The priest gave a speech in Greek to visitors, telling them about the cave, pointing out the sights.

Then everyone drifted away to their meals and their wine and the sunlight. And it was just me sitting there.

Kyrie eleison. Kyrie eleison. Kyrie eleison.

*

I spent the day out on the island. Trying to fix the landscape in my memory. By now it had become an inescapable backdrop to my understanding of the book; the landscape of my Revelation was this island. I cannot read that last book of the Bible now without seeing the lion-coloured stone, the dusty green tamarinds, the deep night-time blueness of the sea, the blessed bright blueness of the sky. And everywhere the tiny white churches, dotting the landscape, but always closed.

One time I arrived at the top of a hill, to find a closed church. I wandered around it, wondering if I could find a window to peer into, and even if I did, whether it was rude to peer. It was only after I had completed my circumnavigation that I realised I was not alone. At the steps of the church there was a man. Grey-haired, wearing a brown leather jacket, he was leaning on the low wall surrounding the church, staring out at the sea in the distance. He was praying. Below, at the end of a stony path which led to the church, I now saw where he'd parked his moped.

He looked up as I approached. We nodded at each other. There were tears in his eyes.

Painfully aware that I was intruding, I stumbled away. What need had driven him to that point? What battle was he facing? What beast was he staring down? I wanted to talk to him, to share something of what I had learned traversing the landscape of this island and this book. I wanted to tell him that the one thing I could be sure of from reading Revelation, is that God is in control, and that the prayers of the saints fill heaven like incense. I wanted to tell him that all around him was another world, as close as the air around him, and that at any moment, the door might open and a strange figure speak out and say, 'Come – I will show you something.'

*

By the time I returned to Chora, dusk was falling. The town had an eerie feel that night. It was like the set of a spy movie. *I will tell you a mystery . . .* That night everything was mysterious. The moon was huge, apricot-coloured. Its light made the white walls of the houses glow. They looked like snowdrifts, the alleys banked with shadows and silence.

Near the main square about twenty rather elderly women emerged from the darkness, cackling and laughing and swaying slightly from side to side. *Hydrophoroi*, perhaps. Here on a weekend break to sacrifice to Artemis.

I sat in the main square and ate a meal of braised goat, scented with rosemary and thyme and lemon, rich with garlic. Eating it is definitely one of the best things you can do with a goat. It's only fair. They try to eat everything else.

At the next table a group of Italians were squabbling and pointing and laughing. I heard the names Socrates, Homer and Vangelis. They must have been working through all the famous Greeks. A woman was smoking a suspiciously thick cigarette in a black holder. A small dog had given up sniffing around the tables and was lying in the middle of the square on a flagstone that still held some heat from the sun.

But everything else seemed colder. For the first time there was a coolness in the air. My arms were almost chilly. Almost. The wind rustled the vines. I had the sense that Patmos was shutting down. Slowing. Preparing for the cooler winds, the end of days.

I walked down the hill one last time, through the scent of pine and dust. As I stood by the harbour in Skala, the moon hung low over the sea like an enormous Chinese lantern.

*

The next day was blustery. The sky was grey, and the wind rattled the trees around the apartment. I packed my stuff, went down to the town and paid my bills.

A friend skyped me. He told me I was looking like Tom Hanks in *Castaway*. I looked in the mirror. There was certainly a lot of beard going on. And the face looked weather-beaten. Weeks alone had changed me. I was not the same person who had landed at Izmir. When you really look closely at yourself, you realise how much of you is unknowable. I am a stranger. I am a foreign land, a lifelong journey of exploration, searching for apocalypse.

Real life had already started to intrude. Diary dates had magically arrived on my computer. A book reading in London. A meeting to 'scope the campaign', whatever that means. Speaking engagements. I was beginning to understand why John had to come to the island to see his vision. It is hard to see clearly in a world so full of distractions.

It had been a tense day. A long wait. Packing. Tidying. Closing things down. Clearing things. Saying farewell to the island. I looked around the flat, trying to store its details in my memory: the roaring of the fridge, the cool feel of the tiled floor on blistered feet, the times when the work went well and carried me late into the night. And the times when my feet carried me elsewhere, out onto the brown hillsides, in search of revelation.

It was late at night when I left the house. Shakira was nowhere to be seen; somewhere down in her field she was dreaming of cantering through the surf. I left a pile of grapes on the wall for her to find in the morning.

By the time I arrived at the port it was a little before midnight. On the quayside at Skala somebody's bag barked at me. Turned out the lady standing next to me had her small dog with her in a blue holdall. Every time the dog barked, the bag jumped. She spent a lot of time soothing her luggage. She could at least have cut holes for his legs to stick out.

I sat waiting at a table by the café. It was so windy that when I put my glasses on the table they blew off. I must have looked anxious. An elderly monk, a visitor to the monastery, presumably, patted me on the shoulder.

'No worry,' he said. 'Is big boat.'

The water looked like beaten pewter in the moonlight. It was rippled, gunmetal grey. Angry, perhaps.

I sipped my coffee. Listed the things I had learnt:

That an island changes your view.

That on Patmos, everywhere is up.

That rocks can be beasts.

That holiness slows down time.

That only in exile can you see your home clearly.

That objects can mean many things.

That all false gods die, but man makes new gods to replace them. And that the new gods are the old gods in different clothing.

That a vision is nothing without action.

That beasts can be defeated.

That there will always be opposition.

Opposition.

Yes. On the day of my departure a suicide bomber blew himself up outside a church in Peshawar, Pakistan, killing himself and fifty-six other people.

On the day of my departure, Islamic extremists killed over fifty people at a shopping mall in Nairobi, shooting anyone who could not prove they were a Muslim.

On the day of my departure I read a piece in a Vancouver newspaper telling how some people were welcoming the destruction of Damascus because they thought it would usher in the millennium.

How do we read Revelation in such a world? We read it as it has always been read. We read it in small, dedicated communities, where to follow the Lamb is to stand against the beast. We read it as ambassadors of the New Jerusalem, demonstrating a new way of life to a world disenchanted with the lies of Babylon. We read it as those prepared to bear witness to the first and last, whatever the cost. We read it as servants, not as masters; as liberators, not oppressors. Too many people have used this book to control; it is time we used it to set people free.

To read Revelation in this way is to read it properly. It is not a map or a timetable. It gives no dates and all the numbers it contains mean something else. It is not a code to be cracked, but a world to be explored, if only we are brave enough to let ourselves be thrilled by its language and imagery, to embrace its wild, dark poetry. If only we have the courage to understand that we will never fully understand this book.

And, most of all, to read Revelation is to glimpse the possibility of a new life, a new citizenship, here and now. John did not see an alien universe, divorced from our reality, but a world that is waiting for us right away. The New Jerusalem is here. Citizenship is waiting. And all we have to do is stand up and be counted.

Who can fight against the beast? *I* can. *You* can. All of us, the witnesses, together.

'The world turns,' I wrote in my notebook. 'The vision and the island remain, until the end of time.'

I stood at the jetty and looked out over the sea. And it seemed to me that the stars began to disappear and the darkness became thicker. And in the distance I was suddenly aware of a monstrous shape coming from the sea, steam pouring from its snorting nostrils, tusks pointing into the dark night sky, eyes blazing with light, and from its mouth came a plaintive, lonely howl.

I thought for a moment it was the beast, come back for another visit.

But it wasn't. It was the ferry to Athens, and it was time to go home.

'The future is already here. It's just unevenly distributed.'

WILLIAM GIBSON

Selected Booklist

Patmos

Sister Anthousa, *Hermits Of Patmos And Hermitages*, trans. Prokes, Kalliopi (Athens: Holy Monastery Evangelismos, 1998)

Boxall, Ian, *Patmos in the Reception History of the Apocalypse* (Oxford: OUP, 2013)

Geil, William Edgar, *The Isle that is Called Patmos* (London: Marshall Brothers, 1897)

Georgirenes, Joseph and Henry Denton, *A description of the present state of Samos, Nicaria, Patmos, and mount Athos, tr. by one that knew the author in Constantinople* (London: 1678)

Graf, Dieter, *Samos, Patmos, Northern Dodecanese: Walking the Greek Islands* (Munich: Graf Editions, 2005)

Grüll, Tibor, *Patmiaka* (Eötvös – füzetek, Új folyam, 12; Budapest: Eötvös, 1989)

Guérin, Victor, *Description de l'Ile de Patmos et de l'Ile de Samos* (Paris: Durand, 1856)

Hill, Aaron, *A Full and Just Account of the Present State of the Ottoman Empire in All Its Branches With the Government, and Policy, Religion, Customs, and Way of Living of the Turks, in General* (London: John Mayo, 1709)

Kellaris, Georgios, 'The Iconography of Sanctuary Doors from Patmos and its Place in the Iconographic program of the Byzantine Iconostasis' (McGill University, 1991)

Kollias, Elias, *Patmos* (Athens: Melissa Pub. House, 1990)

Kominis, Athanasios D., *Patmos: Treasures of the monastery* (Athens: Ekdotike Athenon, 1988)

Levi, Peter, *The Hill of Kronos* (London: Eland, 2007)

McCabe, Donald F. and Mark A. Plunkett, *Patmos Inscriptions: Texts and List* (Princeton: Institute for Advanced Study, 1985)

Oikonomides, Nicolas and Elisavet A. Zachariadou, *Social and Economic Life in Byzantium* (Aldershot: Ashgate Variorum, 2004)

Papadopoulos, Stelios A., *Epigraphes Tes Patmou* (Athens: Genike Dieuthynsis, 1966)

—, *Monastery of St. John the Theologian: Historical-Archaeological Guide* (Patmos: Monastery of St. John the Theologian, 1977)

Terrain Editions, *Patmos Map* (Greece: Terrain Maps, 2009)

Walpole, Robert, et al., *Travels in various countries of the East; being a continuation of Memoirs relating to European and Asiatic Turkey, &c* (London: printed for Longman, Hurst, Rees, Orme, and Brown, 1820)

Revelation

Aune, David E., 'The Influence of Roman Imperial Court Ceremonial on the Apocalypse of John', *Biblical Research*, 18: 5–26, 1983

—, 'The Prophetic Circle of John of Patmos and the Exegesis of Revelation 22:16', *Journal for the Study of the New Testament*, 37: 103–16, 1989

—, *Revelation 1–5* (Dallas: Word Books, 1997)

—, *Revelation 6–16* (Nashville: Thomas Nelson, 1998)

—, *Revelation 17–22* (Nashville: Thomas Nelson, 1999)

Bauckham, Richard, *The Theology of the Book of Revelation* (Cambridge: Cambridge University Press, 1993)

Boesak, Allan Aubrey, *Comfort and Protest: Reflections on the Apocalypse of John of Patmos* (Edinburgh: Saint Andrew, 1987)

Caird, G. B., *A Commentary on the Revelation of St. John the Divine* (London: Adam & Charles Black, 1966)

Collins, Adela Yarbro, *The Apocalypse* (Dublin: Veritas, 1979)

Court, John M., *Myth and History in the Book of Revelation* (London: SPCK, 1979)

Friesen, Steven J., *Imperial Cults and the Apocalypse of John:*

Reading Revelation in the ruins (Oxford: Oxford University Press, 2001)

Garrow, A. J. P., *Revelation* (London: Routledge, 1997)

Gorman, Michael J., *Reading Revelation Responsibly: Uncivil Worship and Witness: Following the Lamb Into the New Creation* (Eugene: Cascade Books, 2011)

Hays, Richard B. and Stefan Alkier, *Revelation and the Politics of Apocalyptic Interpretation* (Waco: Baylor University Press, 2012)

Hemer, Colin J., *The Letters to the Seven Churches of Asia in Their Local Setting* (Sheffield: JSOT, 1986)

Howard-Brook, Wes and Anthony Gwyther, *Unveiling Empire: Reading Revelation then and now* (New York: Orbis, 1999)

Keener, Craig S., *Revelation (NIV Application Commentary)* (Grand Rapids: Zondervan Publishing House, 2000)

Koester, Craig R., 'Revelation's Visionary Challenge to Ordinary Empire', *Interpretation*, 63, 2009

Kovacs, Judith L., Christopher Rowland, and Rebekah Callow, *Revelation: The apocalypse of Jesus Christ* (Oxford: Blackwell, 2004)

Kraybill, J. Nelson, *Apocalypse and Allegiance: Worship, politics, and devotion in the book of Revelation* (Grand Rapids: Brazos Press, 2010)

Lindsey, Hal, *The Late Great Planet Earth* (London: Marshall Pickering, 1987)

Maier, Harry O., *Apocalypse Recalled: The Book of Revelation after Christendom* (Minneapolis: Fortress Press, 2002)

Metzger, Bruce M., *Breaking the Code: Understanding the book of Revelation* (Nashville: Abingdon Press, 1993)

Morris, Leon, *The Revelation of St. John: An Introduction and Commentary* (London: Tyndale, 1969)

Peterson, Eugene H., *Reversed Thunder: The Revelation of John and the Praying Imagination* (San Francisco: HarperSanFrancisco, 1991)

Ramsay, William Mitchell, *The Letters to the Seven Churches of Asia: And Their Place in the Plan of the Apocalypse* (London: Hodder & Stoughton, 1904)

Rhoads, David M., *From Every People and Nation: The book of*

Revelation in intercultural perspective (Edinburgh: Fortress
Alban, 2005)

Thompson, Leonard L., *The Book of Revelation: Apocalypse and
Empire* (Oxford: Oxford University Press, 1990)

Wainwright, Arthur William, *Mysterious Apocalypse:
Interpreting the Book of Revelation* (Nashville: Abingdon
Press, 1993)

Weinrich, William C., *Revelation* (Downers Grove, Ill.:
InterVarsity Press, 2005)

Wilson, Mark, *Charts on the Book of Revelation: Literary,
Historical, and Theological Perspectives* (Grand Rapids: Kregel
Academic, 2007)

Wright, N. T., *Revelation for Everyone* (London: SPCK
Publishing, 2011)

—, 'Farewell to the Rapture', *Bible Review*, 2001

History and background

Ackroyd, Peter, *Blake* (London: Minerva, 1996)

Akurgal, Ekrem, *Ancient Civilizations and Ruins of Turkey: From
Prehistoric Times Until the End of the Roman Empire*
(Istanbul: Turkish Historical Press, 1969)

Balsdon, J. P. V. D., *Romans and Aliens* (Chapel Hill: University
of North Carolina, 1979)

Bean, George Ewart, *Aegean Turkey: An Archaeological Guide*
(London: Benn, 1966)

Benko, Stephen, *Pagan Rome and the Early Christians*
(Bloomington: Indiana University Press, 1984)

Blake, William and Geoffrey Keynes, *Poetry and Prose of William
Blake* (London/New York: The Nonesuch Press/Random
House, 1948)

Boff, Leonardo, Clodovis Boff and Paul Burns, *Introducing
Liberation Theology* (Tunbridge Wells: Burns & Oates, 1987)

Bowring, Jacky, 'Containing Marginal Memories: The Melancholy
Landscapes of Hart Island (New York), Cockatoo Island
(Sydney), and Ripapa Island (Christchurch)', *Memory
Connection Journal*, 1 (1), 2011

Bruce, F. F., *The Acts of the Apostles: The Greek text with introduction and commentary* (London: Tyndale Press, 1952)

Burdon, Christopher, *The Apocalypse in England: Revelation unravelling, 1700–1834* (Basingstoke: Macmillan, 1997)

Cohn, Norman, *Cosmos, Chaos, and the World to Come: The Ancient Roots of Apocalyptic Faith* (New Haven/London: Yale University Press, 1993)

—, *The Pursuit of the Millennium: Revolutionary Millenarians and Mystical Anarchists of the Middle Ages* (London: Paladin, 1970)

DeMar, Gary, *Last Days Madness: Obsession of the Modern Church* (Atlanta: American Vision, 1997)

Eusebius, *The Ecclesiastical History and The Martyrs of Palestine*, trans. Oulton, Hugh Jackson Lawlor and John Ernest Leonard (2 vols; London: SPCK, 1927)

Fant, Clyde E. and Mitchell G. Reddish, *A Guide to Biblical Sites in Greece and Turkey* (Oxford: Oxford University Press, 2003)

Fitzmyer, Joseph A., *The Acts of the Apostles* (New York/London: Doubleday, 1998)

Gempf, Conrad H. and David W. J. Gill, *The Book of Acts in its Graeco-Roman Setting* (Carlisle: Paternoster, 1994)

Gradel, Ittai, *Emperor Worship and Roman Religion* (Oxford: Clarendon Press, 2002)

Herodotus, A. R. Burn and Aubrey De Sélincourt, *Herodotus: The Histories* (London: Penguin Books, 1972)

Holmes, Michael W., *The Apostolic Fathers: Greek Texts and English Translations* (3rd revised edition; Grand Rapids: Baker Academic, 2007)

James, M. R., *The Apocryphal New Testament: being the Apocryphal Gospels, Acts, Epistles and Apocalypses: with other narratives and fragments* (Oxford: Clarendon, 1924)

Koester, Helmut, *Ephesos: Metropolis of Asia: An interdisciplinary approach to its archaeology, religion and culture* (Valley Forge: Trinity Press International, 1995)

McEvedy, Colin and Douglas Stuart Oles, *Cities of the Classical World: An Atlas and Gazetteer of 120 Centres of Ancient Civilization* (London: Allen Lane, 2011)

Milton, Giles, *Paradise Lost: Smyrna 1922: The Destruction of Islam's City of Tolerance* (London: Sceptre, 2009)

Morton, H. V., *In the Steps of St. Paul* (London: Rich & Cowan, 1936)

Nestler, E., 'Was Montanism a Heresy?', *Pneuma*, 6, 1984

Newport, Kenneth G. C., *Apocalypse and Millennium: Studies in Biblical Eisegesis* (Cambridge: Cambridge University Press, 2000)

Price, S. R. F., *Rituals and Power: The Roman imperial cult in Asia Minor* (Cambridge: Cambridge University Press, 1984)

Ramsay, William Mitchell, *St. Paul the Traveller and the Roman Citizen* (London: Hodder & Stoughton, 1908)

—, *The Church in the Roman Empire Before A.D. 170* (Mansfield College Lectures, 1892; London: Hodder & Stoughton, 1893)

Robeck, Jr, Cecil M., 'Montanism and Present Day "Prophets"', *Pneuma*, 32, 2010

Samosata, Lucian of, *Lucian* (Loeb Classical Library, London: Heinemann, 1936)

Stark, Rodney, *Cities of God: The real story of how Christianity became an urban movement and conquered Rome* (San Francisco: HarperSanFrancisco, 2006)

Stewart-Sykes, Alistair, 'The Original Condemnation of Asian Montanism', *Journal of Ecclesiastical History*, 50(1), 1999

Tabbernee, William, 'Portals of the Montanist New Jerusalem: The Discovery of Pepouza and Tymion', *Journal of Early Christian Studies*, 11(1), 2003

Tabbernee, William and Peter Lampe, *Pepouza and Tymion: The discovery and archaeological exploration of a lost ancient city and an imperial estate* (Berlin/New York: W. de Gruyter, 2008)

Thonemann, Peter, *The Maeander Valley: A Historical Geography From Antiquity to Byzantium* (Cambridge: Cambridge University Press, 2011)

Trevett, Christine, *Montanism: Gender, authority and the new prophecy* (Cambridge: Cambridge University Press, 1996)

Weber, Eugen, *Apocalypses: Prophecies, cults and millennial beliefs through the ages* (London: Hutchinson, 1999)

Witherington, Ben, *The Acts of the Apostles: A socio-rhetorical commentary* (Grand Rapids, Eerdmans, 1998)